Systems Programming with Modula-3

Prentice Hall Series in Innovative Technology

Dennis R. Allison, David J. Farber, and Bruce D. Shriver   *Series Advisors*

Johnson	*Superscalar Microprocessor Design*
Kane	*MIPS RISC Architecture*
Nelson, ed.	*Systems Programming with Modula-3*
Rose	*The Open Book: A Practical Perspective on OSI*
Rose	*The Simple Book: An Introduction to Management of TCP/IP-based internets*
Shapiro	*A C++ Toolkit*
Slater	*Microprocessor-Based Design*
Strom, et al.	*Hermes: A Language for Distributed Computing*
Wirfs-Brock, Wilkerson, and Weiner	*Designing Object-Oriented Software*

Systems Programming with Modula-3

Greg Nelson, Editor

PRENTICE HALL, Englewood Cliffs, New Jersey 07632

Library of Congress Cataloging-in-Publication Data

Systems programming with Modula-3 / edited by Greg Nelson.
      p.   cm. -- (Prentice Hall series in innovative technology)
   Includes bibliographical references and index.
   ISBN 0-13-590464-1
   1. Systems programming (Computer science) 2. Modula-3 (Computer
program language)   I. Nelson, Greg (Charles G.) II. Series.
   QA76.66.S87 1991
   005.4'2--dc20   91-14119
                                                              CIP

Editorial/production supervision: Mary P. Rottino
Manufacturing buyers: Kelly Behr and Susan Brunke
Acquisitions editor: Paul Becker
Cover design: L.C., S.C.G., M.S.M., C.G.N., S.E.P.

 © 1991 by Prentice-Hall, Inc.
A Simon & Schuster Company
Englewood Cliffs, New Jersey 07632

The publisher offers discounts on this book when ordered
in bulk quantities. For more information, write:

   Special Sales/College Marketing
   College Technical and Reference Division
   Prentice Hall
   Englewood Cliffs, New Jersey 07632

A previous version of Chapter 2 appeared under copyright by Digital Equipment Corporation, Ing. C. Olivetti
and C., SpA., and the Association for Computing Machinery and appears here with their permission.
   Previous versions of Chapter 4 appeared under copyright by Digital Equipment Corporation and appear here
with permission.

Printed in the United States of America
10 9 8 7 6 5 4 3 2 1

ISBN 0-13-590464-1

Prentice-Hall International (UK) Limited, *London*
Prentice-Hall of Australia Pty. Limited, *Sydney*
Prentice-Hall Canada Inc., *Toronto*
Prentice-Hall Hispanoamericana, S.A., *Mexico*
Prentice-Hall of India Private Limited, *New Delhi*
Prentice-Hall of Japan, Inc., *Tokyo*
Simon & Schuster Asia Pte. Ltd., *Singapore*
Editora Prentice-Hall do Brasil, Ltda., *Rio de Janeiro*

Contents

v

Chapter 8   **How the language got its spots**

Anonymous

Acknowledgments

Modula-3 was designed by Luca Cardelli, Jim Donahue, Mick Jordan, Bill Kalsow, and Greg Nelson, as a joint project by the Digital Equipment Corporation Systems Research Center and the Olivetti Research Center. Paul Rovner made many contributions as a founding member of the design committee. The language specification was written by Lucille Glassman and Greg Nelson, under the watchful supervision of the whole committee.

Maurice Wilkes had the inspiration that sparked the project.

Our technical starting point was Modula-2+, which was designed by Paul Rovner, Roy Levin, John Wick, Andrew Birrell, Butler Lampson, and Garret Swart. We made good use of the ruthlessly complete description of Modula-2+ in Mary-Claire van Leunen's *Modula-2+ User's Manual*. The ideas in the "+" part of Modula-2+ were mostly derived from the Mesa and Cedar languages developed at Xerox PARC.

Niklaus Wirth designed Modula-2, the starting point of our starting point. He also reviewed the evolving design and made many valuable suggestions—not one of which was a suggested addition. Indeed, he inspired us with the courage to pull out a number of deep-rooted weeds.

SRC Modula-3 was implemented by Bill Kalsow and Eric Muller. Olivetti Modula-3 was implemented by Mick Jordan, Trevor Morris, David Chase, Steve Glassman, and Marion Sturtevant.

The language and book were greatly improved by the helpful feedback from Bob Ayers, Andrew Black, Regis Crelier, Dan Craft, Hans Eberle, John Ellis, Stu Feldman, Michel Gangnet, Lucille Glassman, David Goldberg, Stephen Harrison, Sam Harbison, Jim Horning, Solange Karsenty, Mike Kupfer, Butler Lampson, Mark Manasse, Tim Mann, Eliot Moss, Dick Orgass, Sharon Perl, Norman Ramsey, Lyle Ramshaw, Eric Roberts, Peter Robinson, Ed Satterthwaite, Jorge Stolfi, Garret Swart, Chuck Thacker, and Ken Zadeck.

We are grateful for the support of Digital Equipment Corporation in general, and Bob Taylor and Sam Fuller in particular.

Chapter 1

Introduction

Greg Nelson

> *He that will not apply new remedies must expect new evils: for time is the greatest innovator, and if time of course alter things to the worse, and wisdom and counsel shall not alter them to the better, what shall be the end?*
> —*Francis Bacon*

1.1 History

On November 6th, 1986, Maurice Wilkes wrote to Niklaus Wirth proposing that the Modula-2+ language be revised and standardized as a successor to Modula-2. Wirth gave this project his blessing, and the Modula-3 committee was born.

At the first meeting, the committee unanimously agreed to be true to the spirit of Modula-2 by selecting simple, safe, proven features rather than experimenting with our own untried ideas. We found that unanimity was harder to achieve when we got to the details.

Modula-3 supports interfaces, objects, generics, lightweight threads of control, the isolation of unsafe code, garbage collection, exceptions, and subtyping. Some of the more problematical features of Modula-2 have been removed, like variant records and the built-in unsigned numeric data type. Modula-3 is substantially simpler than other languages with comparable power.

Modula-3 is closely based on Modula-2+, which was designed at the Digital Equipment Corporation Systems Research Center and used to build the Topaz system [22, 24]. The

Modula-3 design was a joint project by Digital and Olivetti. The language definition was published in August 1988, and immediately followed by implementation efforts at both companies. In January 1989, the committee revised the language to reflect the experiences of these implementation teams. A few final revisions were made for the publication of this book.

SRC Modula-3 is distributed by the DEC Systems Research Center under a liberal license. The distribution includes a compiler that translates Modula-3 to C, the Modula-3 Abstract Syntax Tree toolkit developed at Olivetti, and a runtime system with configuration files for DEC, IBM, HP, and Sun workstations.

1.2 Perspective

Most systems programming today is done in the BCPL family of languages, which includes B, Bliss, and C. The beauty of these languages is the modest cost with which they were able to take a great leap forward from assembly language. To fully appreciate them, you must consider the engineering constraints of machines in the 1960s. What language designed in the 1980s has a compiler that fits into four thousand 18-bit words, like Ken Thompson's B compiler for the PDP-7? The most successful of these languages was C, which by the early 1970s had almost completely displaced assembly language in the Unix system.

The BCPL-like languages are easy to implement efficiently for the same reason they are attractive to skeptical assembly language programmers: they present a programming model that is close to the target machine. Pointers are identified with arrays, and address arithmetic is ubiquitous. Unfortunately, this low-level programming model is inherently dangerous. Many errors are as disastrous as they would be in machine language. The type system is scanty, and reveals enough quirks of the target machine that even experienced and disciplined programmers sometimes write unportable code simply by accident. The most modern language in this family, C++, has enriched C by adding objects; but it has also given up C's best virtue—simplicity—without relieving C's worst drawback—its low-level programming model.

At the other extreme are languages like Lisp, ML, Smalltalk, and CLU, whose programming models originate from mathematics. Lisp is the hybrid of the lambda calculus and the theory of a pairing function; ML stems from polymorphic type theory; Smalltalk from a theory of objects and inheritance; CLU from a theory of abstract data types. These languages have beautiful programming models, but they tend to be difficult to implement efficiently, because the uniform treatment of values in the programming model invites a runtime system in which values are uniformly represented by pointers. If the implementer doesn't take steps to avoid it, as simple a statement as n := n + 1 could require an allocation, a method lookup, or both. Good implementations avoid most of the cost, and languages in this family have been used successfully for systems programming. But their general disposition towards heap allocation rather than stack allocation remains, and they have not become popular with systems programmers. The runtime systems required to make these languages efficient often isolate them in closed environments that cannot accommodate programs written in other languages. If you are a fan of these languages you may find Modula-3 overly pragmatic; but read on anyway, and give us a chance to show that pragmatic constraints do not exclude attractive solutions.

Between the extremes of BCPL and Lisp is the Algol family of languages, whose modern representatives include Pascal, Ada, Modula-2, and Modula-3. These languages have programming models that reflect the engineering constraints of random-access machines but conceal the details of any particular machine. They give up the beauty and mathematical symmetry of the Lisp family in order to make efficient implementations possible without special tricks; they also have strong type systems that avoid most of the dangerous and machine-dependent features of the BCPL family.

In the 1960s, the trend in the Algol family was toward features for control flow and data structuring. In the 1970s, the trend was toward information-hiding features like interfaces, opaque types, and generics. More recently, the trend in the Algol family has been to adopt a careful selection of techniques from the Lisp and BCPL families. This trend is demonstrated by Modula-3, Oberon, and Cedar, to name three languages that have floated portable implementations in the last few years.

Modula-3, Oberon, and Cedar all provide garbage collection, previously viewed as a luxury available only in the closed runtime systems of the Lisp family. But the world is starting to understand that garbage collection is the only way to achieve an adequate level of safety, and that modern garbage collectors can work in open runtime environments.

At the same time, these three languages allow a small set of unsafe, machine-dependent operations of the sort usually associated with the BCPL family. In Modula-3, unsafe operations are allowed only in modules explicitly labeled unsafe. The combination of garbage collection with the explicit isolation of unsafe features produces a language suitable for programming entire systems from the highest-level applications down to the lowest-level device drivers.

1.3 Overview

The first goal of this book is to describe Modula-3, but its broader purpose is to illustrate the level of programming represented by Modula-3, Oberon, and Cedar. The book is not a programming tutorial, but a medley of lessons and instructive examples derived from our ten years of experience programming with this kind of language. The examples range from tutorial applications of an object-oriented window system toolkit to the machine-dependent part of an input-output streams package. Most of the chapters were written to report on successful system designs rather than to illustrate Modula-3; as a result they introduce the language as no toy examples could. If you are an experienced programmer in any language who would like to see solid examples of how interfaces, objects, garbage collection, and threads help to make programming safe and efficient at the same time, then this book was written for you.

The chapter order was chosen for the reader who wants to master all the courses of the Modula-3 curriculum. If you prefer to read *a la carte*, you may skip or skim Chapters 2 and 3 (the language definition and standard interfaces), and read any of the later chapters independently.

Chapter 4 is an introduction to programming with threads, including recent practical experience on programming a symmetric multiprocessor. Chapter 5 is a formal specification of the Modula-3 thread synchronization primitives. Chapter 6 presents the top-down design and implementation of Modula-3's standard I/O streams package, which illustrates several of Modula-3's novel features, including the partially opaque object type. Before reading it you should read Sections 2.2.9, 2.4.6, and 2.4.7 on objects, opaque types, and revelations. Chapter 7 presents a tutorial on Trestle, a windowing toolkit for Modula-3 programs. Chapter 8 presents an analysis and critique (it is too idiosyncratic to be called a rationale) of some of the closer design decisions in Modula-3.

1.4   Features

The remainder of the introduction is an overview of the most important features of Modula-3.

1.4.1   Interfaces

One of Modula-2's most successful features is the provision for explicit interfaces between modules. Interfaces are retained with essentially no changes in Modula-3. An interface to a module is a collection of declarations that reveal the public parts of a module; things in the module that are not declared in the interface are private. A module *imports* the interfaces it depends on and *exports* the interface (or, in Modula-3, the interfaces) that it implements.

Interfaces make separate compilation type-safe; but it does them an injustice to look at them in such a limited way. Interfaces make it possible to think about large systems without holding the whole system in your head at once.

Programmers who have never used Modula-style interfaces tend to underestimate them, observing, for example, that anything that can be done with interfaces can also be done with C-style include files. This misses the point: many things can be done with include files that cannot be done with interfaces. For example, the meaning of an include file can be changed by defining macros in the environment into which it is included. Include files tempt programmers into shortcuts across abstraction boundaries. To keep large programs well structured, you either need super-human will power, or proper language support for interfaces.

1.4.2 Objects

The better we understand our programs, the bigger the building blocks we use to structure them. After the instruction came the statement, after the statement came the procedure, after the procedure came the interface. The next step seems to be the *abstract type*.

At the theoretical level, an abstract type is a type defined by the specifications of its operations instead of by the representation of its data. As realized in modern programming languages, a value of an abstract type is represented by an "object" whose operations are implemented by a suite of procedure values called the object's "methods". A new object type can be defined as a *subtype* of an existing type, in which case the new type has all the methods of the old type, and possibly new ones as well (inheritance). The new type can provide new implementations for the old methods (overriding).

Objects were invented in the mid-sixties by the farsighted designers of Simula [3]. Objects in Modula-3 are very much like objects in Simula: they are always references, they have both data fields and methods, and they have single inheritance but not multiple inheritance.

Small examples are often used to get across the basic idea: truck as a subtype of vehicle; rectangle as a subtype of polygon. This book aims at larger examples that illustrate how object types provide structure for large programs. Chapter 6 describes an I/O streams package, and Chapter 7 a windowing toolkit. These are practical examples of a useful methodology: the main design effort is concentrated into specifying the properties of a single abstract type—a stream of characters, a window on the screen. Then dozens of interfaces and modules are coded that provide useful subtypes of the central abstraction. The abstract type provides the blueprint for a whole family of interfaces and modules. If the central abstraction is well-designed then useful subtypes can be produced easily, and the original design cost will be repaid with interest.

The combination of object types with Modula-2 opaque types produces something new: the *partially opaque type*, where some of an object's fields are visible in a scope and others are hidden. Because the committee had no experience with partially opaque types, the first version of Modula-3 restricted them severely; but after a year of experience it was clear that they were a good thing, and the language was revised to remove the restrictions. Chapter 6 on I/O streams contains an extended example.

It is possible to use object-oriented techniques even in languages that were not designed to support them, by explicitly allocating the data records and method suites. This approach works reasonably smoothly when there are no subtypes; however it is through subtyping that object-oriented techniques offer the most leverage. The approach works badly when subtyping is needed: either you allocate the data records for the different parts of the object individually (which is expensive and notationally cumbersome) or you must rely on unchecked type transfers, which is unsafe. Whichever approach is taken, the subtype relations are all in the programmer's head: only with an object-oriented language is it possible to get object-oriented static typechecking.

1.4.3 Generics

A generic module is a template in which some of the imported interfaces are regarded as formal parameters, to be bound to actual interfaces when the generic is instantiated. For example, a generic hash table module could be instantiated to produce tables of integers, tables of text strings, or tables of any desired type. The different generic instances are compiled independently: the source program is reused, but the compiled code will generally be different for different instances.

To keep Modula-3 generics simple, they are confined to the module level: generic procedures and types do not exist in isolation, and generic parameters must be entire interfaces.

In the same spirit of simplicity, there is no separate typechecking associated with generics. Implementations are expected to expand the generic and typecheck the result. The alternative would be to invent a polymorphic type system flexible enough to express the constraints on the parameter interfaces that are necessary in order for the generic body to compile. This has been achieved for ML and CLU, but it has not yet been achieved satisfactorily in the Algol family of languages, where the type systems are less uniform. (The rules associated with Ada generics are too complicated for our taste.)

1.4.4 Threads

Dividing a computation into concurrent processes (or threads of control) is a fundamental method of separating concerns. For example, suppose you are programming a terminal emulator with a blinking cursor: the most satisfactory way to separate the cursor blinking code from the rest of the program is to make it a separate thread. Or suppose you are augmenting a program with a new module that communicates over a buffered channel. Without threads, the rest of the program will be blocked whenever the new module blocks on its buffer, and conversely, the new module will be unable to service the buffer whenever any other part of the program blocks. If this is unacceptable (as it almost always is) there is no way to add the new module without finding and modifying every statement of the program that might block. These modifications destroy the structure of the program by introducing undesirable dependencies between what would otherwise be independent modules.

The provisions for threads in Modula-2 are weak, amounting essentially to coroutines. Hoare's monitors [12] are a sounder basis for concurrent programming. Monitors were used in Mesa, where they worked well; except that the requirement that a monitored data structure be an entire module was irksome. For example, it is often useful for a monitored data structure to be an object instead of a module. Mesa relaxed this requirement, made a slight change in the details of the semantics of Hoare's `Signal` primitive, and introduced the `Broadcast` primitive as a convenience [18]. The Mesa primitives were simplified in the Modula-2+ design, and the result was successful enough to be incorporated with no substantial changes in Modula-3.

A threads package is a tool with a very sharp edge. A common programming error is to access a shared variable without obtaining the necessary lock. This introduces a race condition that can lie dormant throughout testing and strike after the program is shipped. Theoretical work on process algebra has raised hopes that the rendezvous model of concurrency may be safer than the shared memory model, but the experience with Ada, which adopted the rendezvous, lends at best equivocal support for this hope—Ada still allows shared variables, and apparently they are widely used.

Chapter 4 is a tutorial on programming with the Modula-3 thread interface. Chapter 5 presents a formal specification for the thread synchronization primitives.

1.4.5 Safety

A language feature is *unsafe* if its misuse can corrupt the runtime system so that further execution of the program is not faithful to the language semantics. An example of an unsafe feature is array assignment without bounds checking: if the index is out of bounds, then an arbitrary location can be clobbered and the address space can become fatally corrupted. An error in a safe program can cause the computation to abort with a run-time error message or to give the wrong answer, but it can't cause the computation to crash in a rubble of bits.

Safe programs can share the same address space, each safe from corruption by errors in the others. To get similar protection for unsafe programs requires placing them in separate address spaces. As large address spaces become available, and programmers use them to produce tightly-coupled applications, safety becomes more and more important.

Unfortunately, it is generally impossible to program the lowest levels of a system with complete safety. Neither the compiler nor the runtime system can check the validity of a bus address for an I/O controller, nor can they limit the ensuing havoc if it is invalid. This presents the language designer with a dilemma. If he holds out for safety, then low level code will have to be programmed in another language. But if he adopts unsafe features, then his safety guarantee becomes void everywhere.

The languages of the BCPL family are full of unsafe features; the languages of the Lisp family generally have none (or none that are documented). In this area Modula-3 follows the lead of Cedar by adopting a small number of unsafe features that are allowed only in modules explicitly labeled unsafe. In a safe module, the compiler prevents any errors that could corrupt the runtime system; in an unsafe module, it is the programmer's responsibility to avoid them.

Chapter 6 provides a realistic example of the isolation of unsafe code in the depths of the I/O streams package.

1.4.6   Garbage Collection

A classic unsafe runtime error is to free a data structure that is still reachable by active references (or "dangling pointers"). The error plants a time bomb that explodes later, when the storage is reused. If on the other hand the programmer fails to free records that have become unreachable, the result will be a "storage leak" and the computation space will grow without bound. Problems due to dangling pointers and storage leaks tend to persist long after other errors have been found and removed. The only sure way to avoid these problems is the automatic freeing of unreachable storage, or garbage collection.

Modula-3 therefore provides "traced references", which are like Modula-2 pointers except that the storage they point to is kept in the "traced heap" where it will be freed automatically when all references to it are gone.

Another great benefit of garbage collection is that it simplifies interfaces. Without garbage collection, an interface must specify whether the client or the implementation has the responsibility for freeing each allocated reference, and the conditions under which it is safe to do so. This can swamp the interface in complexity. For example, Modula-3 supports text strings by a simple required interface Text, rather than with a built-in type. Without garbage collection, this approach would not be nearly as attractive.

New refinements in garbage collection have appeared continually for more than twenty years, but it is still difficult to implement efficiently. For many programs, the programming time saved by simplifying interfaces and eliminating storage leaks and dangling pointers makes garbage collection a bargain, but the lowest levels of a system may not be able to afford it. For example, in SRC's Topaz system, the part of the operating system that manages files and heavy-weight processes relies on garbage collection, but the inner "nub" that implements virtual memory and thread context switching does not. Essentially all Topaz application programs rely on garbage collection.

For programs that cannot afford garbage collection, Modula-3 provides a set of reference types that are not traced by the garbage collector. In most other respects, traced and untraced references behave identically.

1.4.7   Exceptions

An exception is a control construct that exits many scopes at once. Raising an exception exits active scopes repeatedly until a handler is found for the exception, and transfers control to the handler. If there is no handler, the computation terminates in some system-dependent way—for example, by entering the debugger.

There are many arguments for and against exceptions, most of which revolve around inconclusive issues of style and taste. One argument in their favor that has the weight of experience behind it is that exceptions are a good way to handle any runtime error that is usually, but not necessarily, fatal. If exceptions are not available, each procedure that might encounter a runtime error must return an additional code to the caller to identify whether an error has occurred. This can be clumsy, and has the practical drawback that even careful programmers may inadvertently omit the test for the error return code. The frequency with which returned error codes are ignored has become something of a standing joke in the Unix/C world. Raising an exception is more robust, since it stops the program unless there is an explicit handler for it.

1.4.8 Type system

Like all languages in the Algol family, Modula-3 is strongly typed. The basic idea of strong typing is to partition the value space into types, restrict variables to hold values of a single type, and restrict operations to apply to operands of fixed types. In actuality, strong typing is rarely so simple. For example, each of the following complications is present in at least one language of the Algol family: a variable of type [0..9] may be safely assigned to an INTEGER, but not vice-versa (subtyping). Operations like absolute value may apply both to REALs and to INTEGERs instead of to a single type (overloading). The types of literals (for example, NIL) can be ambiguous. The type of an expression may be determined by how it is used (target-typing). Type mismatches may cause automatic conversions instead of errors (as when a fractional real is rounded upon assignment to an integer).

We adopted several principles in order to make Modula-3's type system as uniform as possible. First, there are no ambiguous types or target-typing: the type of every expression is determined by its subexpressions, not by its use. Second, there are no automatic conversions. In some cases the *representation* of a value changes when it is assigned (for example, when assigning to a packed field of a record type) but the abstract value itself is transferred without change. Third, the rules for type compatibility are defined in terms of a single subtype relation. The subtype relation is required for treating objects with inheritance, but it is also useful for defining the type compatibility rules for conventional types.

1.4.9 Simplicity

In the early days of the Ada project, a general in the Ada Program Office opined that "obviously the Department of Defense is not interested in an artificially simplified language such as Pascal". Modula-3 represents the opposite point of view. We used every artifice that we could find or invent to make the language simple.

C. A. R. Hoare has suggested that as a rule of thumb a language is too complicated if it can't be described precisely and readably in fifty pages. The Modula-3 committee elevated this to a design principle: we gave ourselves a "complexity budget" of fifty pages, and chose the most useful features that we could accommodate within this budget. In the end, we were over budget by six lines plus the syntax equations. This policy is a bit arbitrary, but there are so many good ideas in programming language design that some kind of arbitrary budget seems necessary to keep a language from getting too complicated.

In retrospect, the features that made the cut were directed toward two main goals. Interfaces, objects, generics, and threads provide fundamental patterns of abstraction that help to structure large programs. The isolation of unsafe code, garbage collection, and exceptions help make programs safer and more robust. Of the techniques that we used to keep the language internally consistent, the most important was the definition of a clean type system based on a subtype relation. There is no special novelty in any one of these features individually, but there is simplicity and power in their combination.

Chapter 2

Language Definition

Luca Cardelli, James Donahue, Lucille Glassman,
Mick Jordan, Bill Kalsow, Greg Nelson

> *The language designer should be familiar with many alternative*
> *features designed by others, and should have excellent judgment in*
> *choosing the best and rejecting any that are mutually inconsistent...*
> *One thing he should not do is to include untried ideas of his own.*
> *His task is consolidation, not innovation.*
> *—C.A.R. Hoare*

2.1 Definitions

A Modula-3 program specifies a computation that acts on a sequence of digital components called *locations*. A *variable* is a set of locations that represents a mathematical value according to a convention determined by the variable's *type*. If a value can be represented by some variable of type T, then we say that the value is a *member* of T and T *contains* the value.

An *identifier* is a symbol declared as a name for a variable, type, procedure, etc. The region of the program over which a declaration applies is called the *scope* of the declaration. Scopes can be nested. The meaning of an identifier is determined by the smallest enclosing scope in which the identifier is declared.

11

An *expression* specifies a computation that produces a value or variable. Expressions that produce variables are called *designators*. A designator can denote either a variable or the value of that variable, depending on the context. Some designators are *readonly*, which means that they cannot be used in contexts that might change the value of the variable. A designator that is not readonly is called *writable*. Expressions whose values can be determined statically are called *constant expressions*; they are never designators.

A *static error* is an error that the implementation must detect before program execution. Violations of the language definition are static errors unless they are explicitly classified as runtime errors.

A *checked runtime error* is an error that the implementation must detect and report at runtime. The method for reporting such errors is implementation-dependent. (If the implementation maps them into exceptions, then a program could handle these exceptions and continue.)

An *unchecked runtime error* is an error that is not guaranteed to be detected, and can cause the subsequent behavior of the computation to be arbitrary. Unchecked runtime errors can occur only in unsafe modules.

2.2   Types

> *I am the voice of today, the herald of tomorrow...*
> *I am the leaden army that conquers the world—I am TYPE.*
> *—Frederic William Goudy*

Modula-3 uses structural equivalence, instead of the name equivalence of Modula-2. Two types are the same if their definitions become the same when expanded; that is, when all constant expressions are replaced by their values and all type names are replaced by their definitions. In the case of recursive types, the expansion is the infinite limit of the partial expansions. A type expression is generally allowed wherever a type is required.

A type is *empty* if it contains no values. For example, [1..0] is an empty type. Empty types can be used to build non-empty types (for example, SET OF [1..0], which is not empty because it contains the empty set). It is a static error to declare a variable of an empty type.

Every expression has a statically-determined type, which contains every value that the expression can produce. The type of a designator is the type of the variable it produces.

Assignability and type compatibility are defined in terms of a single syntactically specified subtype relation with the property that if T is a subtype of U, then every member of T is a member of U. The subtype relation is reflexive and transitive.

Every expression has a unique type, but a value can be a member of many types. For example, the value 6 is a member of both [0..9] and INTEGER. It would be ambiguous to talk about "the type of a value". Thus the phrase "type of x" means "type of the expression x", while "x is a member of T" means "the value of x is a member of T".

However, there is one sense in which a value can be said to have a type: every object or traced reference value includes a code for a type, called the *allocated type* of the reference value. The allocated type is tested by TYPECASE (Section 2.3.18, page 35).

2.2.1 Ordinal types

There are three kinds of ordinal types: enumerations, subranges, and INTEGER. An enumeration type is declared like this:

TYPE T = {id_1, id_2, ..., id_n}

where the id's are distinct identifiers. The type T is an ordered set of n values; the expression T.id_i denotes the i'th value of the type in increasing order. The empty enumeration { } is allowed.

Integers and enumeration elements are collectively called *ordinal values*. The *base type* of an ordinal value v is INTEGER if v is an integer, otherwise it is the unique enumeration type that contains v.

A subrange type is declared like this:

TYPE T = [Lo..Hi]

where Lo and Hi are two ordinal values with the same base type, called the base type of the subrange. The values of T are all the values from Lo to Hi inclusive. Lo and Hi must be constant expressions (Section 2.6.15, page 59). If Lo exceeds Hi, the subrange is empty.

The operators ORD and VAL convert between enumerations and integers. The operators FIRST, LAST, and NUMBER applied to an ordinal type return the first element, last element, and number of elements, respectively (Section 2.6.13, page 57).

Here are the predeclared ordinal types:

INTEGER	All integers represented by the implementation
CARDINAL	The subrange [0..LAST(INTEGER)]
BOOLEAN	The enumeration {FALSE, TRUE}
CHAR	An enumeration containing at least 256 elements

The first 256 elements of type CHAR represent characters in the ISO-Latin-1 code, which is an extension of ASCII. The language does not specify the names of the elements of the CHAR enumeration. FALSE and TRUE are predeclared synonyms for BOOLEAN.FALSE and BOOLEAN.TRUE.

Each distinct enumeration type introduces a new collection of values, but a subrange type reuses the values from the underlying type. For example:

```
TYPE
  T1 = {A, B, C};
  T2 = {A, B, C};
  U1 = [T1.A..T1.C];
  U2 = [T1.A..T2.C]; (* sic *)
  V  = {A, B}
```

T1 and T2 are the same type, since they have the same expanded definition. In particular, T1.C = T2.C and therefore U1 and U2 are also the same type. But the types T1 and U1 are distinct, although they contain the same values, because the expanded definition of T1 is an enumeration while the expanded definition of U1 is a subrange. The type V is a third type whose values V.A and V.B are not related to the values T1.A and T1.B.

2.2.2 Floating-point types

There are three floating point types, which in order of increasing range and precision are REAL, LONGREAL, and EXTENDED. The properties of these types are specified by required interfaces in Section 3.4, page 72.

2.2.3 Arrays

An *array* is an indexed collection of component variables, called the *elements* of the array. The indexes are the values of an ordinal type, called the *index type* of the array. The elements all have the same size and the same type, called the *element type* of the array.

There are two kinds of array types, *fixed* and *open*. The length of a fixed array is determined at compile time. The length of an open array type is determined at runtime, when it is allocated or bound. The length cannot be changed thereafter.

The *shape* of a multi-dimensional array is the sequence of its lengths in each dimension. More precisely, the shape of an array is its length followed by the shape of any of its elements; the shape of a non-array is the empty sequence.

Arrays are assignable if they have the same element type and shape. If either the source or target of the assignment is an open array, a runtime shape check is required.

A fixed array type declaration has the form:

```
TYPE T = ARRAY Index OF Element
```

where Index is an ordinal type and Element is any type other than an open array type. The values of type T are arrays whose element type is Element and whose length is the number of elements of the type Index.

If a has type T, then a[i] designates the element of a whose position corresponds to the position of i in Index. For example, consider the declarations:

```
VAR a := ARRAY [1..3] OF REAL {1.0, 2.0, 3.0};
VAR b: ARRAY [-1..1] OF REAL := a;
```

Now a = b is TRUE; yet a[1] = 1.0 while b[1] = 3.0. The interpretation of indexes is determined by an array's type, not its value; the assignment b := a changes b's value, not its type. (This example uses variable initialization, page 38, and array constructors, page 52.)

An expression of the form:

```
ARRAY Index₁, ..., Indexₙ OF Element
```

is shorthand for:

```
ARRAY Index₁ OF ... OF ARRAY Indexₙ OF Element
```

This shorthand is eliminated from the expanded type definition used to define structural equivalence. An expression of the form $a[i_1, \ldots, i_n]$ is shorthand for $a[i_1]\ldots[i_n]$.

An open array type declaration has the form:

```
TYPE T = ARRAY OF Element
```

where Element is any type. The values of T are arrays whose element type is Element and whose length is arbitrary. The index type of an open array is the integer subrange [0..n-1], where n is the length of the array.

An open array type can be used only as the type of a formal parameter, the referent of a reference type, the element type of another open array type, or as the type in an array constructor.

Examples of array types:

```
TYPE
  Transform = ARRAY [1..3], [1..3] OF REAL;
  Vector = ARRAY OF REAL;
  SkipTable = ARRAY CHAR OF INTEGER
```

2.2.4 Records

A *record* is a sequence of named variables, called the *fields* of the record. Different fields can have different types. The name and type of each field is statically determined by the record's type. The expression r.f designates the field named f in the record r.

A record type declaration has the form:

```
TYPE T = RECORD FieldList END
```

where `FieldList` is a list of field declarations, each of which has the form:

```
fieldName: Type := default
```

where `fieldName` is an identifier, `Type` is any non-empty type other than an open array type, and `default` is a constant expression. The field names must be distinct. A record is a member of `T` if it has fields with the given names and types, in the given order, and no other fields. Empty records are allowed.

The constant `default` is a default value used when a record is constructed (page 52) or allocated (page 53). Either ":= default" or ": Type" can be omitted, but not both. If `Type` is omitted, it is taken to be the type of `default`. If both are present, the value of `default` must be a member of `Type`.

When a series of fields shares the same type and default, any `fieldName` can be a list of identifiers separated by commas. Such a list is shorthand for a list in which the type and default are repeated for each identifier. That is:

```
f₁, ..., fₘ: Type := default
```

is shorthand for:

$$f_1: \text{Type} := \text{default}; \ldots; f_m: \text{Type} := \text{default}$$

This shorthand is eliminated from the expanded definition of the type. The default values are included.

Examples of record types:

```
TYPE
  Time = RECORD seconds: INTEGER; milliseconds: [0..999] END;
  Alignment = {Left, Center, Right};
  TextWindowStyle = RECORD
    align := Alignment.Center;
    font := Font.Default;
    foreground := Color.Black;
    background := Color.White;
    margin, border := 2
  END
```

2.2.5   Packed types

A declaration of a packed type has the form:

```
TYPE T = BITS n FOR Base
```

where Base is a type and n is an integer-valued constant expression. The values of type T are the same as the values of type Base, but variables of type T that occur in records, objects, or arrays will occupy exactly n bits and be packed adjacent to the preceding field or element. For example, a variable of type

```
ARRAY [0..255] OF BITS 1 FOR BOOLEAN
```

is an array of 256 booleans, each of which occupies one bit of storage.

The values allowed for n are implementation-dependent. An illegal value for n is a static error. The legality of a packed type can depend on its context; for example, an implementation could prohibit packed integers from spanning word boundaries.

2.2.6 Sets

A *set* is a collection of values taken from some ordinal type. A set type declaration has the form:

```
TYPE T = SET OF Base
```

where Base is an ordinal type. The values of T are all sets whose elements have type Base. For example, a variable whose type is SET OF [0..1] can assume the following values:

```
{}    {0}    {1}    {0,1}
```

Implementations are expected to use the same representation for a SET OF T as for an ARRAY T OF BITS 1 FOR BOOLEAN. Hence, programmers should expect SET OF [0..1023] to be practical, but not SET OF INTEGER.

2.2.7 References

A *reference* value is either NIL or the address of a variable, called the referent.

A reference type is either *traced* or *untraced*. When all traced references to a piece of allocated storage are gone, the implementation reclaims the storage. Two reference types are of the same *reference class* if they are both traced or both untraced. A general type is traced if it is a traced reference type, a record type any of whose field types is traced, an array type whose element type is traced, or a packed type whose underlying unpacked type is traced.

A declaration for a traced reference type has the form:

```
TYPE T = REF Type
```

where Type is any type. The values of T are traced references to variables of type Type, which is called the *referent type* of T.

A declaration for an untraced reference type has the form:

    TYPE T = UNTRACED REF Type

where Type is any untraced[1] type. The values of T are the untraced references to variables of type Type.

In both the traced and untraced cases, the keyword REF can optionally be preceded by "BRANDED b" where b is a text constant called the *brand*. Brands distinguish types that would otherwise be the same; they have no other semantic effect. All brands in a program must be distinct. If BRANDED is present and b is absent, the implementation automatically supplies a unique value for b. Explicit brands are useful for persistent data storage.

The following reference types are predeclared:

    REFANY   Contains all traced references
    ADDRESS   Contains all untraced references
    NULL   Contains only NIL

The TYPECASE statement (Section 2.3.18, page 35) can be used to test the referent type of a REFANY or object, but there is no such test for an ADDRESS.

Examples of reference types:

    TYPE TextLine = REF ARRAY OF CHAR;
      ControllerHandle = UNTRACED REF RECORD
        status: BITS 8 FOR [0..255];
        filler: BITS 12 FOR [0..0];
        pc: BITS 12 FOR [0..4095]
      END;
      T = BRANDED "ANSI-M3-040776" REF INTEGER;
      Apple = BRANDED REF INTEGER;
      Orange = BRANDED REF INTEGER;

2.2.8 Procedures

A *procedure* is either NIL or a triple consisting of:

- the *body*, which is a statement,

- the *signature*, which specifies the procedure's formal arguments, result type, and raises set (the set of exceptions that the procedure can raise),

- the *environment*, which is the scope with respect to which variable names in the body will be interpreted.

---

[1]This restriction is lifted in unsafe modules.

A procedure that returns a result is called a *function procedure*; a procedure that does not return a result is called a *proper procedure*. A *top-level* procedure is a procedure declared in the outermost scope of a module. Any other procedure is a *local* procedure. A local procedure can be passed as a parameter but not assigned, since in a stack implementation a local procedure becomes invalid when the frame for the procedure containing it is popped.

A *procedure constant* is an identifier declared as a procedure. (As opposed to a procedure variable, which is a variable declared with a procedure type.)

A procedure type declaration has the form:

```
TYPE T = PROCEDURE sig
```

where `sig` is a signature specification, which has the form:

```
(formal₁; ...; formalₙ): R RAISES S
```

where

- Each `formal`$_i$ is a formal parameter declaration, as described below.

- `R` is the result type, which can be any type but an open array type. The ": R" can be omitted, making the signature that of a proper procedure.

- `S` is the raises set, which is either an explicit set of exceptions with the syntax $\{E_1, \ldots, E_n\}$, or the symbol `ANY` representing the set of all exceptions. If "RAISES S" is omitted, "RAISES {}" is assumed.

A formal parameter declaration has the form

```
Mode Name: Type := Default
```

where

- `Mode` is a parameter mode, which can be `VALUE`, `VAR`, or `READONLY`. If `Mode` is omitted, it defaults to `VALUE`.

- `Name` is an identifier that names the parameter. The parameter names must be distinct.

- `Type` is the type of the parameter.

- `Default` is a constant expression, the default value for the parameter. If `Mode` is `VAR`, ":= `Default`" must be omitted, otherwise either ":= `Default`" or ": `Type`" can be omitted, but not both. If `Type` is omitted, it is taken to be the type of `Default`. If both are present, the value of `Default` must be a member of `Type`.

When a series of parameters share the same mode, type, and default, name$_i$ can be a list of identifiers separated by commas. Such a list is shorthand for a list in which the mode, type, and default are repeated for each identifier. That is:

```
Mode v₁, ..., vₙ: Type := Default
```

is shorthand for:

```
Mode v₁: Type := Default; ...; Mode vₙ: Type := Default
```

This shorthand is eliminated from the expanded definition of the type. The default values are included.

A procedure value P is a member of the type T if it is NIL or its signature is *covered* by the signature of T, where signature₁ covers signature₂ if:

- They have the same number of parameters, and corresponding parameters have the same type and mode.

- They have the same result type, or neither has a result type.

- The raises set of signature₁ contains the raises set of signature₂.

The parameter names and defaults affect the type of a procedure, but not its value. For example, consider the declarations:

```
PROCEDURE P(txt: TEXT := "P") =
  BEGIN
    Wr.PutText(Stdio.stdout, txt)
  END P;

VAR q: PROCEDURE(txt: TEXT := "Q") := P;
```

Now P = q is TRUE, yet P() prints "P" and q() prints "Q". The interpretation of defaulted parameters is determined by a procedure's type, not its value; the assignment q := P changes q's value, not its type.

Examples of procedure types:

```
TYPE
  Integrand = PROCEDURE (x: REAL): REAL;
  Integrator = PROCEDURE(f: Integrand; lo, hi: REAL): REAL;
  TokenIterator = PROCEDURE(VAR t: Token) RAISES {TokenError};
  RenderProc = PROCEDURE(
    scene: REFANY;
    READONLY t: Transform := Identity)
```

In a procedure type, RAISES binds to the closest preceding PROCEDURE. That is, the parentheses are required in:

```
TYPE T = PROCEDURE (): (PROCEDURE ()) RAISES {}
```

2.2.9 Objects

An *object* is either NIL or a reference to a data record paired with a method suite, which is a record of procedures that will accept the object as a first argument.

An object type determines the types of a prefix of the fields of the data record, as if "OBJECT" were "REF RECORD". But in the case of an object type, the data record can contain additional fields introduced by subtypes of the object type. Similarly, the object type determines a prefix of the method suite, but the suite can contain additional methods introduced by subtypes.

If o is an object, then o.f designates the data field named f in o's data record. If m is one of o's methods, an invocation of the form o.m(...) denotes an execution of o's m method (Section 2.3.2). An object's methods can be invoked, but not read or written.

If T is an object type and m is the name of one of T's methods, then T.m denotes T's m method. This notation makes it convenient for a subtype method to invoke the corresponding method of one of its supertypes.

A field or method in a subtype masks any field or method with the same name in the supertype. To access such a masked field, use NARROW to view the subtype variable as a member of the supertype, as illustrated on page 23.

Object assignment is reference assignment. Objects cannot be dereferenced, since the static type of an object variable does not determine the type of its data record. To copy the data record of one object into another, the fields must be assigned individually.

There are two predeclared object types:

ROOT	The traced object type with no fields or methods
UNTRACED ROOT	The untraced object type with no fields or methods

The declaration of an object type has the form:

```
TYPE T =
  ST OBJECT Fields METHODS Methods OVERRIDES Overrides END
```

where ST is an optional supertype, Fields is a list of field declarations, exactly as in a record type, Methods is a list of *method declarations* and Overrides is a list of *method overrides*. The fields of T consist of the fields of ST followed by the fields declared in Fields. The methods of T consist of the methods of ST modified by Overrides and followed by the methods declared in Methods. T has the same reference class as ST.

The names introduced in Fields and Methods must be distinct from one another and from the names overridden in Overrides. If ST is omitted, it defaults to ROOT. If ST is untraced, then the fields must not include traced types.[2] If ST is declared as an opaque type

---

[2]This restriction is lifted in unsafe modules.

(Section 2.4.6, page 39), the declaration of T is legal only in scopes where ST's concrete type is known to be an object type.

The keyword OBJECT can optionally be preceded by "BRANDED" or by "BRANDED b", where b is a text literal. The meaning is the same as in non-object reference types.

A method declaration has the form:

```
m sig := proc
```

where m is an identifier, `sig` is a procedure signature, and `proc` is a top-level procedure constant. It specifies that T's m method has signature `sig` and value `proc`. If ":= proc" is omitted, ":= NIL" is assumed. If `proc` is non-nil, its first parameter must have mode VALUE and type some supertype of T, and dropping its first parameter must result in a signature that is covered by `sig`.

A method override has the form:

```
m := proc
```

where m is the name of a method of the supertype ST and `proc` is a top-level procedure constant. It specifies that the m method for T is proc, rather than ST.m. If `proc` is non-nil, its first parameter must have mode VALUE and type some supertype of T, and dropping its first parameter must result in a signature that is covered by the signature of ST's m method.

Examples. Consider the following declarations:

```
TYPE
  A = OBJECT a: INTEGER; METHODS p() END;
  AB = A OBJECT b: INTEGER END;

PROCEDURE Pa(self: A) = ... ;
PROCEDURE Pab(self: AB) = ... ;
```

The procedures Pa and Pab are candidate values for the p methods of objects of types A and AB. For example:

```
TYPE T1 = AB OBJECT OVERRIDES p := Pab END
```

declares a type with an AB data record and a p method that expects an AB. T1 is a valid subtype of AB. Similarly,

```
TYPE T2 = A OBJECT OVERRIDES p := Pa END
```

declares a type with an A data record and a method that expects an A. T2 is a valid subtype of A. A more interesting example is:

```
TYPE T3 = AB OBJECT OVERRIDES p := Pa END
```

which declares a type with an AB data record and a p method that expects an A. Since every AB is an A, the method is not too choosy for the objects in which it will be placed. T3 is a valid subtype of AB. In contrast,

```
TYPE T4 = A OBJECT OVERRIDES p := Pab END
```

attempts to declare a type with an A data record and a method that expects an AB; since not every A is an AB, the method is too choosy for the objects in which it would be placed. The declaration of T4 is a static error.

The following example illustrates the difference between declaring a new method and overriding an existing method. After the declarations

```
TYPE
  A = OBJECT METHODS m() := P END;
  B = A OBJECT OVERRIDES m := Q END;
  C = A OBJECT METHODS m() := Q END;

VAR
  a := NEW(A); b := NEW(B); c := NEW(C);
```

we have that

```
a.m() activates P(a)
b.m() activates Q(b)
c.m() activates Q(c)
```

So far there is no difference between overriding and extending. But c's method suite has two methods, while b's has only one, as can be revealed if b and c are viewed as members of type A:

```
NARROW(b, A).m() activates Q(b)
NARROW(c, A).m() activates P(c)
```

Here NARROW is used to view a variable of a subtype as a value of its supertype. It is more often used for the opposite purpose, when it requires a runtime check (see Section 2.6.13, page 57).

The last example uses object subtyping to define reusable queues. First the interface:

```
TYPE
  Queue = RECORD head, tail: QueueElem END;
  QueueElem = OBJECT link: QueueElem END;

PROCEDURE Insert(VAR q: Queue; x: QueueElem);
PROCEDURE Delete(VAR q: Queue): QueueElem;
PROCEDURE Clear(VAR q: Queue);
```

Then an example client:

```
TYPE
  IntQueueElem = QueueElem OBJECT val: INTEGER END;
VAR
  q: Queue;
  x: IntQueueElem;

  ...
  Clear(q);
  x := NEW(IntQueueElem, val := 6);
  Insert(q, x);
  ...
  x := Delete(q)
```

Passing x to Insert is safe, since every IntQueueElem is a QueueElem. Assigning the result of Delete to x cannot be guaranteed valid at compile-time, since other subtypes of QueueElem can be inserted into q, but the assignment will produce a checked runtime error if the source value is not a member of the target type. Thus IntQueueElem bears the same relation to QueueElem as [0..9] bears to INTEGER.

2.2.10 Subtyping rules

We write T <: U to indicate that T is a subtype of U and U is a supertype of T.

If T <: U, then every value of type T is also a value of type U. The converse does not hold: for example, a record or array type with packed fields contains the same values as the corresponding type with unpacked fields, but there is no subtype relation between them. This section presents the rules that define the subtyping relation.

```
[u..v] <: B            if u and v have base type B
[u..v] <: [u'..v']     if [u..v] is a (possibly empty) subset of [u'..v']
```

That is, subtyping on ordinal types reflects the subset relation on the value sets.

$$(\text{ARRAY OF})^m \text{ ARRAY } J_1 \text{ OF } \ldots \text{ ARRAY } J_n \text{ OF}$$
$$\text{ARRAY } K_1 \text{ OF } \ldots \text{ ARRAY } K_p \text{ OF T}$$
$$<: (\text{ARRAY OF})^m (\text{ARRAY OF})^n$$
$$\text{ARRAY } I_1 \text{ OF } \ldots \text{ ARRAY } I_p \text{ OF T}$$

if NUMBER(I_i) = NUMBER(K_i) for $i = 1, \ldots, p$.

That is, an array type A is a subtype of an array type A' if they have the same ultimate element type, the same number of dimensions, and, for each dimension, either both are open (as in the first m dimensions above), or A is fixed and A' is open (as in the next n dimensions above), or they are both fixed and have the same size (as in the last p dimensions above).

```
NULL <: REF T <: REFANY
NULL <: UNTRACED REF T <: ADDRESS
```

That is, REFANY and ADDRESS contain all traced and untraced references, respectively, and NIL is a member of every reference type. These rules also apply to branded types.

    NULL <: PROCEDURE(A): R RAISES S for any A, R, and S.

That is, NIL is a member of every procedure type.

    PROCEDURE(A): Q RAISES E <: PROCEDURE(B): R RAISES F
    if signature (B): R RAISES F   covers signature (A): Q RAISES E.

That is, for procedure types, T <: T′ if they are the same except for parameter names, defaults, and the raises set, and the raises set for T is contained in the raises set for T′.

    ROOT <: REFANY
    UNTRACED ROOT <: ADDRESS
    NULL <: T OBJECT ... END <: T

That is, every object is a reference, NIL is a member of every object type, and every subtype is included in its supertype. The third rule also applies to branded types.

    BITS n FOR T <: T and T <: BITS n FOR T

That is, BITS FOR T has the same values as T.

    T <: T for all T
    T <: U and U <: V implies T <: V for all T, U, V.

That is, <: is reflexive and transitive.

Note that T <: U and U <: T does not imply that T and U are the same, since the subtype relation is unaffected by parameter names, default values, and packing.

For example, consider:

    TYPE
      T = [0..255];
      U = BITS 8 FOR [0..255];
      AT = ARRAY OF T;
      AU = ARRAY OF U;

The types T and U are subtypes of one another but are not the same. The types AT and AU are unrelated by the subtype relation.

2.2.11 Predeclared opaque types

The language predeclares the two types:

    TEXT <: REFANY
    MUTEX <: ROOT

which represent text strings and mutual exclusion semaphores, respectively. These are opaque types as defined in Section 2.4.6, page 39. Their properties are specified in the required interfaces Text (Section 3.1) and Thread (Section 3.2).

2.3   Statements

> *Look into any carpenter's tool-bag and see how many different*
> *hammers, chisels, planes and screw-drivers he keeps there—not for*
> *ostentation or luxury, but for different sorts of jobs.*
> *—Robert Graves and Alan Hodge*

Executing a statement produces a computation that can halt (normal outcome), raise an exception, cause a checked runtime error, or loop forever. If the outcome is an exception, it can optionally be paired with an argument.

We define the semantics of EXIT and RETURN with exceptions called the *exit-exception* and the *return-exception*. The exit-exception takes no argument; the return-exception takes an argument of arbitrary type. Programs cannot name these exceptions explicitly.

Implementations should speed up normal outcomes at the expense of exceptions (except for the return-exception and exit-exception). Expending a thousand instructions per exception raised to save one instruction per procedure call would be reasonable.

If an expression is evaluated as part of the execution of a statement, and the evaluation raises an exception, then the exception becomes the outcome of the statement.

The empty statement is a no-op. In this report, empty statements are written (*skip*).

2.3.1   Assignment

To specify the typechecking of assignment statements we need to define "assignable", which is a relation between types and types, between expressions and variables, and between expressions and types.

A type T is *assignable* to a type U if:

- T <: U, or

- U <: T and T is an array or a reference type other than ADDRESS[3], or

- T and U are ordinal types with at least one member in common.

An expression e is *assignable* to a variable v if:

---

[3]This restriction is lifted in unsafe modules.

- the type of e is assignable to the type of v, and

- the value of e is a member of the type of v, is not a local procedure, and if it is an array, then it has the same shape as v.

The first point can be checked statically; the others generally require runtime checks. Since there is no way to determine statically whether the value of a procedure parameter is local or global, assigning a local procedure is a runtime rather than a static error.

An expression e is *assignable* to a type T if e is assignable to some variable of type T. (If T is not an open array type, this is the same as saying that e is assignable to any variable of type T.)

An assignment statement has the form:

```
v := e
```

where v is a writable designator and e is an expression assignable to the variable designated by v. The statement sets v to the value of e. The order of evaluation of v and e is undefined, but e will be evaluated before v is updated. In particular, if v and e are overlapping subarrays (Section 2.6.3, page 50), the assignment is performed in such a way that no element is used as a target before it is used as a source.

Examples of assignments:

```
VAR
    x: REFANY;
    a: REF INTEGER;
    b: REF BOOLEAN;

    a := b; (* static error *)
    x := a; (* no possible error *)
    a := x  (* possible checked runtime error *)
```

The same comments would apply if x had an ordinal type with non-overlapping subranges a and b, or if x had an object type and a and b had incompatible subtypes. The type ADDRESS is treated differently from other reference types, since a runtime check cannot be performed on the assignment of raw addresses. For example:

```
VAR
    x: ADDRESS;
    a: UNTRACED REF INTEGER;
    b: UNTRACED REF BOOLEAN;

    a := b; (* static error *)
    x := a; (* no possible error *)
    a := x  (* static error in safe modules *)
```

2.3.2 Procedure call

A procedure call has the form:

```
P(Bindings)
```

where P is a procedure-valued expression and `Bindings` is a list of *keyword* or *positional* bindings. A keyword binding has the form `name := actual`, where `actual` is an expression and `name` is an identifier. A positional binding has the form `actual`, where actual is an expression. When keyword and positional bindings are mixed in a call, the positional bindings must precede the keyword bindings. If the list of bindings is empty, the parentheses are still required.

The list of bindings is rewritten to fit the signature of P's type as follows: First, each positional binding `actual` is converted and added to the list of keyword bindings by supplying the name of the i'th formal parameter, where `actual` is the i'th binding in `Bindings`. Second, for each parameter that has a default and is not bound after the first step, the binding `name := default` is added to the list of bindings, where `name` is the name of the parameter and `default` is its default value. The rewritten list of bindings must bind only formal parameters and must bind each formal parameter exactly once. For example,, suppose that the type of P is

```
PROCEDURE(ch: CHAR; n: INTEGER := 0)
```

Then the following calls are all equivalent:

```
P('a', 0)
P('a')
P(ch := 'a')
P(n := 0, ch := 'a')
P('a', n := 0)
```

The call `P()` is illegal, since it doesn't bind ch. The call `P(n := 0, 'a')` is illegal, since it has a keyword parameter before a positional parameter.

For a READONLY or VALUE parameter, the actual can be any expression assignable to the type of the formal (except that the prohibition against assigning local procedures is relaxed). For a VAR parameter, the actual must be a writable designator whose type is the same as that of the formal, or, in case of a VAR array parameter, assignable to that of the formal.

A VAR formal is bound to the variable designated by the corresponding actual; that is, it is aliased. A VALUE formal is bound to a variable with an unused location and initialized to the value of the corresponding actual. A READONLY formal is treated as a VAR formal if the actual is a designator and the type of the actual is the same as the type of the formal (or an array type that is assignable to the type of the formal); otherwise it is treated as a VALUE formal.

Implementations are allowed to forbid VAR or READONLY parameters of packed types.

To execute the call, the procedure P and its arguments are evaluated, the formal parameters are bound, and the body of the procedure is executed. The order of evaluation of P and its actual arguments is undefined. It is a checked runtime error to call an undefined or NIL procedure.

It is a checked runtime error for a procedure to raise an exception not included in its raises set[4] or for a function procedure to fail to return a result.

A procedure call is a statement only if the procedure is proper. To call a function procedure and discard its result, use EVAL.

A procedure call can also have the form:

```
o.m(Bindings)
```

where o is an object and m names one of o's methods. This is equivalent to:

```
(o's m method) (o, Bindings)
```

2.3.3 Eval

An EVAL statement has the form:

```
EVAL e
```

where e is an expression. The effect is to evaluate e and ignore the result. For example:

```
EVAL Thread.Fork(p)
```

2.3.4 Block statement

A block statement has the form:

```
Decls BEGIN S END
```

where Decls is a sequence of declarations and S is a statement. The block introduces the constants, types, variables, and procedures declared in Decls and then executes S. The scope of the declared names is the block. (See Section 2.4, page 37.)

---

[4]If an implementation maps this runtime error into an exception, the exception is implicitly included in all RAISES clauses.

2.3.5 Sequential composition

A statement of the form:

S_1 ; S_2

executes S_1, and then if the outcome is normal, executes S_2. If the outcome of S_1 is an exception, S_2 is ignored.[5]

2.3.6 Raise

A RAISE statement without an argument has the form:

RAISE e

where e is an exception that takes no argument. The outcome of the statement is the exception e. A RAISE statement with an argument has the form:

RAISE e(x)

where e is an exception that takes an argument and x is an expression assignable to e's argument type. The outcome is the exception e paired with the argument x.

2.3.7 Try Except

A TRY-EXCEPT statement has the form:

```
TRY
  Body
EXCEPT
  id₁ (v₁) => Handler₁
| ...
| idₙ (vₙ) => Handlerₙ
ELSE Handler₀
END
```

where Body and each Handler are statements, each id names an exception, and each v_i is an identifier. The "ELSE Handler$_0$" and each "(v_i)" are optional. It is a static error for an exception to be named more than once in the list of id's.

The statement executes Body. If the outcome is normal, the except clause is ignored. If Body raises any listed exception id_i, then Handler$_i$ is executed. If Body raises any other exception and "ELSE Handler$_0$" is present, then it is executed. In either case, the outcome

---

[5]Some programmers use the semicolon as a statement terminator, some as a statement separator. Similarly, some use the vertical bar in case statements as a case initiator, some as a separator. Modula-3 allows both styles. This report uses both operators as separators.

of the TRY statement is the outcome of the selected handler. If Body raises an unlisted exception and "ELSE $Handler_0$" is absent, then the outcome of the TRY statement is the exception raised by Body.

Each (v_i) declares a variable whose type is the argument type of the exception id_i and whose scope is $Handler_i$. When an exception id_i paired with an argument x is handled, v_i is initialized to x before $Handler_i$ is executed. It is a static error to include (v_i) if exception id_i does not take an argument.

If (v_i) is absent, then id_i can be a list of exceptions separated by commas, as shorthand for a list in which the rest of the handler is repeated for each exception. That is:

```
id_1, ..., id_n => Handler
```

is shorthand for:

```
id_1 => Handler; ...; id_n => Handler
```

It is a checked runtime error to raise an exception outside the dynamic scope of a handler for that exception. A "TRY EXCEPT ELSE" counts as a handler for all exceptions.

2.3.8 Try Finally

A statement of the form:

```
TRY S_1 FINALLY S_2 END
```

executes statement S_1 and then statement S_2. If the outcome of S_1 is normal, the TRY statement is equivalent to S_1; S_2. If the outcome of S_1 is an exception and the outcome of S_2 is normal, the exception from S_1 is re-raised after S_2 is executed. If both outcomes are exceptions, the outcome of the TRY is the exception from S_2.

2.3.9 Loop

A statement of the form:

```
LOOP S END
```

repeatedly executes S until it raises the exit-exception. Informally it is like:

```
TRY S; S; S; ... EXCEPT exit-exception => (*skip*) END
```

2.3.10 Exit

The statement

```
EXIT
```

raises the exit-exception. An EXIT statement must be textually enclosed by a LOOP, WHILE, REPEAT, or FOR statement.

We define EXIT and RETURN in terms of exceptions in order to specify their interaction with the exception handling statements. As a pathological example, consider the following code, which is an elaborate infinite loop:

```
LOOP
  TRY
    TRY EXIT FINALLY RAISE E END
  EXCEPT
    E: (*skip*)
  END
END
```

2.3.11   Return

A RETURN statement for a proper procedure has the form:

```
RETURN
```

The statement raises the return-exception without an argument. It is allowed only in the body of a proper procedure.

A RETURN statement for a function procedure has the form:

```
RETURN Expr
```

where Expr is an expression assignable to the result type of the procedure. The statement raises the return-exception with the argument Expr. It is allowed only in the body of a function procedure.

Failure to return a value from a function procedure is a checked runtime error.

The effect of raising the return exception is to terminate the current procedure activation. To be precise, a call on a proper procedure with body B is equivalent (after binding the arguments) to:

```
TRY B EXCEPT return-exception => (*skip*) END
```

A call on a function procedure with body B is equivalent to:

```
TRY
    B; (error: no returned value)
EXCEPT
    return-exception (v) => (the result becomes v)
END
```

2.3.12   If

An IF statement has the form:

```
IF     B₁ THEN S₁
ELSIF B₂ THEN S₂
   ...
ELSIF Bₙ THEN Sₙ
ELSE S₀
END
```

where the B's are boolean expressions and the S's are statements. The "ELSE S_0" and each "ELSIF B_i THEN S_i" are optional.

The statement evaluates the B's in order until some B_i evaluates to TRUE, and then executes S_i. If none of the expressions evaluates to TRUE and "ELSE S_0" is present, S_0 is executed. If none of the expressions evaluates to TRUE and "ELSE S_0" is absent, the statement is a no-op (except for any side-effects of the B's).

2.3.13   While

If B is an expression of type BOOLEAN and S is a statement:

```
WHILE B DO S END
```

is shorthand for:

```
LOOP IF B THEN S ELSE EXIT END END
```

2.3.14   Repeat

If B is an expression of type BOOLEAN and S is a statement:

```
REPEAT S UNTIL B
```

is shorthand for:

```
LOOP S; IF B THEN EXIT END END
```

2.3.15   With

A WITH statement has the form:

```
WITH id = e DO S END
```

where id is an identifier, e an expression, and S a statement. The statement declares id with scope S as an alias for the variable e or as a readonly name for the value e. The expression e is evaluated once, at entry to the WITH statement.

The statement is like the procedure call P(e), where P is declared as:

```
PROCEDURE P(mode id: type of e) = BEGIN S END P;
```

If e is a writable designator, mode is VAR; otherwise, mode is READONLY. The only difference between the WITH statement and the call P(e) is that free variables, RETURNs, and EXITs that occur in the WITH statement are interpreted in the context of the WITH statement, not in the context of P.

A single WITH can contain multiple bindings, which are evaluated sequentially. That is: WITH id_1 = e_1, id_2 = e_2, ... is equivalent to: WITH id_1 = e_1 DO WITH id_2 = e_2 DO ....

2.3.16   For

A FOR statement has the form:

```
FOR id := first TO last BY step DO S END
```

where id is an identifier, first and last are ordinal expressions with the same base type, step is an integer-valued expression, and S is a statement. "BY step" is optional; if omitted, step defaults to 1.

The identifier id denotes a readonly variable whose scope is S and whose type is the common basetype of first and last.

If id is an integer, the statement steps id through the values first, first+step, first+2*step, ..., stopping when the value of id passes last. S executes once for each value; if the sequence of values is empty, S never executes. The expressions first, last, and step are evaluated once, before the loop is entered. If step is negative, the loop iterates downward.

The case in which id is an element of an enumeration is similar. In either case, the semantics are defined precisely by the following rewriting, in which T is the type of id and in which i, done, and delta stand for variables that do not occur in the FOR statement:

```
VAR
  i := ORD(first); done := ORD(last); delta := step;
BEGIN
  IF delta >= 0 THEN
    WHILE i <= done DO
      WITH id = VAL(i, T) DO S END; INC(i, delta)
    END
  ELSE
    WHILE i >= done DO
      WITH id = VAL(i, T) DO S END; INC(i, delta)
    END
  END
END
```

If the upper bound of the loop is LAST(INTEGER), it should be rewritten as a WHILE loop to avoid overflow.

2.3.17 Case

A CASE statement has the form:

```
CASE Expr OF
  L_1 => S_1
| ...
| L_n => S_n
ELSE S_0
END
```

where Expr is an expression whose type is an ordinal type and each L is a list of constant expressions or ranges of constant expressions denoted by "$e_1..e_2$", which represent the values from e_1 to e_2 inclusive. If e_1 exceeds e_2, the range is empty. It is a static error if the sets represented by any two L's overlap or if the value of any of the constant expressions is not a member of the type of Expr. The "ELSE S_0" is optional.

The statement evaluates Expr. If the resulting value is in any L_i, then S_i is executed. If the value is in no L_i and "ELSE S_0" is present, then it is executed. If the value is in no L_i and "ELSE S_0" is absent, a checked runtime error occurs.

2.3.18 Typecase

A TYPECASE statement has the form:

```
TYPECASE Expr OF
  T_1 (v_1) => S_1
| ...
| T_n (v_n) => S_n
ELSE S_0
END
```

where Expr is an expression whose type is a reference type, the S's are statements, the T's are reference types, and the v's are identifiers. It is a static error if Expr has type ADDRESS or if any T is not a subtype of the type of Expr. The "ELSE S_0" and each "(v)" are optional.

The statement evaluates Expr. If the resulting reference value is a member of any listed type T_i, then S_i is executed, for the minimum such i. (Thus a NULL case is useful only if it comes first.) If the value is a member of no listed type and "ELSE S_0" is present, then it is executed. If the value is a member of no listed type and "ELSE S_0" is absent, a checked runtime error occurs.

Each (v_i) declares a variable whose type is T_i and whose scope is S_i. If v_i is present, it is initialized to the value of Expr before S_i is executed.

If (v_i) is absent, then T_i can be a list of type expressions separated by commas, as shorthand for a list in which the rest of the branch is repeated for each type expression. That is:

```
T₁, ..., Tₙ => S
```

is shorthand for:

```
T₁ => S | ... | Tₙ => S
```

For example:

```
PROCEDURE ToText(r: REFANY): TEXT =
    (* Assume r = NIL or r^ is a BOOLEAN or INTEGER. *)
  BEGIN
    TYPECASE r OF
      NULL => RETURN "NIL"
    | REF BOOLEAN (rb) => RETURN Fmt.Bool(rb^)
    | REF INTEGER (ri) => RETURN Fmt.Int(ri^)
    END
  END ToText;
```

2.3.19   Lock

A LOCK statement has the form:

```
LOCK mu DO S END
```

where S is a statement and mu is an expression whose type is MUTEX. It is equivalent to:

```
WITH m = mu DO
  Thread.Acquire(m);
  TRY S FINALLY Thread.Release(m) END
END
```

where m stands for a variable that does not occur in S. (The Thread interface is presented in Section 3.2, page 69.)

2.3.20   Inc and Dec

INC and DEC statements have the form:

```
INC(v, n)
DEC(v, n)
```

where v designates a variable of an ordinal type[6] and n is an optional integer-valued argument. If omitted, n defaults to 1. The statements increment and decrement v by n, respectively. The statements are equivalent to:

```
WITH x = v DO x := VAL(ORD(x) + n, T) END
WITH x = v DO x := VAL(ORD(x) - n, T) END
```

where T is the type of v and x stands for a variable that does not appear in n. As a consequence, the statements check for range errors.

2.4 Declarations

> *There are two basic methods of declaring high or low before the showdown in all High-Low Poker games. They are (1) simultaneous declarations, and (2) consecutive declarations .... It is a sad but true fact that the consecutive method spoils the game.*
> *—John Scarne's Guide to Modern Poker*

A declaration introduces a name for a constant, type, variable, exception, or procedure. The scope of the name is the block containing the declaration. A block has the form:

```
Decls BEGIN S END
```

where Decls is a sequence of declarations and S is a statement, the executable part of the block. A block can appear as a statement or as the body of a module or procedure. The declarations of a block can introduce a name at most once, though a name can be redeclared in nested blocks, and a procedure declared in an interface can be redeclared in a module exporting the interface (Section 2.5, page 41). The order of declarations in a block does not matter, except to determine the order of initialization of variables.

2.4.1 Types

If T is an identifier and U a type (or type expression, since a type expression is allowed wherever a type is required), then:

```
TYPE T = U
```

declares T to be the type U.

2.4.2 Constants

If id is an identifier, T a type, and C a constant expression, then:

---

[6]In unsafe modules, INC and DEC are extended to ADDRESS.

```
CONST id: T = C
```

declares id as a constant with the type T and the value of C. The ": T" can be omitted, in which case the type of id is the type of C. If T is present it must contain C.

2.4.3 Variables

If id is an identifier, T a non-empty type other than an open array type, and E an expression, then:

```
VAR id: T := E
```

declares id as a variable of type T whose initial value is the value of E. Either ":= E" or ": T" can be omitted, but not both. If T is omitted, it is taken to be the type of E. If E is omitted, the initial value is an arbitrary value of type T. If both are present, E must be assignable to T.

The initial value is a shorthand that is equivalent to inserting the assignment id := E at the beginning of the executable part of the block. If several variables have initial values, their assignments are inserted in the order they are declared. For example:

```
VAR i: [0..5] := j; j: [0..5] := i; BEGIN S END
```

initializes i and j to the same arbitrary value in [0..5]; it is equivalent to:

```
VAR i: [0..5]; j: [0..5]; BEGIN i := j; j := i; S END
```

If a sequence of identifiers share the same type and initial value, id can be a list of identifiers separated by commas. Such a list is shorthand for a list in which the type and initial value are repeated for each identifier. That is:

```
VAR v₁, ..., vₙ: T := E
```

is shorthand for:

```
VAR v₁: T := E; ...; VAR vₙ: T := E
```

This means that E is evaluated n times.

2.4.4 Procedures

There are two forms of procedure declaration:

```
PROCEDURE id sig = B id

PROCEDURE id sig
```

where id is an identifier, sig is a procedure signature, and B is a block. In both cases, the type of id is the procedure type determined by sig. The first form is allowed only in modules; the second form is allowed only in interfaces.

The first form declares id as a procedure constant whose signature is sig, whose body is B, and whose environment is the scope containing the declaration. The parameter names are treated as if they were declared at the outer level of B; the parameter types and default values are evaluated in the scope containing the procedure declaration. The procedure name id must be repeated after the END that terminates the body.

The second form declares id to be a procedure constant whose signature is sig. The procedure body is specified in a module exporting the interface, by a declaration of the first form.

2.4.5 Exceptions

If id is an identifier and T a type other than an open array type, then:

        EXCEPTION id(T)

declares id as an exception with argument type T. If "(T)" is omitted, the exception takes no argument. An exception declaration is allowed only in an interface or in the outermost scope of a module. All declared exceptions are distinct.

2.4.6 Opaque types

An *opaque type* is a name that denotes an unknown subtype of some given reference type. For example, an opaque subtype of REFANY is an unknown traced reference type; an opaque subtype of UNTRACED ROOT is an unknown untraced object type. The actual type denoted by an opaque type name is called its *concrete type*.

Different scopes can reveal different information about an opaque type. For example, what is known in one scope only to be a subtype of REFANY could be known in another scope to be a subtype of ROOT.

An opaque type declaration has the form:

        TYPE T <: U

where T is an identifier and U an expression denoting a reference type. It introduces the name T as an opaque type and reveals that U is a supertype of T. The concrete type of T must be revealed elsewhere in the program.

2.4.7   Revelations

A *revelation* introduces information about an opaque type into a scope. Unlike other declarations, revelations introduce no new names.

There are two kinds of revelations, *partial* and *complete*. A program can contain any number of partial revelations for an opaque type; it must contain exactly one complete revelation.

A partial revelation has the form:

    REVEAL T <: V

where V is a type expression (possibly just a name) and T is an identifier (possibly qualified, as on page 42) declared as an opaque type. It reveals that V is a supertype of T.

In any scope, the revealed supertypes of an opaque type must be linearly ordered by the subtype relation. That is, if it is revealed that T <: U1 and T <: U2, it must also be revealed either that U1 <: U2 or that U2 <: U1.

A complete revelation has the form:

    REVEAL T = V

where V is a type expression (not just a name) whose outermost type constructor is a branded reference or object type and T is an identifier (possibly qualified) that has been declared as an opaque type. The revelation specifies that V is the concrete type for T. It is a static error if any type revealed in any scope as a supertype of T is not a supertype of V. Generally this error is detected at link time.

Distinct opaque types have distinct concrete types, since V includes a brand and all brands in a program are distinct.

A revelation is allowed only in an interface or in the outermost scope of a module. A revelation in an interface can be imported into any scope where it is required, as illustrated by the stack example on page 44.

For example, consider:

    INTERFACE I; TYPE T <: ROOT; PROCEDURE P(x:T): T; END I.

    INTERFACE IClass; IMPORT I; REVEAL I.T <: MUTEX; END IClass.

    INTERFACE IRep; IMPORT I;
      REVEAL I.T = MUTEX BRANDED OBJECT count: INTEGER END;
    END IRep.

An importer of I sees I.T as an opaque subtype of ROOT, and is limited to allocating objects of type I.T, passing them to I.P, or declaring subtypes of I.T. An importer of IClass sees that every I.T is a MUTEX, and can therefore lock objects of type I.T. Finally, an importer of IRep sees the concrete type, and can access the count field.

2.4.8 Recursive declarations

A constant, type, or procedure declaration N = E, a variable declaration N : E, an exception declaration N(E), or a revelation N = E is *recursive* if N occurs in any partial expansion of E. A variable declaration N := I where the type is omitted is recursive if N occurs in any partial expansion of the type E of I. Such declarations are allowed if every occurrence of N in any partial expansion of E is (1) within some occurrence of the type constructor REF or PROCEDURE, (2) within a field or method type of the type constructor OBJECT, or (3) within a procedure body.

Examples of legal recursive declarations:

```
TYPE
  List = REF RECORD x: REAL; link: List END;
  T = PROCEDURE(n: INTEGER; p: T);
  XList = X OBJECT link: XList END;
CONST N = BYTESIZE(REF ARRAY [0..N] OF REAL);
PROCEDURE P(b: BOOLEAN) = BEGIN IF b THEN P(NOT b) END END P;
EXCEPTION E(PROCEDURE () RAISES {E});
VAR v: REF ARRAY [0..BYTESIZE(v)] OF INTEGER;
```

Examples of illegal recursive declarations:

```
TYPE
  T = RECORD x: T END;
  U = OBJECT METHODS m() := U.m END;
CONST N = N+1;
REVEAL I.T = I.T BRANDED OBJECT END;
VAR v := P(); PROCEDURE P(): ARRAY [0..LAST(v)] OF T;
```

Examples of legal non-recursive declarations:

```
VAR n := BITSIZE(n);
REVEAL T <: T;
```

2.5 Modules and interfaces

> *Art, it seems to me, should simplify. That, indeed, is very nearly the whole of the higher artistic process; finding what conventions of form and what detail one can do without and yet preserve the spirit of the whole.*
> —*Willa Cather*

A *module* is like a block, except for the visibility of names. An entity is visible in a block if it is declared in the block or in some enclosing block; an entity is visible in a module if it is declared in the module or in an interface that is imported or exported by the module.

An *interface* is a group of declarations. Declarations in interfaces are the same as in blocks, except that any variable initializations must be constant, and procedure declarations must specify only the signature, not the body.

A module X *exports* an interface I to supply bodies for one or more of the procedures declared in the interface. A module or interface X *imports* an interface I to make the entities declared in I visible in X.

A *program* is a collection of modules and interfaces that contains every interface imported or exported by any of its modules or interfaces, and in which no procedure, module, or interface is multiply defined. The effect of executing a program is to execute the bodies of each of its modules. The order of execution of the modules is constrained by the initialization rule on page 47.

The module whose body is executed last is called the *main module*. Implementations are expected to provide a way to specify the main module, in case the initialization rule does not determine it uniquely. The recommended rule is that the main module be the one that exports the interface Main, whose contents are implementation-dependent.

Program execution terminates when the body of the main module terminates, even if concurrent threads of control are still executing.

The names of the modules and interfaces of a program are called *global* names. The method for looking up global names—for example, by file system search paths—is implementation-dependent.

2.5.1 Import statements

There are two forms of import statements. All imports of both forms are interpreted simultaneously: their order doesn't matter.

The first form is

```
IMPORT I AS J
```

which imports the interface whose global name is I and gives it the local name J. The entities and revelations declared in I become accessible in the importing module or interface, but the entities and revelations imported into I do not. To refer to the entity declared with name N in the interface I, the importer must use the *qualified identifier* J.N.

The statement IMPORT I is short for IMPORT I AS I.

The second form is

```
FROM I IMPORT N
```

which introduces N as the local name for the entity declared as N in the interface I. A local binding for I takes precedence over a global binding. For example,

```
IMPORT I AS J, J AS I; FROM I IMPORT N
```

simultaneously introduces local names J, I, and N for the entities whose global names are
I, J, and J.N, respectively.

It is illegal to use the same local name twice:

```
IMPORT J AS I, K AS I;
```

is a static error, and would be even if J and K were the same.

2.5.2 Interfaces

An interface has the form:

```
INTERFACE id; Imports; Decls END id.
```

where id is an identifier that names the interface, Imports is a sequence of import
statements, and Decls is a sequence of declarations that contains no procedure bodies
or non-constant variable initializations. The names declared in Decls and the visible
imported names must be distinct. It is a static error for two or more interfaces to form an
import cycle.

2.5.3 Modules

A module has the form:

```
MODULE id EXPORTS Interfaces; Imports; Block id.
```

where id is an identifier that names the module, Interfaces is a list of distinct names of
interfaces exported by the module, Imports is a list of import statements, and Block is a
block, the *body* of the module. The name id must be repeated after the END that terminates
the body. "EXPORTS Interfaces" can be omitted, in which case Interfaces defaults
to id.

If module M exports interface I, then all declared names in I are visible without qualification
in M. Any procedure declared in I can be redeclared in M, with a body. The signature in M
must be covered by the signature in I (as defined in Section 2.2.8, page 18.) To determine
the interpretation of keyword bindings in calls to the procedure, the signature in M is used
within M; the signature in I is used everywhere else.

Except for the redeclaration of exported procedures, the names declared at the top level
of Block, the visible imported names, and the names declared in the exported interfaces
must be distinct.

For example, the following is illegal, since two names in exported interfaces coincide:

```
INTERFACE I;          INTERFACE J;          MODULE M EXPORTS I, J;
  PROCEDURE X();        PROCEDURE X();          PROCEDURE X() = ...;
```

The following is also illegal, since the visible imported name X coincides with the top-level name X:

```
INTERFACE I;          MODULE M EXPORTS I; FROM I IMPORT X;
  PROCEDURE X();        PROCEDURE X() = ...;
```

But the following is legal, although peculiar:

```
INTERFACE I;          MODULE M EXPORTS I; IMPORT I;
  PROCEDURE X(...);      PROCEDURE X(...) = ...;
```

since the only visible imported name is I, and the coincidence between X as a top-level name and X as a name in an exported interface is allowed, assuming the interface signature covers the module signature. Within M, the interface declaration determines the signature of I.X and the module declaration determines the signature of X.

2.5.4 Example module and interface

Here is the canonical example of a public stack with hidden representation:

```
INTERFACE Stack;
  TYPE T <: REFANY;
  PROCEDURE Create(): T;
  PROCEDURE Push(VAR s: T; x: REAL);
  PROCEDURE Pop(VAR s: T): REAL;
END Stack.

MODULE Stack;
  REVEAL T = BRANDED OBJECT item: REAL; link: T END;
  PROCEDURE Create(): T = BEGIN RETURN NIL END Create;
  PROCEDURE Push(VAR s: T; x: REAL) =
    BEGIN
      s := NEW(T, item := x, link := s)
    END Push;
  PROCEDURE Pop(VAR s: T): REAL =
    VAR res: REAL;
    BEGIN
      res := s.item; s := s.link; RETURN res
    END Pop;
BEGIN
END Stack.
```

If the representation of stacks is required in more than one module, it should be moved to a private interface, so that it can be imported wherever it is required:

```
INTERFACE Stack (* ... as before ... *) END Stack.

INTERFACE StackRep; IMPORT Stack;
   REVEAL Stack.T = BRANDED OBJECT item: REAL; link: Stack.T END
END StackRep.

MODULE Stack; IMPORT StackRep;
   (* Push, Pop, and Create as before *)
BEGIN
END Stack.
```

2.5.5   Generics

In a generic interface or module, some of the imported interface names are treated as formal parameters, to be bound to actual interfaces when the generic is instantiated.

A generic interface has the form

```
GENERIC INTERFACE G(F₁, ..., Fₙ); Body END G.
```

where G is an identifier that names the generic interface, $F_1, \ldots, F_n$ is a list of identifiers, called the formal imports of G, and Body is a sequence of imports followed by a sequence of declarations, exactly as in a non-generic interface.

An instance of G has the form

```
INTERFACE I = G(A₁, ..., Aₙ) END I.
```

where I is the name of the instance and $A_1, \ldots, A_n$ is a list of actual interfaces to which the formal imports of G are bound. The instance I is equivalent to an ordinary interface defined as follows:

```
INTERFACE I; IMPORT A₁ AS F₁, ..., Aₙ AS Fₙ; Body END I.
```

A generic module has the form

```
GENERIC MODULE G(F₁, ..., Fₙ); Body END G.
```

where G is an identifier that names the generic module, $F_1, \ldots, F_n$ is a list of identifiers, called the formal imports of G, and Body is a sequence of imports followed by a block, exactly as in a non-generic module.

An instance of G has the form

```
MODULE I EXPORTS E = G(A₁, ..., Aₙ) END I.
```

where I is the name of the instance, E is a list of interfaces exported by I, and $A_1, \ldots, A_n$ is a list of actual interfaces to which the formal imports of G are bound. "EXPORTS E" can be omitted, in which case it defaults to "EXPORTS I". The instance I is equivalent to an ordinary module defined as follows:

```
MODULE I EXPORTS E; IMPORT A₁ AS F₁, ..., Aₙ AS Fₙ; Body END I.
```

Notice that the generic module itself has no exports; they are supplied only when it is instantiated.

For example, here is a generic stack package:

```
GENERIC INTERFACE Stack(Elem);
  (* Stacks of Elem.T, which can be any type
     except an open array type. *)
  TYPE T <: REFANY;
  PROCEDURE Create(): T;
  PROCEDURE Push(VAR s: T; x: Elem.T);
  PROCEDURE Pop(VAR s: T): Elem.T;
END Stack.


GENERIC MODULE Stack(Elem);

  REVEAL
    T = BRANDED OBJECT n: INTEGER; a: REF ARRAY OF Elem.T END;

  PROCEDURE Create(): T = BEGIN RETURN NEW(T, 0, NIL) END Create;

  PROCEDURE Push(VAR s: T; x: Elem.T) =
    BEGIN
      IF s.a = NIL THEN
        s.a := NEW(REF ARRAY OF Elem.T, 5)
      ELSIF s.n > LAST(s.a^) THEN
        WITH temp = NEW(REF ARRAY OF Elem.T, 2 * NUMBER(s.a^)) DO
          FOR i := 0 TO LAST(s.a^) DO temp[i] := s.a[i] END;
          s.a := temp
        END
      END;
      s.a[s.n] := x;
      INC(s.n)
    END Push;

  PROCEDURE Pop(VAR s: T): Elem.T =
    BEGIN DEC(s.n); RETURN s.a[s.n] END Pop;

  BEGIN END Stack.
```

To instantiate these generics to produce stacks of integers:

```
INTERFACE Integer; TYPE T = INTEGER END Integer.
INTERFACE IntStack = Stack(Integer) END IntStack.
MODULE IntStack = Stack(Integer) END IntStack.
```

Implementations are not expected to share code between different instances of a generic module, since this will not be possible in general.

Implementations are not required to typecheck uninstantiated generics, but they must typecheck their instances. For example, if one made the following mistake:

```
INTERFACE String; TYPE T = ARRAY OF CHAR END String.
INTERFACE StringStack = Stack(String) END StringStack.
MODULE StringStack = Stack(String) END StringStack.
```

everything would go well until the last line, when the compiler would attempt to compile a version of Stack in which the element type was an open array. It would then complain that the NEW call in Push does not have enough parameters.

2.5.6 Initialization

The order of execution of the modules in a program is constrained by the following rule:

If module M depends on module N and N does not depend on M, then N's body will be executed before M's body, where:

- A module M *depends on* a module N if M uses an interface that N exports or if M depends on a module that depends on N.

- A module M *uses* an interface I if M imports or exports I or if M uses an interface that imports I.

Except for this constraint, the order of execution is implementation-dependent.

2.5.7 Safety

The keyword UNSAFE can precede the declaration of any interface or module to indicate that it is *unsafe*; that is, uses the unsafe features of the language (Section 2.7, page 59). An interface or module not explicitly labeled UNSAFE is called *safe*.

An interface is *intrinsically safe* if there is no way to produce an unchecked runtime error by using the interface in a safe module. If all modules that export a safe interface are safe, the compiler guarantees the intrinsic safety of the interface. If any of the modules that export a safe interface are unsafe, it is the programmer, rather than the compiler, who makes the guarantee.

It is a static error for a safe interface to import an unsafe one or for a safe module to import or export an unsafe interface.

2.6   Expressions

> *The rules of logical syntax must follow of themselves,*
> *if we only know how every single sign signifies.*
> —*Ludwig Wittgenstein*

An expression prescribes a computation that produces a value or variable. Syntactically, an expression is either an operand, or an operation applied to arguments, which are themselves expressions. Operands are identifiers, literals, or types. An expression is evaluated by recursively evaluating its arguments and performing the operation. The order of argument evaluation is undefined for all operations except AND and OR.

2.6.1   Conventions for describing operations

To describe the argument and result types of operations, we use a notation like procedure signatures. But since most operations are too general to be described by a true procedure signature, we extend the notation in several ways.

The argument to an operation can be required to have a type in a particular class, such as an ordinal type, set type, etc. In this case the formal specifies a type class instead of a type. For example:

```
ORD (x: Ordinal): INTEGER
```

The formal type Any specifies an argument of any type.

A single operation name can be overloaded, which means that it denotes more than one operation. In this case, we write a separate signature for each of the operations. For example:

```
ABS (x: INTEGER)   : INTEGER
    (x: Float)     : Float
```

The particular operation will be selected so that each actual argument type is a subtype of the corresponding formal type or a member of the corresponding formal type class.

The argument to an operation can be an expression denoting a type. In this case, we write Type as the argument type. For example:

```
BYTESIZE (T: Type): CARDINAL
```

The result type of an operation can depend on its argument values (although the result type can always be determined statically). In this case, the expression for the result type contains the appropriate arguments. For example:

```
FIRST (T: FixedArrayType): IndexType(T)
```

`IndexType(T)` denotes the index type of the array type `T` and `IndexType(a)` denotes the index type of the array `a`. The definitions of `ElemType(T)` and `ElemType(a)` are similar.

2.6.2 Operation syntax

The operators that have special syntax are classified and listed in order of decreasing binding power in the following table:

`x.a`	infix dot
`f(x)  a[i]  T{x}`	applicative (, [, {
`p^`	postfix ^
`+ -`	prefix arithmetics
`* / DIV MOD`	infix arithmetics
`+ - &`	infix arithmetics
`= # < <= >= > IN`	infix relations
`NOT`	prefix NOT
`AND`	infix AND
`OR`	infix OR

All infix operators are left associative. Parentheses can be used to override the precedence rules. Here are some examples of expressions together with their fully parenthesized forms:

`M.F(x)`	`(M.F)(x)`	dot before application
`Q(x)^`	`(Q(x))^`	application before ^
`- p^`	`- (p^)`	^ before prefix -
`- a * b`	`(- a) * b`	prefix - before *
`a * b - c`	`(a * b) - c`	* before infix -
`x IN s - t`	`x IN (s - t)`	infix - before IN
`NOT x IN s`	`NOT (x IN s)`	IN before NOT
`NOT p AND q`	`(NOT p) AND q`	NOT before AND
`A OR B AND C`	`A OR (B AND C)`	AND before OR

Operators without special syntax are *procedural*. An application of a procedural operator has the form `op(args)`, where `op` is the operation and `args` is the list of argument expressions. For example, `MAX` and `MIN` are procedural operators.

2.6.3 Designators

An identifier is a writable designator if it is declared as a variable, is a `VAR` or `VALUE` parameter, is a local of a `TYPECASE` or `TRY EXCEPT` statement, or is a `WITH` local that is bound to a writable designator. An identifier is a readonly designator if it is a `READONLY` parameter, a local of a `FOR` statement, or a `WITH` local bound to a non-designator or readonly designator.

The only operations that produce designators are dereferencing, subscripting, selection, and SUBARRAY.[7] This section defines these operations and specifies the conditions under which they produce designators.

r^   denotes the the referent of r; this operation is called *dereferencing*. The expression r^ is always a writable designator. It is a static error if the type of r is REFANY, ADDRESS, NULL, an object type, or an opaque type, and a checked runtime error if r is NIL. The type of r^ is the referent type of r.

a[i]   denotes the $(i + 1 - \texttt{FIRST(a)})^{\text{th}}$ element of the array a. The expression a[i] is a designator if a is, and is writable if a is. The expression i must be assignable to the index type of a. The type of a[i] is the element type of a.

An expression of the form a[i_1, ..., i_n] is shorthand for a[i_1]...[i_n]. If a is a reference to an array, then a[i] is shorthand for a^[i].

r.f, o.f, I.x, T.m, E.id

If r denotes a record, r.f denotes its f field. In this case r.f is a designator if r is, and is writable if r is. The type of r.f is the declared type of the field.

If r is a reference to a record, then r.f is shorthand for r^.f.

If o denotes an object and f names a data field specified in the type of o, then o.f denotes that data field of o. In this case o.f is a writable designator whose type is the declared type of the field.

If I denotes an imported interface, then I.x denotes the entity named x in the interface I. In this case I.x is a designator if x is declared as a variable; such a designator is always writable.

If T is an object type and m is the name of one of T's methods, then T.m denotes the m method of type T. In this case T.m is not a designator. Its type is the procedure type whose first argument has mode VALUE and type T, and whose remaining arguments are determined by the method declaration for m in T. The name of the first argument is unspecified; thus in calls to T.m, this argument must be given positionally, not by keyword. T.m is a procedure constant.

If E is an enumerated type, then E.id denotes its value named id. In this case E.id is not a designator. The type of E.id is E.

SUBARRAY(a: Array; from, for: CARDINAL): ARRAY OF ElemType(a)

SUBARRAY produces a subarray of a. It does not copy the array; it is a designator if a is, and is writable if a is. If a is a multi-dimensional array, SUBARRAY applies only to the top-level array.

---

[7]In unsafe modules, LOOPHOLE can also produce a designator.

The operation returns the subarray that skips the first from elements of a and contains the next for elements. Note that if from is zero, the subarray is a prefix of a, whether the type of a is zero-based or not. It is a checked runtime error if from+for exceeds NUMBER(a).

Implementations may restrict or prohibit the SUBARRAY operation for arrays with packed element types.

2.6.4 Numeric literals

Numeric literals denote constant non-negative integers or reals. The types of these literals are INTEGER, REAL, LONGREAL, and EXTENDED.

A literal INTEGER has the form base_digits, where base is one of "2", "3", ..., "16", and digits is a non-empty sequence of the decimal digits 0 through 9 plus the hexadecimal digits A through F. The "base_" can be omitted, in which case base defaults to 10. The digits are interpreted in the given base. Each digit must be less than base. For example, 16_FF and 255 are equivalent integer literals.

If no explicit base is present, the value of the literal must be at most LAST(INTEGER). If an explicit base is present, the value of the literal must be less than $2^{\text{Word.Size}}$, and its interpretation uses the convention of the Word interface (page 71). For example, on a sixteen-bit two's complement machine, 16_FFFF and −1 represent the same value.

A literal REAL has the form decimal E exponent, where decimal is a non-empty sequence of decimal digits followed by a decimal point followed by a non-empty sequence of decimal digits, and exponent is a non-empty sequence of decimal digits optionally beginning with a + or −. The literal denotes decimal times 10^{exponent}. If "E exponent" is omitted, exponent defaults to 0.

LONGREAL and EXTENDED literals are like REAL literals, but instead of E they use D and X respectively.

Case is not significant in digits, prefixes or scale factors. Embedded spaces are not allowed.

For example, 1.0 and 0.5 are valid, 1. and .5 are not; 6.624E-27 is a REAL, and 3.1415926535d0 a LONGREAL.

2.6.5 Text and character literals

A character literal is a pair of single quotes enclosing either a single ISO-Latin-1 printing character (excluding single quote) or an escape sequence. The type of a character literal is CHAR.

A text literal is a pair of double quotes enclosing a sequence of ISO-Latin-1 printing characters (excluding double quote) and escape sequences. The type of a text literal is TEXT.

Here are the legal escape sequences and the characters they denote:

\n	newline (linefeed)	\f	form feed
\t	tab	\\	backslash
\r	carriage return	\"	double quote
\'	single quote	\nnn	char with code 8_nnn

A \ followed by exactly three octal digits specifies the character whose code is that octal value. A \ that is not a part of one of these escape sequences is a static error.

For example, 'a' and '\'' are valid character literals, ''' is not; "" and "Don't\n" are valid text literals, """ is not.

2.6.6 Nil

The literal "NIL" denotes the value NIL. Its type is NULL.

2.6.7 Function application

A procedure call is an expression if the procedure returns a result. The type of the expression is the result type of the procedure.

2.6.8 Set, array, and record constructors

A set constructor has the form:

```
S{e₁, ..., eₙ}
```

where S is a set type and the e's are expressions or ranges of the form lo..hi. The constructor denotes a value of type S containing the listed values and the values in the listed ranges. The e's, lo's, and hi's must be assignable to the element type of S.

An array constructor has the form:

```
A{e₁, ..., eₙ}
```

where A is an array type and the e's are expressions. The constructor denotes a value of type A containing the listed elements in the listed order. The e's must be assignable to the element type of A. This means that if A is a multi-dimensional array, the e's must themselves be array-valued expressions.

If A is a fixed array type and n is at least 1, then e_n can be followed by ", .." to indicate that the value of e_n will be replicated as many times as necessary to fill out the array. It is a static error to provide too many or too few elements for a fixed array type.

A record constructor has the form:

    R{Bindings}

where R is a record type and `Bindings` is a list of keyword or positional bindings, exactly as in a procedure call (Section 2.3.2). The list of bindings is rewritten to fit the list of fields and defaults of R, exactly as for a procedure call; the record field names play the role of the procedure formal parameters. The expression denotes a value of type R whose field values are specified by the rewritten binding.

The rewritten binding must bind only field names and must bind each field name exactly once. Each expression in the binding must be assignable to the type of the corresponding record field.

2.6.9 New

An allocation operation has the form:

    NEW(T, ...)

where T is a reference type other than REFANY, ADDRESS, or NULL. The operation returns the address of a newly-allocated variable of T's referent type; or if T is an object type, a newly-allocated data record paired with a method suite. The reference returned by NEW is distinct from all existing references. The allocated type of the new reference is T.

It is a static error if T's referent type is empty. If T is declared as an opaque type, NEW(T) is legal only in scopes where T's concrete type is known completely, or is known to be an object type.

The initial state of the referent generally represents an arbitrary value of its type. If T is an object type or a reference to a record or open array then NEW takes additional arguments to control the initial state of the new variable.

If T is a reference to an array with k open dimensions, the NEW operation has the form:

    NEW(T, n_1, ..., n_k)

where the n's are integer-valued expressions that specify the lengths of the new array in its first k dimensions. The values in the array will be arbitrary values of their type.

If T is an object type or a reference to a record, the NEW operation has the form:

    NEW(T, Bindings)

where `Bindings` is a list of keyword bindings used to initialize the new fields. Positional bindings are not allowed.

Each binding f := v initializes the field f to the value v. Fields for which no binding is supplied will be initialized to their defaults if they have defaults; otherwise they will be initialized to arbitrary values of their types.

If T is an object type then Bindings can also include method overrides of the form m := P, where m is a method of T and P is a top-level procedure constant. This is syntactic sugar for the allocation of a subtype of T that includes the given overrides. For example, NEW(T, m := P) is sugar for NEW(T OBJECT OVERRIDES m := P END).

The order of the bindings and overrides makes no difference.

2.6.10 Arithmetic operations

The basic arithmetic operations are built into the language; additional operations are provided by the required interfaces in Section 3.4.

To test or set the implementation's behavior for overflow, underflow, rounding, and division by zero, see the required interface FloatMode (page 75). Modula-3 arithmetic was designed to support the IEEE floating-point standard, but not to require it.

To perform arithmetic operations modulo the word size, programs should use the routines in the required interface Word (Section 3.3).

Implementations must not rearrange the computation of expressions in a way that could affect the result. For example, (x+y)+z generally cannot be computed as x+(y+z), since addition is not associative either for bounded integers or for floating-point values.

```
prefix     +   (x: INTEGER)      : INTEGER
           +   (x: Float)        : Float

infix      +   (x,y: INTEGER)    : INTEGER
           +   (x,y: Float)      : Float
               (x,y: Set)        : Set
```

As a prefix operator, +x returns x. As an infix operator on numeric arguments, + denotes addition. On sets, + denotes set union. That is, e IN (x + y) if and only if (e IN x) OR (e IN y). The types of x and y must be the same, and the result is the same type as both. In unsafe modules, + is extended to ADDRESS.

```
prefix     -   (x: INTEGER)      : INTEGER
               (x: Float)        : Float

infix      -   (x,y: INTEGER)    : INTEGER
               (x,y: Float)      : Float
               (x,y: Set)        : Set
```

As a prefix operator, -x is the negative of x. As an infix operator on numeric arguments, - denotes subtraction. On sets, - denotes set difference. That is, e IN (x - y) if and only if (e IN x) AND NOT (e IN y). The types of x and y must be the same, and the result is the same type as both. In unsafe modules, - is extended to ADDRESS.

infix   *   (x,y: INTEGER)   : INTEGER
                    (x,y: Float)   : Float
                    (x,y: Set)   : Set

On numeric arguments, * denotes multiplication. On sets, * denotes intersection. That is, e IN (x * y) if and only if (e IN x) AND (e IN y). The types of x and y must be the same, and the result is the same type as both.

infix   /   (x,y: Float)   : Float
                    (x,y: Set)   : Set

On reals, / denotes division. On sets, / denotes symmetric difference. That is, e IN (x / y) if and only if (e IN x) # (e IN y). The types of x and y must be the same, and the result is the same type as both.

infix   DIV (x,y: INTEGER): INTEGER
infix   MOD (x,y: INTEGER): INTEGER
              MOD (x, y: Float): Float

The value x DIV y is the floor of the quotient of x and y; that is, the maximum integer not exceeding the real number z such that z * y = x. For integers x and y, the value of x MOD y is defined to be x - y * (x DIV y).

This means that for positive y, the value of x MOD y lies in the interval [0 .. y-1], regardless of the sign of x. For negative y, the value of x MOD y lies in the interval [y+1 .. 0], regardless of the sign of x.

If x and y are floats, the value of x MOD y is x - y * FLOOR(x / y). This may be computed as a Modula-3 expression, or by a method that avoids overflow if x is much greater than y. The types of x and y must be the same, and the result is the same type as both.

        ABS (x: INTEGER)   : INTEGER
             (x: Float)   : Float

ABS(x) is the absolute value of x. If x is a float, the type of ABS(x) is the same as the type of x.

      FLOAT (x: INTEGER; T: Type := REAL)   : T
             (x: Float; T: Type := REAL)   : T

FLOAT(x, T) is the nearest floating-point value of type T to x. The type T must be a floating-point type; it defaults to REAL. Ties are broken according to the thread's current rounding mode, as defined in the required interface FloatMode (page 75).

```
FLOOR    (x: Float)  : INTEGER

CEILING  (x: Float)  : INTEGER
```

FLOOR(x) is the greatest integer not exceeding x. CEILING(x) is the least integer not less than x.

```
ROUND  (r: Float)  : INTEGER

TRUNC  (r: Float)  : INTEGER
```

ROUND(r) is the nearest integer to r; ties are broken according to the constant RoundDefault in the required interface FloatMode (page 75). TRUNC(r) rounds r toward zero; it equals FLOOR(r) for positive r and CEILING(r) for negative r.

```
MAX, MIN  (x,y: Ordinal)  : Ordinal
          (x,y: Float)     : Float
```

MAX returns the greater of the two values x and y; MIN returns the lesser. If x and y are ordinals, they must have the same base type, which is the type of the result. If x and y are floats, they must have the same type, and the result is the same type as both.

2.6.11 Relations

infix   =, # (x, y: Any): BOOLEAN

The operator = returns TRUE if x and y are equal. The operator # returns TRUE if x and y are not equal. It is a static error if the type of x is not assignable to the type of y or vice versa.

Ordinals are equal if they have the same value. Floats are equal if the underlying implementation defines them to be; for example, on an IEEE implementation, +0 equals −0 and NaN does not equal itself. References are equal if they address the same location. Procedures are equal if they agree as closures; that is, if they refer to the same procedure body and environment. Sets are equal if they have the same elements. Arrays are equal if they have the same length and corresponding elements are equal. Records are equal if they have the same fields and corresponding fields are equal.

```
infix     <=, >=  (x,y: Ordinal)  : BOOLEAN
                  (x,y: Float)     : BOOLEAN
                  (x,y: ADDRESS)   : BOOLEAN
                  (x,y: Set)       : BOOLEAN
```

In the first three cases, <= returns TRUE if x is at most as large as y. In the last case, <= returns TRUE if every element of x is an element of y. In all cases, it is a static error if the type of x is not assignable to the type of y, or vice versa. The expression x >= y is equivalent to y <= x.

```
infix    >, <  (x,y: Ordinal)   : BOOLEAN
               (x,y: Float)      : BOOLEAN
               (x,y: ADDRESS)    : BOOLEAN
               (x,y: Set)        : BOOLEAN
```

In all cases, x < y means (x <= y) AND (x # y), and x > y means y < x. It is a static error if the type of x is not assignable to the type of y, or vice versa.

Warning: with IEEE floating-point, x <= y is not the same as NOT x > y.

```
infix    IN   (e: Ordinal; s: Set): BOOLEAN
```

Returns TRUE if e is an element of the set s. It is a static error if the type of e is not assignable to the element type of s. If the value of e is not a member of the element type, no error occurs, but IN returns FALSE.

2.6.12 Boolean operations

```
prefix    NOT  (p: BOOLEAN)     : BOOLEAN
infix     AND  (p,q: BOOLEAN)   : BOOLEAN
infix     OR   (p,q: BOOLEAN)   : BOOLEAN
```

NOT p is the complement of p.

p AND q is TRUE if both p and q are TRUE. If p is FALSE, q is not evaluated.

p OR q is TRUE if at least one of p and q is TRUE. If p is TRUE, q is not evaluated.

2.6.13 Type operations

```
        ISTYPE  (x: Reference; T: RefType)   : BOOLEAN
```

ISTYPE(x, T) is TRUE if and only if x is a member of T. T must be an object type or traced reference type, and x must be assignable to T.

```
        NARROW  (x: Reference; T: RefType): T
```

NARROW(x, T) returns x after checking that x is a member of T. If the check fails, a runtime error occurs. T must be an object type or traced reference type, and x must be assignable to T.

```
        TYPECODE  (T: RefType)           : CARDINAL
                  (r: REFANY)            : CARDINAL
                  (r: UNTRACED ROOT)     : CARDINAL
```

Every object type or traced reference type (including NULL) has an associated integer code. Different types have different codes. The code for a type is constant for any single execution of a program, but may differ for different executions. TYPECODE(T) returns the code for the type T and TYPECODE(r) returns the code for the allocated type of r. It is a static error if T is REFANY or is not an object type or traced reference type.

```
ORD   (element: Ordinal): INTEGER
VAL   (i: INTEGER; T: OrdinalType): T
```

ORD converts an element of an enumeration to the integer that represents its position in the enumeration order. The first value in any enumeration is represented by zero. If the type of element is a subrange of an enumeration T, the result is the position of the element within T, not within the subrange.

VAL is the inverse of ORD; it converts from a numeric position i into the element that occupies that position in an enumeration. If T is a subrange, VAL returns the element with the position i in the original enumeration type, not the subrange. It is a checked runtime error for the value of i to be out of range for T.

If n is an integer, ORD(n) = VAL(n, INTEGER) = n.

```
NUMBER  (T: OrdinalType)     : CARDINAL
        (A: FixedArrayType)  : CARDINAL
        (a: Array)           : CARDINAL
```

For an ordinal type T, NUMBER(T) returns the number of elements in T. For a fixed array type A, NUMBER(A) is defined by NUMBER(IndexType(A)). Similarly, for an array a, NUMBER(a) is defined by NUMBER(IndexType(a)). In this case, the expression a will be evaluated only if it denotes an open array.

```
FIRST  (T: OrdinalType)     : BaseType(T)
       (T: FloatType)       : T
       (A: FixedArrayType)  : BaseType(IndexType(A))
       (a: Array)           : BaseType(IndexType(a))

LAST   (T: OrdinalType)     : BaseType(T)
       (T: FloatType)       : T
       (A: FixedArrayType)  : BaseType(IndexType(A))
       (a: Array)           : BaseType(IndexType(a))
```

For a non-empty ordinal type T, FIRST returns the smallest value of T and LAST returns the largest value. If T is the empty enumeration, FIRST(T) and LAST(T) are static errors. If T is any other empty ordinal type, the values returned are implementation-dependent, but they satisfy FIRST(T) > LAST(T).

For a floating-point type T, FIRST(T) and LAST(T) are the smallest and largest values of the type, respectively. On IEEE implementations, these are minus and plus infinity.

For a fixed array type A, FIRST(A) is defined by FIRST(IndexType(A)) and LAST(A) by LAST(IndexType(A)). Similarly, for an array a, FIRST(a) and LAST(a) are defined by

FIRST(IndexType(a)) and LAST(IndexType(a)). The expression a will be evaluated only if it is an open array. Note that if a is an open array, FIRST(a) and LAST(a) have type INTEGER.

```
BITSIZE    (x: Any)    : CARDINAL
           (T: Type)   : CARDINAL

BYTESIZE   (x: Any)    : CARDINAL
           (T: Type)   : CARDINAL

ADRSIZE    (x: Any)    : CARDINAL
           (T: Type)   : CARDINAL
```

These operations return the size of the variable x or of variables of type T. BITSIZE returns the number of bits, BYTESIZE the number of 8-bit bytes, and ADRSIZE the number of addressable locations. In all cases, x must be a designator and T must not be an open array type. A designator x will be evaluated only if its type is an open array type.

2.6.14 Text operations

infix & (a,b: TEXT): TEXT

The concatenation of a and b, as defined by Text.Cat. (Section 3.1, page 68.)

2.6.15 Constant Expressions

Constant expressions are a subset of the general class of expressions, restricted by the requirement that it be possible to evaluate the expression statically. All operations are legal in constant expressions except for ADR, LOOPHOLE, TYPECODE, NARROW, ISTYPE, SUBARRAY, NEW, dereferencing (explicit or implicit), and the only procedures that can be applied are the functions in the Word interface (Section 3.3).

A variable can appear in a constant expression only as an argument to FIRST, LAST, NUMBER, BITSIZE, BYTESIZE, or ADRSIZE, and such a variable must not have an open array type. Literals and top-level procedure constants are legal in constant expressions.

2.7 Unsafe operations

> *There are some cases that no law can be framed to cover.*
> *—Aristotle*

The features defined in this section can potentially cause unchecked runtime errors and are thus forbidden in safe modules.

An unchecked type transfer operation has the form:

    LOOPHOLE(e, T)

where e is an expression whose type is not an open array type and T is a type. It denotes e's bit pattern interpreted as a variable or value of type T. It is a designator if e is, and is writable if e is. An unchecked runtime error can occur if e's bit pattern is not a legal T, or if e is a designator and some legal bit pattern for T is not legal for e.

If T is not an open array type, BITSIZE(e) must equal BITSIZE(T). If T is an open array type, its element type must not be an open array type, and e's bit pattern is interpreted as an array whose length is BITSIZE(e) divided by BITSIZE(the element type of T). The division must come out even.

The following operations are primarily used for address arithmetic:

       ADR   (VAR x: Any)   : ADDRESS

       +   (x: ADDRESS, y:INTEGER)   : ADDRESS
       -     (x: ADDRESS, y:INTEGER)   : ADDRESS
       -     (x,y: ADDRESS)   : INTEGER

ADR(x) is the address of the variable x. The actual argument must be a designator but need not be writable. The operations + and - treat addresses as integers. The validity of the addresses produced by these operations is implementation-dependent. For example, the address of a variable in a local procedure frame is probably valid only for the duration of the call. The address of the referent of a traced reference is probably valid only as long as traced references prevent it from being collected (and not even that long if the implementation uses a compacting collector).

In unsafe modules the INC and DEC statements apply to addresses as well as ordinals:

            INC (VAR x: ADDRESS; n: INTEGER := 1)
            DEC (VAR x: ADDRESS; n: INTEGER := 1)

These are short for x := x + n and x := x - n, except that x is evaluated only once.

A DISPOSE statement has the form:

            DISPOSE (v)

where v is a writable designator whose type is not REFANY, ADDRESS, or NULL. If v is untraced, the statement frees the storage for v's referent and sets v to NIL. Freeing storage to which active references remain is an unchecked runtime error. If v is traced, the statement is equivalent to v := NIL. If v is NIL, the statement is a no-op.

In unsafe modules the definition of "assignable" for types is extended: two reference types T and U are assignable if T <: U or U <: T. The only effect of this change is to allow a value of type ADDRESS to be assigned to a variable of type UNTRACED REF T. It is an unchecked runtime error if the value does not address a variable of type T.

In unsafe modules the type constructor UNTRACED REF T is allowed for traced as well as untraced T, and the fields of untraced objects can be traced. If u is an untraced reference to a traced variable t, then the validity of the traced references in t is implementation-dependent, since the garbage collector probably will not trace them through u.

2.8 Syntax

> *Care should be taken, when using colons and semicolons in the same sentence,*
> *that the reader understands how far the force of each sign carries.*
> *—Robert Graves and Alan Hodge*

2.8.1 Keywords

AND	DO	FROM	NOT	REPEAT	UNTIL
ANY	ELSE	GENERIC	OBJECT	RETURN	UNTRACED
ARRAY	ELSIF	IF	OF	REVEAL	VALUE
AS	END	IMPORT	OR	ROOT	VAR
BEGIN	EVAL	IN	OVERRIDES	SET	WHILE
BITS	EXCEPT	INTERFACE	PROCEDURE	THEN	WITH
BRANDED	EXCEPTION	LOCK	RAISE	TO	
BY	EXIT	LOOP	RAISES	TRY	
CASE	EXPORTS	METHODS	READONLY	TYPE	
CONST	FINALLY	MOD	RECORD	TYPECASE	
DIV	FOR	MODULE	REF	UNSAFE	

2.8.2 Reserved identifiers

ABS	BYTESIZE	EXTENDED	INTEGER	MIN	NUMBER	TEXT
ADDRESS	CARDINAL	FALSE	ISTYPE	MUTEX	ORD	TRUE
ADR	CEILING	FIRST	LAST	NARROW	REAL	TRUNC
ADRSIZE	CHAR	FLOAT	LONGREAL	NEW	REFANY	TYPECODE
BITSIZE	DEC	FLOOR	LOOPHOLE	NIL	ROUND	VAL
BOOLEAN	DISPOSE	INC	MAX	NULL	SUBARRAY	

2.8.3 Operators

+	<	#	=	;	..	:
–	>	{	}	|	:=	<:
*	<=	(	)	^	,	=>
/	>=	[	]	.	&	

2.8.4 Comments

A comment is an arbitrary character sequence opened by (* and closed by *). Comments can be nested and can extend over more than one line.

2.8.5 Pragmas

A pragma is an arbitrary character sequence opened by <* and closed by *>. Pragmas can be nested and can extend over more than one line. Pragmas are hints to the implementation; they do not affect the language semantics.

We recommend supporting the two pragmas <*INLINE*> and <*EXTERNAL*>. The pragma <*INLINE*> precedes a procedure declaration to indicate that the procedure should be expanded at the point of call. The pragma <* EXTERNAL N:L *> precedes an interface or a declaration in an interface to indicate that the entity it precedes is implemented by the language L, where it has the name N. If ":L" is omitted, then the implementation's default external language is assumed. If "N" is omitted, then the external name is determined from the Modula-3 name in some implementation-dependent way.

2.8.6 Conventions for syntax

We use the following notation for defining syntax:

X Y	X followed by Y
X|Y	X or Y.
[X]	X or empty
{X}	A possibly empty sequence of X's
X&Y	X or Y or X Y

"Followed by" has greater binding power than | or &; parentheses are used to override this precedence rule. Non-terminals begin with an upper-case letter. Terminals are either keywords or quoted operators. The symbols Ident, Number, TextLiteral, and CharLiteral are defined in the token grammar on page 65. Each production is terminated by a period. The syntax does not reflect the restrictions that revelations and exceptions can be declared only at the top level; nor does it include explicit productions for NEW, INC, and DEC, which parse like procedure calls.

2.8.7   Compilation unit productions

```
Compilation = [UNSAFE] (Interface | Module) | GenInf | GenMod.

Interface   = INTERFACE Id ";" {Import} {Decl} END Id ".".
            | INTERFACE Id "=" Id GenActls END Id ".".
Module      = MODULE Id [EXPORTS IdList] ";" {Import} Block Id ".".
            | MODULE Id [EXPORTS IdList] "=" Id GenActls END Id ".".

GenInf = GENERIC INTERFACE Id GenFmls ";" {Import} {Decl} END Id ".".
GenMod = GENERIC MODULE Id GenFmls ";" {Import} Block Id ".".

Import      = AsImport | FromImport.
AsImport    = IMPORT ImportItem {"," ImportItem} ";".
FromImport  = FROM Id IMPORT IdList ";".
Block       = {Decl} BEGIN S END.
Decl = CONST {ConstDecl ";"}
     | TYPE {TypeDecl ";"}
     | EXCEPTION {ExceptionDecl ";"}
     | VAR {VariableDecl ";"}
     | ProcedureHead ["=" Block Id] ";"
     | REVEAL {QualId ("=" | "<:") Type ";"}.

GenFmls       = "(" [IdList] ")".
GenActls      = "(" [IdList] ")".
ImportItem    = Id | Id AS Id.
ConstDecl     = Id [":" Type] "=" ConstExpr.
TypeDecl      = Id ("=" | "<:") Type.
ExceptionDecl = Id ["(" Type ")"].
VariableDecl  = IdList (":" Type & ":=" Expr).
ProcedureHead = PROCEDURE Id Signature.

Signature     = "(" Formals ")" [":" Type] [RAISES Raises].
Formals       = [ Formal {";" Formal} [";"] ].
Formal        = [Mode] IdList (":" Type & ":=" ConstExpr).
Mode          = VALUE | VAR | READONLY.
Raises        = "{" [ QualId {"," QualId} ] "}" | ANY.
```

2.8.8   Statement productions

```
Stmt = AssignSt | Block | CallSt | CaseSt | ExitSt | EvalSt | ForSt
     | IfSt | LockSt | LoopSt | RaiseSt | RepeatSt | ReturnSt
     | TCaseSt | TryXptSt | TryFinSt | WhileSt | WithSt.

S =  [ Stmt {";" Stmt} [";"] ].
```

```
AssignSt = Expr ":=" Expr.
CallSt   = Expr "(" [Actual {"," Actual}] ")".
CaseSt   = CASE Expr OF [Case] {"|" Case} [ELSE S] END.
ExitSt   = EXIT.
EvalSt   = EVAL Expr.
ForSt    = FOR Id ":=" Expr TO Expr [BY Expr] DO S END.
IfSt     = IF Expr THEN S {ELSIF Expr THEN S} [ELSE S] END.
LockSt   = LOCK Expr DO S END.
LoopSt   = LOOP S END.
RaiseSt  = RAISE QualId ["(" Expr ")"].
RepeatSt = REPEAT S UNTIL Expr.
ReturnSt = RETURN [Expr].
TCaseSt  = TYPECASE Expr OF [TCase] {"|" TCase} [ELSE S] END.
TryXptSt = TRY S EXCEPT [Handler] {"|" Handler} [ELSE S] END.
TryFinSt = TRY S FINALLY S END.
WhileSt  = WHILE Expr DO S END.
WithSt   = WITH Binding {"," Binding} DO S END.

Case    = Labels {"," Labels} "=>" S.
Labels  = ConstExpr [".." ConstExpr].
Handler = QualId {"," QualId} ["(" Id ")"] "=>" S.
TCase   = Type {"," Type} ["(" Id ")"] "=>" S.
Binding = Id "=" Expr.
Actual  = Type | [Id ":="] Expr .
```

2.8.9 Type productions

```
Type = TypeName | ArrayType | PackedType | EnumType | ObjectType
     | ProcedureType | RecordType | RefType | SetType | SubrangeType
     | "(" Type ")".

ArrayType     = ARRAY [Type {"," Type}] OF Type.
PackedType    = BITS ConstExpr FOR Type.
EnumType      = "{" [IdList] "}".
ObjectType    = [TypeName | ObjectType] [Brand] OBJECT Fields
                    [METHODS Methods] [OVERRIDES Overrides] END.
ProcedureType = PROCEDURE Signature.
RecordType    = RECORD Fields END.
RefType       = [UNTRACED] [Brand] REF Type.
SetType       = SET OF Type.
SubrangeType  = "[" ConstExpr ".." ConstExpr "]".

Brand   = BRANDED [TextLiteral].
Fields  = [ Field {";" Field} [";"] ].
```

```
Field     = IdList (":" Type & ":=" ConstExpr).
Methods   = [ Method {";" Method} [";"] ].
Method    = Id Signature [":=" ConstExpr].
Overrides = [ Override {";" Override} [";"] ].
Override  = Id ":=" ConstExpr .
```

2.8.10 Expression productions

```
ConstExpr = Expr.

Expr = E1 {OR E1}.
  E1 = E2 {AND E2}.
  E2 = {NOT} E3.
  E3 = E4 {Relop E4}.
  E4 = E5 {Addop E5}.
  E5 = E6 {Mulop E6}.
  E6 = {"+" | "-"} E7.
  E7 = E8 {Selector}.
  E8 = Id | Number | CharLiteral | TextLiteral
     | Constructor | "(" Expr ")".

Relop =  "=" | "#" | "<"  | "<=" | ">" | ">=" | IN.
Addop =  "+" | "-" | "&".
Mulop =  "*" | "/" | DIV | MOD.

Selector = "^"  |  "." Id  |  "[" Expr {"," Expr} "]"
     | "(" [ Actual {"," Actual} ] ")".

Constructor = Type "{" [ SetCons | RecordCons | ArrayCons ] "}".

SetCons = SetElt {"," SetElt}.
SetElt = Expr [".." Expr].
RecordCons = RecordElt {"," RecordElt}.
RecordElt = [Id ":="] Expr.
ArrayCons =  Expr {"," Expr} ["," ".."] .
```

2.8.11 Miscellaneous productions

```
IdList   = Id {"," Id}.
QualId   = Id ["." Id].
TypeName = QualId | ROOT | UNTRACED ROOT.
```

2.8.12 Token productions

To read a token, first skip all blanks, tabs, newlines, carriage returns, vertical tabs, form feeds, comments, and pragmas. Then read the longest sequence of characters that forms an operator (as defined in Section 2.8.3, page 62) or an Id or Literal, as defined here.

An Id is a case-significant sequence of letters, digits, and underscores that begins with a letter. An Id is a keyword if it appears in Section 2.8.1, a reserved identifier if it appears in Section 2.8.2, and an ordinary identifier otherwise.

In the following grammar, terminals are characters surrounded by double-quotes and the special terminal DQUOTE represents double-quote itself.

```
Id = Letter {Letter | Digit | "_"}.

Literal = Number | CharLiteral | TextLiteral.

CharLiteral = "'"  (PrintingChar | Escape | DQUOTE) "'".

TextLiteral = DQUOTE {PrintingChar | Escape | "'"} DQUOTE.

Escape = "\" "n"   | "\" "t"    | "\" "r"   | "\" "f"
       | "\" "\"   | "\" "'"    | "\" DQUOTE
       | "\" OctalDigit OctalDigit OctalDigit.

Number = Digit {Digit}
       | Digit {Digit} "_" HexDigit {HexDigit}
       | Digit {Digit} "." Digit {Digit} [Exp].

Exp = ("E" | "e" | "D" | "d" | "X" | "x") ["+" | "-"] Digit {Digit}.

PrintingChar = Letter | Digit | OtherChar.

HexDigit = Digit | "A" | "B" | "C" | "D" | "E" | "F"
                 | "a" | "b" | "c" | "d" | "e" | "f".

Digit = "0" | "1" | ... | "9".

OctalDigit = "0" | "1" | ... | "7".

Letter = "A"  | "B"  | ... | "Z"  | "a"  | "b"  | ... | "z".

OtherChar = " " | "!" | "#" | "$" | "%" | "&" | "(" | ")"
          | "*" | "+" | "," | "-" | "." | "/" | ":" | ";"
          | "<" | "=" | ">" | "?" | "@" | "[" | "]" | "^"
          | "_" | "'" | "{" | "|" | "}" | " "
          | ExtendedChar

ExtendedChar = any char with ISO-Latin-1 code in [8_240..8_377].
```

Chapter 3

Standard Interfaces

Greg Nelson

> *C++ has a host of operators that will be explained if and where needed.*
> *—The C++ Programming Language*

This chapter presents several fundamental interfaces that every Modula-3 implementation must provide:

Text provides operations on text strings.

Thread provides synchronization primitives for multiple threads of control.

Word provides operations on unsigned words.

Real, LongReal, and ExtendedReal define the properties of the three floating point types; for example, their bases and ranges.

RealFloat, LongRealFloat, and ExtendedFloat provide numerical operations related to the floating-point representation; for example, extracting the exponent of a number.

FloatMode provides operations for testing (and possibly setting) the behavior of the implementation in response to numeric conditions; for example, overflow.

Implementations are free to extend the required interfaces, provided they do not invalidate clients of the unextended interfaces.

This chapter also presents several interfaces that are provided by SRC Modula-3 and recommended to other implementers, but not required:

Fmt provides for textual formatting of numbers and other data.

Pkl provides type-safe persistent storage via binary files called "pickles".

Table provides generic hash tables.

SRC Modula-3 also provides interfaces for text input and output and window-oriented user interfaces; these are the subjects of Chapters 6 and 7.

3.1   The Text interface

```
INTERFACE Text;

TYPE
  T = TEXT;
```

A non-nil TEXT represents a zero-based sequence of characters. NIL does not represent any sequence of characters, it will not be returned from any procedure in the interface, and it is a checked runtime error to pass it to any procedure in the interface.

```
PROCEDURE Cat(t, u: T): T;
```

The concatenation of t and u.

```
PROCEDURE Equal(t, u: T): BOOLEAN;
```

TRUE if t and u have the same length and (case-sensitive) contents.

```
PROCEDURE GetChar(t: T; i: CARDINAL): CHAR;
```

Character i of t. A checked runtime error if i >= Length(t).

```
PROCEDURE Length(t: T): CARDINAL;
```

The number of characters in t.

```
PROCEDURE Empty(t: T): BOOLEAN;
```

TRUE if Length(t) = 0.

```
PROCEDURE Sub(t: T; start, length: CARDINAL): T;
```

Return a subsequence of t: empty if start >= Length(t) or length = 0; otherwise the subsequence ranging from start to the minimum of start+length-1 and Length(t)-1.

```
PROCEDURE SetChars(VAR a: ARRAY OF CHAR; t: T);
```

For each i from 0 to MIN(LAST(a), Length(t)-1), set a[i] to GetChar(t, i).

```
PROCEDURE FromChar(ch: CHAR): T;
```

A text containing the single character ch.

```
PROCEDURE FromChars(READONLY a: ARRAY OF CHAR): T;
```

A text containing the characters of a.

```
PROCEDURE Hash(t: T): INTEGER;
```

Return a hash function of the contents of t.

```
END Text.
```

3.2 The Thread interface

If a shared variable is written concurrently by two threads, or written by one and read concurrently by another, the effect is to set the variable to an implementation-dependent value of its type. For example, if one thread writes a[0] while another concurrently writes a[1], one of the writes might be lost. Thus, portable programs must use the Thread interface to provide mutual exclusion for shared variables. Chapter 5 contains the formal specification of this interface; Chapter 4 contains an introductory tutorial. The comments in this section give terse summaries of the semantics.

```
INTERFACE Thread;

TYPE
  T <: REFANY;
  Mutex = MUTEX;
  Condition <: ROOT;
  Closure = OBJECT METHODS apply(): REFANY END;
```

A Thread.T is a handle on a thread. A Mutex is locked by some thread, or unlocked. A Condition is a set of waiting threads. A newly-allocated Mutex is unlocked; a newly-allocated Condition is empty. It is a checked runtime error to pass the NIL Mutex, Condition, or T to any procedure in this interface.

```
PROCEDURE Fork(cl: Closure): T;
```

A handle on a newly-created thread executing cl.apply().

```
PROCEDURE Join(t: T): REFANY;
```

Wait until t has terminated and return its result. It is a checked error to call this more than once for any t.

```
PROCEDURE Wait(m: Mutex; c: Condition);
```

The calling thread must have m locked. Atomically unlocks m and waits on c. Then relocks m and returns.

```
PROCEDURE Acquire(m: Mutex);
```

Wait until m is unlocked and then lock it.

```
PROCEDURE Release(m: Mutex);
```

The calling thread must have m locked. Unlocks m.

```
PROCEDURE Broadcast(c: Condition);
```

All threads waiting on c become eligible to run.

```
PROCEDURE Signal(c: Condition);
```

One or more threads waiting on c become eligible to run.

```
PROCEDURE Self(): T;
```

Return the handle of the calling thread.

```
EXCEPTION Alerted;
```

Used to approximate asynchronous interrupts.

```
PROCEDURE Alert(t: T);
```

Mark t as an alerted thread.

```
PROCEDURE TestAlert(): BOOLEAN;
```

TRUE if the calling thread has been marked alerted.

```
PROCEDURE AlertWait(m: Mutex; c: Condition) RAISES {Alerted};
```

Like Wait, but if the thread is marked alerted at the time of call or sometime during the wait, lock m and raise Alerted.

```
PROCEDURE AlertJoin(t: T): REFANY RAISES {Alerted};
```

Like Join, but if t is marked alerted at the time of call or sometime during the wait, raise Alerted.

```
CONST
  AtomicSize = ...;
```

An implementation-dependent integer constant: the number of bits in a memory-coherent block. If two components of a record or array fall in different blocks, they can be accessed concurrently by different threads without locking.

```
END Thread.
```

3.3 The Word interface

```
INTERFACE Word;

TYPE T = INTEGER;

CONST Size = BITSIZE(T);
```

A Word.T w represents a sequence of Word.Size bits $w_0, \ldots, w_{Word.Size-1}$. It also represents the unsigned number $\sum_i w_i \cdot 2^i$. Finally, it also represents a signed INTEGER by some implementation-dependent encoding (for example, two's complement). The built-in operations of the language deal with the signed value; the operations in this interface deal with the unsigned value or with the bit sequence.

Here are the arithmetic operations on unsigned words:

```
PROCEDURE Plus  (x,y: T): T;      (* (x + y) MOD 2^Word.Size *)

PROCEDURE Times (x,y: T): T;      (* (x * y) MOD 2^Word.Size *)

PROCEDURE Minus (x,y: T): T;      (* (x - y) MOD 2^Word.Size *) .

PROCEDURE Divide(x,y: T): T;      (* x DIV y *)

PROCEDURE Mod(x,y: T): T;         (* x MOD y *)

PROCEDURE LT(x,y: T): BOOLEAN;    (* x < y *)

PROCEDURE LE(x,y: T): BOOLEAN;    (* x <= y *)

PROCEDURE GT(x,y: T): BOOLEAN;    (* x > y *)

PROCEDURE GE(x,y: T): BOOLEAN;    (* x >= y *)
```

And here are the logical operations on bit sequences:

```
PROCEDURE And(x,y: T): T;   (* Bitwise AND of x and y *)

PROCEDURE Or (x,y: T): T;   (* Bitwise OR of x and y *)

PROCEDURE Xor(x,y: T): T;   (* Bitwise XOR of x and y *)

PROCEDURE Not (x: T):  T;   (* Bitwise complement of x *)
```

And here are additional operations on bit sequences:

```
PROCEDURE Shift(x: T; n: INTEGER): T;
```

> For all i such that both i and $i - n$ are in the range $[0 .. \texttt{Word.Size} - 1]$, bit i of the result equals bit $i - n$ of x. The other bits of the result are 0. Thus shifting by n > 0 is like multiplying by 2^n.

Since Modula-3 has no exponentiation operator, Word.Shift(1, n) is the usual way of writing 2^n in a constant expression.

```
PROCEDURE Rotate(x: T; n: INTEGER): T;
```

> Bit i of the result is bit $((i - n) \texttt{ MOD Word.Size})$ of x.

```
PROCEDURE Extract(x: T; i, n: CARDINAL): T;
```

> Take n bits from x, with bit i as the least significant bit, and return them as the least significant n bits of a word whose other bits are 0. A checked runtime error if n + i > Word.Size.

```
PROCEDURE Insert(x: T; y: T; i, n: CARDINAL): T;
```

> Result of replacing n bits of x, with bit i as the least significant bit, by the least significant n bits of y. The other bits of x are unchanged. A checked runtime error if n + i > Word.Size.

```
END Word.
```

3.4 Floating-point interfaces

For definitions of the terms used in these interfaces, see the ANSI/IEEE Standard 754-1985 for floating-point arithmetic.

The first three interfaces define constant attributes of the three built-in floating-point types:

```
INTERFACE Real; TYPE T = REAL;
CONST
  Base: INTEGER = ...;
  Precision: INTEGER = ...;
  MaxFinite: T = ...;
  MinPos: T = ...;
  MinPosNormal: T = ...;
END Real.

INTERFACE LongReal; TYPE T = LONGREAL;
CONST
  Base: INTEGER = ...;
  Precision: INTEGER = ...;
  MaxFinite: T = ...;
  MinPos: T = ...;
  MinPosNormal: T = ...;
END LongReal.

INTERFACE Extended; TYPE T = EXTENDED;
CONST
  Base: INTEGER = ...;
  Precision: INTEGER = ...;
  MaxFinite: T = ...;
  MinPos: T = ...;
  MinPosNormal: T = ...;
END Extended.
```

The specification is the same for all three interfaces:

Base is the radix of the floating-point representation for T.

Precision is the number of base-Base digits of precision for T.

MaxFinite is the maximum finite value in T. For non-IEEE implementations, this is the same as LAST(T).

MinPos is the minimum positive value in T.

MinPosNormal is the minimum positive normal value in T; it differs from MinPos only for implementations (like IEEE) with denormalized numbers.

The next three interfaces define operations that depend on the floating-point representation. They are all are instances of a generic interface Float:

```
INTERFACE RealFloat = Float(Real) END RealFloat.
INTERFACE LongFloat = Float(LongReal) END LongFloat.
INTERFACE ExtendedFloat = Float(Extended) END ExtendedFloat.
```

```
GENERIC INTERFACE Float(R); TYPE T = R.T;
```

This generic interface provides access to the floating-point operations required or recommended by the IEEE floating-point standard. Consult the standard for the precise specifications of the procedures, including when their arguments are NaNs, infinities, and signed zeros, and including what exceptions they can raise. The comments here specify their effect when the arguments are ordinary numbers and no exception is raised. Implementations on non-IEEE machines that have values similar to NaNs and infinities should explain how those values behave in an implementation guide.

```
PROCEDURE Scalb(x: T; n: INTEGER): T;
```

Return $x \cdot 2^n$.

```
PROCEDURE Logb(x: T): T;
```

Return the exponent of x. More precisely, return the unique n such that the ratio `ABS(x) / Base`^{n} is in the range `[1..Base-1]`, unless x is denormalized, in which case return `MinExp-1`, where `MinExp` is the minimum exponent value for T.

```
PROCEDURE ILogb(x: T): INTEGER;
```

Like Logb, but returns an integer, never raises an exception, and always returns the n such that `ABS(x) / Base`^{n} is in the range `[1..Base-1]`, even for denormalized numbers.

```
PROCEDURE NextAfter(x, y: T): T;
```

Return the next representable neighbor of x in the direction towards y. If x = y, return x.

```
PROCEDURE CopySign(x, y: T): T;
```

Return x with the sign of y.

```
PROCEDURE Finite(x: T): BOOLEAN;
```

Return TRUE if x is strictly between minus infinity and plus infinity. This always returns TRUE on non-IEEE machines.

```
PROCEDURE IsNaN(x: T): BOOLEAN;
```

Return FALSE if x represents a numerical (possibly infinite) value, and TRUE if x does not represent a numerical value. For example, on IEEE implementations, returns TRUE if x is a NaN, FALSE otherwise.

```
PROCEDURE Sign(x: T): [0..1];
```

Return the sign bit x. For non-IEEE implementations, this is the same as ORD(x >= 0); for IEEE implementations, Sign(-0) = 1 and Sign(+0) = 0.

```
PROCEDURE Differs(x, y: T): BOOLEAN;
```

Return (x < y OR y < x). Thus, for IEEE implementations, Differs(NaN,x) is always FALSE; for non-IEEE implementations, Differs(x,y) is the same as x # y.

```
PROCEDURE Unordered(x, y: T): BOOLEAN;
```

Return NOT (x <= y OR y <= x).

```
PROCEDURE Sqrt(x: T): T;
```

Return the square root of T. This must be correctly rounded if FloatMode.IEEE is TRUE.

```
TYPE IEEEClass =
  {SignalingNaN, QuietNaN, Infinity, Normal, Denormal, Zero};
```

```
PROCEDURE Class(x: T): IEEEClass;
```

Return the IEEE number class containing x.

```
END Float.
```

The final interface FloatMode allows you to test the behavior of rounding and of numerical exceptions. On some implementations it also allows you to change the behavior, on a per-thread basis.

```
INTERFACE FloatMode;
```

```
CONST IEEE: BOOLEAN = ...;
```

TRUE for fully-compliant IEEE implementations.

```
EXCEPTION Failure;
```

Raised by attempts to set modes that are not supported by the implementation.

```
TYPE RoundingMode =
  {MinusInfinity, PlusInfinity, Zero, Nearest, Vax, IBM370, Other};
```

Rounding modes. The first four are the IEEE modes.

```
CONST RoundDefault: RoundingMode = ...;
```

Implementation-dependent: the default mode for rounding arithmetic operations, used by a newly forked thread. This also specifies the behavior of the ROUND operation in half-way cases.

```
PROCEDURE SetRounding(md: RoundingMode) RAISES {Failure};
```

Change the rounding mode for the calling thread to md, or raise the exception if this cannot be done. This affects the implicit rounding in floating-point operations; it does not affect the ROUND operation. Generally this can be done only on IEEE implementations and only if md is an IEEE mode.

```
PROCEDURE GetRounding(): RoundingMode;
```

Return the rounding mode for the calling thread.

```
TYPE Flag =
  {Invalid, Inexact, Overflow, Underflow, DivByZero, IntOverflow,
   IntDivByZero};
```

Associated with each thread is a set of boolean status flags recording whether the condition represented by the flag has occurred in the thread since the flag was last reset. The meaning of the first five flags is defined precisely in the IEEE floating point standard; roughly they mean:

Invalid = invalid argument to an operation.

Inexact = an operation produced an inexact result.

Overflow = a floating-point operation produced a result whose absolute value is too large to be represented.

Underflow = a floating-point operation produced a result whose absolute value is too small to be represented.

DivByZero = floating-point division by zero.

The meaning of the last two flags is:

IntOverflow = an integer operation produced a result whose absolute value is too large to be represented.

IntDivByZero = integer DIV or MOD by zero.

```
CONST NoFlags = SET OF Flags {};
```

```
PROCEDURE GetFlags(): SET OF Flag;
```

Return the set of flags for the current thread.

```
PROCEDURE SetFlags(s: SET OF Flag): SET OF Flag;
```

Set the flags for the current thread to s, and return their previous values.

```
PROCEDURE ClearFlag(f: Flag);
```

Turn off the flag f for the current thread.

```
EXCEPTION
  Trap(Flag);
```

```
TYPE
  Behavior = {Trap, SetFlag, Ignore};
```

The behavior of an operation that causes one of the flag conditions is either

Ignore = return some result and do nothing.

SetFlag = return some result and set the condition flag. For IEEE implementations, the result of the operation is defined by the standard.

Trap = possibly set the condition flag; in any case raise the Trap exception with the appropriate flag as the argument.

```
PROCEDURE SetBehavior(f: Flag; b: Behavior) RAISES Failure;
```

Set the behavior of the current thread for the flag f to be b, or raise Failure if this cannot be done.

```
PROCEDURE GetBehavior(f: Flag): Behavior;
```

Return the behavior of the current thread for the flag f.

```
END FloatMode.
```

3.5 The Fmt interface

The Fmt interface provides procedures for formatting numbers and other data as text.

```
INTERFACE Fmt;
```

```
TYPE
  Align = {Left, Right};
  Base = [2..16];
  Style = {Flo, AltFlo, Sci, AltSci, Mix};
```

Style parameters control the formatting of floating-point numbers. The Sci and AltSci formats are "decimal E exponent"; the Flo and AltFlo formats are simply "decimal". In the Alt formats, trailing zeros are suppressed in the decimal part; in both formats, a decimal point is always printed. The Mix format is AltFlo unless AltSci is shorter; if

AltFlo is selected and there are no digits after the decimal point, the decimal point is suppressed.

```
PROCEDURE Bool(b: BOOLEAN): TEXT;
```

Format b as "TRUE" or "FALSE".

```
PROCEDURE Int(n: INTEGER; base: Base := 10): TEXT;
```

Format n in the given base.

```
PROCEDURE Addr(n: ADDRESS; base: Base := 16): TEXT;
```

Format n in the given base. Return "NIL" if n = NIL.

```
PROCEDURE Ref(r: REFANY; base: Base := 16): TEXT;
```

Format r in the given base. Return "NIL" if r = NIL.

```
PROCEDURE Real
  (x: REAL; precision: CARDINAL := 6; style := Style.Mix): TEXT;
```

Format x in the given style. The precision is the number of fractional digits in the decimal, or the maximum number for the Alt formats.

```
PROCEDURE LongReal(
  x: LONGREAL;
  precision: CARDINAL := 6;
  style := Style.Mix)
  : TEXT;
```

Format x in the given style. The precision is the number of fractional digits in the decimal, or the maximum number for the Alt formats.

```
PROCEDURE Extended(
  x: EXTENDED;
  precision: CARDINAL := 6;
  style := Style.Mix):
  TEXT;
```

Format x in the given style. The precision is the number of fractional digits in the decimal, or the maximum number for the Alt formats.

```
PROCEDURE Char(c: CHAR): TEXT;
```

Return a text containing the character c.

```
PROCEDURE Pad(
  text: TEXT;
  length: CARDINAL;
  padChar: CHAR := ' ';
  align := Align.Right)
  : TEXT;
```

> If Text.Length(text) >= length, then text is returned unchanged. Otherwise, text is padded with padChar until it has the given length. The text goes to the right or left, according to align.

```
PROCEDURE F(fmt: Text.T; t1,t2,t3,t4,t5: Text.T := NIL): Text.T;
```

> Use fmt as a format string. The result is a copy of fmt in which all format specifiers have been replaced, in order, by the text arguments t1, t2, etc.

A format specifier contains a field width, alignment and one of two padding characters. The procedure Fmt.F evaluates the specifier and replaces it by the corresponding text argument padded as it would be by a call to Pad with the specified field width, padding character and alignment.

The syntax of a format specifier is:

$$\%[-]\{0-9\}s$$

that is, a percent character followed by an optional minus sign, an optional number and a compulsory terminating s.

If the minus sign is present the alignment is Align.Left, otherwise it is Align.Right. The alignment corresponds to the align argument to Pad.

The number specifies the field width (this corresponds to the length argument to Pad). If the number is omitted it defaults to zero.

If the number is present and starts with zero the padding character is '0'; otherwise it is the space character. The padding character corresponds to the padChar argument to Pad.

It is a checked runtime error if fmt is NIL or the number of format specifiers in fmt is not equal to the number of non-nil arguments to Fmt.F.

Non-nil arguments to Fmt.F must precede any NIL arguments; it is a checked runtime error if they do not.

If t1 to t5 are all NIL and fmt contains no format specifiers, the result is fmt.

Examples:

```
F("%s", Int(3))      returns   "3"
F("%2s", Int(3))     returns   " 3"
F("%-2s", Int(3))    returns   "3 "
```

```
F("%02s", Int(3))        returns  "03"
F("%-02s", Int(3))       returns  "30"
F("%s", "%s")            returns  "%s"
F("%s% tax", Int(3))     returns  "3% tax"
```

The following examples are legal but pointless:

```
F("%-s", Int(3))         returns  "3"
F("%0s", Int(3))         returns  "3"
F("%-0s", Int(3))        returns  "3"
```

PROCEDURE FN(fmt: Text.T; READONLY texts: ARRAY OF Text.T): Text.T;

> Similar to F but accepts an array of text arguments. It is a checked runtime error if the number of format specifiers in fmt is not equal to NUMBER(texts) or if any element of texts is NIL.

> If NUMBER(texts) = 0 and fmt contains no format specifiers the result is fmt.

> Example:

```
FN("%s %s %s %s %s %s %s",
   ARRAY OF TEXT{"Too", "many", "arguments",
     "for", "F", "to", "handle"})
```

> returns "Too many arguments for F to handle".

END Fmt.

3.6   The Pkl interface

A "pickle" is a binary file storing a Modula-3 data structure. Pkl.Write(r, wr) writes a pickle for the data structure referenced by the traced reference r to the file writer wr. Pkl.Read(rd) read a pickle from a file reader rd and returns it as a REFANY. (File readers and writers are explained in Chapter 6.)

Pickles are optimized for reading. The format of the pickle file matches the runtime layout of the traced heap, so that Pkl.Read just copies the data and relocates the internal references, without allocating each reference individually. It's like linking, but for data instead of programs. The pickle format is machine-dependent, like the binary format for compiled programs.

The call Pkl.Write(r, wr) uses depth-first graph search to visit everything reachable from r via traced references, make a compact copy, and write the copy to wr. Pickling preserves shared substructures and circular data structures.

The type of the reference returned by Pkl.Read is the same as the type of the reference passed to Pkl.Write, even if these types have different names in the reading and writing program. For example, if we compile and run the program P1:

```
MODULE P1 EXPORTS Main;
  IMPORT Pkl, FileStream;
  TYPE T = REF RECORD val: INTEGER END;
  VAR r := NEW(T, val := 6);
    wr := FileStream.OpenWrite("A.pickle");
  Pkl.Write(r, wr);
  Wr.Close(wr)
END P1.
```

And then in the same directory run program P2:

```
MODULE P2 EXPORTS Main;
  IMPORT Pkl, FileStream, Wr, Stdio, Fmt;
  TYPE U = REF RECORD val: INTEGER END;
  VAR r: U := Pkl.Read(FileStream.OpenRead("A.pickle"));
  Wr.PutText(Stdio.stdout, Fmt.Int(r.val))
END P2.
```

then P2 will print "6". The fact that the type has different names in the two programs doesn't matter.

Pkl.Read will raise an exception if the pickle to be read contains any types that are not present in the reading program. For example, if after writing A.pickle as above, you run P3:

```
MODULE P3 EXPORTS Main;
  IMPORT Pkl, FileStream;
  TYPE T = REF RECORD newVal: INTEGER END;
  VAR r: T := Pkl.Read(FileStream.OpenRead("A.pickle"));
END P3.
```

the call to Pkl.Read will raise an exception, since the type in the pickle is not present anywhere in P3. The fact that P3 contains a different type with the same name and a similar structure doesn't matter.

If you pickle a BRANDED REF INTEGER, there is no guarantee that you will be able to read it back as a BRANDED REF INTEGER, since the implicit brand can vary from program to program. Therefore you should use explicit brands in types that will be pickled.

When Pkl.Write encounters a procedure, it writes the procedure's qualified name and signature into the pickle. The program reading the pickle must contain a procedure with the same qualified name and signature, or else Pkl.Read will raise an exception. Different programs reading the pickle could have different compiled code for the procedure. Methods are treated the same way.

`Pkl.Write` uses the same runtime information that the garbage collector uses. Therefore, it is only able to follow traced references. If it encounters any untraced references it pickles them as `NIL`.

It is a good idea to use object types in pickles instead of `REF RECORDS`, since you might need to subtype them later. For example, suppose that you have implemented a data storage system involving objects with the following type:

```
TYPE
  Employee = OBJECT
    name, phoneNumber, office: TEXT
  END
```

A few years later you decide that it would be nice to start storing electronic mail addresses as well. But you have thousands of old pickles that (we suppose) you cannot arrange to convert. You therefore change the program to

```
TYPE
  Employee = OBJECT
    name, phoneNumber, office: TEXT
  END;
  NewEmployee = OldEmployee OBJECT
    email: TEXT
  END;
```

The parts of the program that use only the old fields will not need to be changed. The parts of the program that use the new field can use `TYPECASE` to distinguish old pickles from new pickles.

You can register procedures to control the behavior of the pickles package. For example, consider the following "Atom" interface, which hashes texts into unique atoms:

```
INTERFACE Atom;
  TYPE T <: REFANY;
  PROCEDURE FromText(txt:TEXT): T;
  PROCEDURE ToText(atm: T): TEXT;
  (* ToText(FromText(txt)) = txt *)
  (* Text.Equal(ToText(a), ToText(b)) => a = b. *)
END Atom.
```

A simple implementation would represent an `Atom.T` by a reference to an element of a bucket of a global chained hash table. If an `Atom.T` were then pickled and unpickled, the result would be a copy of a fragment of a bucket of the hash table, which wouldn't be of any use to anybody.

Instead, when `Pkl.Write` encounters an `Atom.T` (say `atm`), we would like it to write `Atom.ToText(atm)` into the pickle; and when `Pkl.Read` encounters this text (say `txt`), we would like it to call `Atom.FromText(txt)` to reconstruct the atom for that text. The initialization code for Atom can arrange for this the happen by registering "byte specials" as follows:

```
PROCEDURE WriteAtom(r: REFANY): TEXT =
  BEGIN RETURN Atom.ToText(r) END WriteAtom;

PROCEDURE ReadAtom(READONLY bytes: ARRAY OF CHAR): REFANY =
  BEGIN
    RETURN Atom.FromText(Text.FromChars(bytes))
  END ReadAtom;

Pkl.RegisterBytes(TYPECODE(Atom.T), WriteAtom, ReadAtom);
```

The call to Pkl.RegisterBytes causes Pkl.Write to use WriteAtom to pickle each Atom.T that it encounters, and causes Pkl.Read to use ReadAtom to unpickle each Atom.T that it finds in the pickle. ReadAtom is applied to whatever sequence of bytes was returned by WriteAtom.

It is also possible to register "convert" procedures for a type, which will be applied whenever a member of that type is pickled or unpickled. A convert procedure takes the object to be converted as a VAR parameter and modifies it in place. For example, a parse tree that has been decorated by the front end of a compiler might contain redundant information than is not worth storing in a pickle. In this case convert procedures could be used to prune away the redundant information when the pickle is written and recompute it when the pickle is read.

Pkl.Write always copies an object before applying a convert procedure to it, to avoid modifying the data structure being pickled. Pkl.Read applies the convert procedure to the copy that it constructs.

To summarize, the two important differences between convert procedures and bytes procedures are:

- A bytes procedure produces raw data that Pkl.Write stores in the pickle without further ado; a convert procedure produces a modified copy of an object that Pkl.Write traces as though it were part of the original data structure. Any references to the original object encountered during tracing are pickled as though they were references to the copy.

- When an object is pickled or unpickled, the convert procedures for its type and all its supertypes are invoked. But the bytes procedure is only invoked for an object's allocated type: any bytes procedures for its supertypes are ignored.

```
INTERFACE Pkl;

IMPORT Rd, Wr, Thread;

EXCEPTION Error(Code);
```

```
PROCEDURE Write(r: REFANY; wr: Wr.T)
  RAISES {Wr.Failure, Thread.Alerted, Error};
```

Trace the data structure reachable via traced references from r, convert it into a pickle, and write the pickle to wr, which must be seekable. The order in which the data structure is traced is unspecified.

```
PROCEDURE Read(rd: Rd.T): REFANY RAISES Error;
```

Read a pickle from rd, reconstruct a copy of the pickled data structure, and return it.

```
TYPE
  ConvertProc = PROCEDURE(r: REFANY);
```

```
PROCEDURE RegisterConvertProcs(
  tc: INTEGER;
  wrproc: ConvertProc;
  rdproc: ConvertProc);
```

Register wrproc and rdproc as the write and read conversion procedures for the type with code tc. It is a checked error to call this more than once for the same type, unless wrproc and rdproc are the same as they were on the previous calls (in which case it has no effect).

Whenever Pkl.Write traces a reference r, if there are conversion procedures registered for any type that contains r, then r is copied, the conversion procedures are applied to the copy, and tracing continues using the copy in place of the original. The conversion procedures are applied in supertype-to-subtype order. References to the original will be pickled as though they were references to the copy.

Whenever Pkl.Read reconstructs a reference r the read conversion procedures for the types that contain r will be applied to r. The read conversion procedures for any particular reference will be applied in supertype-to-subtype order, but the order in which the different references are converted is unspecified.

```
TYPE
  WriteBytesProc = PROCEDURE(r: REFANY): TEXT;
  ReadBytesProc = PROCEDURE(READONLY bytes: ARRAY OF CHAR): REFANY;
```

```
PROCEDURE RegisterBytesProcs(
  tc: INTEGER;
  wrproc: WriteBytesProc;
  rdproc: ReadBytesProc);
```

Register wrproc and rdproc as the write and read bytes procedures for the type with code tc. It is a checked error to call this more than once for the same type, unless wrproc and rdproc are the same as they were on the previous calls (in which case it has no effect).

Whenever `Pkl.Write` traces a reference `r`, if `r`'s type has a `WriteBytesProc`, then the procedure is applied, the resulting text is written into the pickle, and `r` is otherwise ignored.

Whenever `Pkl.Read` encounters a sequence of bytes in a pickle that were written by a `WriteBytes` special for type `t`, then the `ReadBytesProc` for type `t` is applied to those bytes and the result is included in the data structure in place of the original reference `r`.

In `Pkl.Write`, the convert procedures are all applied before any of the bytes procedures. In `Pkl.Read`, the bytes procedures are all applied before any of the convert procedures. A convert procedure and a bytes procedure can be registered for the same type, in which case both will be applied.

```
TYPE
  Code = {Malformed, UnknownType, UnknownProc, NoReadBytesProc,
  WrongType, Unseekable};
```

`Malformed` is raised by `Pkl.Read` on malformed pickles.

`UnknownType` is raised by `Pkl.Read` if the pickle contains some type that is not present in the reading program.

`UnknownProc` is raised by `Pkl.Read` if the pickle contains some procedure that is not present in the reading program.

`NoReadBytesProc` is raised by `Pkl.Read` if the pickle contains a sequence of bytes written by a `WriteBytesProc` registered for type T, but there is no `ReadBytesProc` registered for T in the reading program.

`WrongType` is raised by `Pkl.Read` if a `ReadBytesProc` registered for type T returns a result that is not a member of type T.

`Unseekable` is raised by `Pkl.Write` if given an unseekable writer.

```
END Pkl.
```

3.7 The Table interface

The basic generic table interface takes two parameters `Key` and `Value`, which provide the key and value types for the particular table being defined. The table type declared in the generic interface is an object type whose methods operate on the table. A stylized comment immediately after the generic header identifies the restrictions on the parameters:

```
GENERIC INTERFACE Table(Key, Value);
(* where Key.T and Value.T are types *)
```

A Table.T is a partial map from keys to values. That is, if tbl is a Table.T, then for each k in the set domain(tbl), k is a Key.T and tbl(k) is a Value.T.

```
TYPE T <: OBJECT
  METHODS
    get(key: Key.T; VAR val: Value.T): BOOLEAN;
    put(key: Key.T; val: Value.T): BOOLEAN;
    delete(key: Key.T; VAR val: Value.T): BOOLEAN;
    clear();
    copy(): T;
    size(): CARDINAL;
    map(cl: Closure) RAISES ANY;
    init(size: CARDINAL): T
  END;
```

Here are the specifications of the methods:

tbl.get(key, val): If key is in domain(tbl), set val := tbl(key) and return TRUE, else return FALSE.

tbl.put(key, val): Set tbl(key) := val. Return TRUE if key was already in domain(tbl), FALSE if it was not. This method will expand the table if necessary.

tbl.delete(key, val): If key is in domain(tbl), set val := tbl(key), remove (key, val) from tbl, and return TRUE; else return FALSE.

tbl.clear(): Remove all entries from tbl.

tbl.copy(): Make and return a copy of tbl.

tbl.size(): Return the number of key-value pairs in tbl.

tbl.map(cl): Map cl over tbl until it returns TRUE. (See the definition of the type Closure below.) More precisely, tbl.map(cl) is equivalent to the following:

```
FOR EACH (key, value) such that tbl(key) = value
  IF cl.apply(key, value) THEN EXIT END
END
```

The only exceptions raised by Map are those raised by cl.apply.

tbl.init(n): Initialize tbl to an empty table that has room for at least n key-value pairs before it is rehashed. This must be called before the table is used.

The only other declaration in the interface is for the closure type passed to the apply method:

```
TYPE Closure = OBJECT
  METHODS
    apply(key: Key.T; value: Value.T): BOOLEAN RAISES ANY
  END;

END Table.
```

The parameters to the corresponding generic module are Key, Value, and also the particular instance of Table that is to be implemented. The generic module imposes the additional constraint that the Key interface must supply procedures for hashing and comparing keys:

```
GENERIC MODULE Table(Key, Value, Tbl);
(* where Tbl = Table(Key, Value)
   and Key.Hash(k: Key.T): INTEGER,
   and Key.Equal(k1, k2: Key.T): BOOLEAN. *)
...
END Table.
```

We will omit the body of the generic module, which is a straightforward table implementation using double hashing.

As an example of the use of Table, a client would create interfaces and modules for mapping TEXTs to TEXTs like this:

```
INTERFACE TextTable = Table(Text, Text) END TextTable.

MODULE TextTable = Table(Text, Text, TextTable) END TextTable.
```

and then use them in some other program like this:

```
    IMPORT TextTable;
    ...
    capital := NEW(TextTable.T).init(50);
    EVAL capital.put("California", "Sacramento");
    EVAL capital.put("Hawaii", "Honolulu");
    EVAL capital.put("Alaska", "Juneau");
    ...
```

SRC Modula-3 provides other generic table implementations that are specialized to particular key types, such as scalars. These use the same Table interface; the only difference is the comment that expresses the restriction on the parameters to the generic module. SRC Modula-3 also provides special types of tables with additional functionality. For example, there is a sorted table that uses balanced trees and provides methods for enumerating subranges of the table. In this case, there is a new generic interface SortedTable, that defines SortedTable.T as an opaque subtype of Table.T, with additional methods for enumerating subranges.

We will not describe these specialized tables further, but we mention them as examples of the flexibility that can be achieved by object types together with generics.

Chapter 4

An Introduction to Programming with Threads

A. D. Birrell

The advent of parallel programming may do something to revive the
pioneer spirit in programming, which seems to be degenerating
into a rather dull and routine occupation.
—S. Gill, 1958

This chapter provides an introduction to writing concurrent programs using the Modula-3 Thread interface, which allows you to write programs with multiple simultaneous points of execution, synchronizing through shared memory. It describes the basic thread and synchronization primitives, then for each primitive provides a tutorial on how to use it. The tutorial sections provide advice on the best ways to use the primitives, give warnings about what can go wrong, and offer hints about how to avoid these pitfalls. The chapter is aimed at experienced programmers who want to acquire practical expertise in writing concurrent programs.

4.1   Introduction

Many experimental operating systems, and some commercial ones, have recently included support for concurrent programming. The most popular mechanism for this is some provision for allowing multiple lightweight "threads" within a single address space, used from within a single program.[1]

Programming with threads introduces new difficulties even for experienced programmers. Concurrent programming has techniques and pitfalls that do not occur in sequential programming. Many of the techniques are obvious, but some are obvious only with hindsight. Some of the pitfalls are comfortable (for example, deadlock is a pleasant sort of bug—your program stops with all the evidence intact), but some take the form of insidious performance problems.

The purpose of this chapter is to give you an introduction to programming techniques that work well with threads, and to warn you about techniques or interactions that work out badly. It should provide the experienced sequential programmer with enough hints to be able to build a substantial multi-threaded program that works—correctly, efficiently, and with a minimum of surprises.

A "thread" is a straightforward concept: a single sequential flow of control. In a high-level language you normally program a thread using procedures, where the procedure calls follow the traditional stack discipline. Within a single thread, there is at any instant a single point of execution. The programmer need learn nothing new to use a single thread.

Having "multiple threads" in a program means that at any instant the program has multiple points of execution, one in each of its threads. The programmer can mostly view the threads as executing simultaneously, as if the computer were endowed with as many processors as there are threads. The programmer is required to decide when and where to create multiple threads, or to accept such decisions made for him by implementers of existing library packages or runtime systems. Additionally, the programmer must occasionally be aware that the computer might not in fact execute all his threads simultaneously.

Having the threads execute within "a single address space" means that the computer's addressing hardware is configured so as to permit the threads to read and write the same memory locations. In other words, the off-stack (global) variables are shared among all the threads of the program. Each thread executes on a separate call stack with its own separate local variables. The programmer is responsible for using the synchronization mechanisms of the thread facility to ensure that the shared memory is accessed in a manner that will give the correct answer.

The Thread interface is designed to be "lightweight". This means that thread creation, existence, destruction and synchronization primitives are cheap enough that you can use them for all your concurrency needs.

Please be aware that I am presenting you with a selective and idiosyncratic collection of techniques. Selective, because an exhaustive survey would be premature, and would be too exhausting to serve as an introduction—I will be discussing only the most important

---

[1]Throughout this chapter I use the word "process" only when I mean a single flow of control associated one-to-one with an address space, since this now seems to be the most common usage of that word.

thread primitives, omitting features such as per-thread context information. Idiosyncratic, because the techniques presented here derive from my personal experience of programming with threads over the last ten years—I have not attempted to represent colleagues who might have different opinions about which programming techniques are good or important. Nevertheless, I believe that an understanding of the ideas presented here will serve as a sound basis for programming with concurrent threads. I will frequently cite our experience with Threads in the Topaz system at Digital's Systems Research Center (SRC).

Threads are not a tool for automatic parallel decomposition, where a compiler will take an apparently sequential program and generate object code to utilize multiple processors. That is an entirely different art, which I will not discuss here.

4.2   Why use concurrency?

Life would be simpler if you didn't need to use concurrency. But there are a variety of forces pushing towards its use. The most recent is the advent of multiprocessors. With these machines, there really are multiple simultaneous points of execution, and threads are an attractive tool for allowing a program to take advantage of the available hardware. The alternative, with most conventional operating systems, is to configure your program as multiple separate processes, running in separate address spaces. This tends to be expensive to set up, and the costs of communicating between address spaces are often high, even in the presence of shared segments. By using a lightweight multi-threading facility, the programmer can utilize the processors cheaply. This seems to work well in systems having up to about ten processors, but not so well in those having thousands.

A second area where threads are useful is in driving slow devices such as disks, networks, terminals and printers. In these cases an efficient program should be doing some useful work while waiting for the device to produce its next event (such as the completion of a disk transfer or the receipt of a packet from the network). As we will see later, this can be programmed quite easily with threads by adopting an attitude that device requests are all sequential (i.e. they suspend execution of the invoking thread until the request completes), and that the program meanwhile does other work in other threads.

A third source of concurrency is human users. Humans are actually quite good at doing two or three things at a time, and seem to get offended if their computer cannot. Again, threads are a convenient way of programming this. The typical arrangement of a modern window system is that each time the user invokes an action (by clicking a button with the mouse, for example), a separate thread is used to implement the action. If the user invokes multiple actions, multiple threads will perform them concurrently. (Note that the implementation of the window system probably also uses a thread to watch the mouse actions themselves, since the mouse is an example of a slow device.)

A final source of concurrency appears when building a distributed system. Here we frequently encounter shared network servers (such as a file server or a spooling print server), that are willing to service requests from multiple clients. Use of multiple threads allows the server to handle clients' requests in parallel, instead of artificially serializing them (or creating one server process per client, at great expense).

Sometimes you can deliberately add concurrency to your program in order to reduce the latency of operations (the elapsed time between start and completion). Often, some of the work incurred by a procedure can be deferred, since it does not affect the result of the procedure. For example, when you add or remove something in a balanced tree you can happily return to the caller before re-balancing the tree. With threads you can achieve this easily: do the re-balancing in a separate thread. If the separate thread is scheduled at a lower priority, then the work can be done at a time when the system is less busy (for example, when waiting for user input). Adding threads to defer work is a powerful technique, even on a uni-processor. Even if the same total work is done, reducing latency can improve the responsiveness of your program.

4.3   The design of a thread facility

The Thread interface provides four major mechanisms: thread creation, mutual exclusion, waiting for events, and getting a thread out of an unwanted long-term wait.

A thread is created by calling Fork(cl), where cl is a *closure*, that is, an object with an *apply* method:

```
TYPE Closure = OBJECT METHODS apply (): REFANY END

PROCEDURE Fork(cl: Closure): Thread.T;
```

The call Fork(cl) creates a new thread that computes cl.apply(). Fork returns a handle on the new thread. The handle can be passed to Thread.Join, which waits for the thread to finish its computation, and returns the result:

```
PROCEDURE Join(th: Thread.T): REFANY;
```

As a simple example of the use of Fork and Join, suppose that we are given a numerical procedure F and want to compute the sum F(0) + F(1) by evaluating both terms concurrently. First we declare a closure whose apply method will compute an application of F:

```
TYPE
  FClosure = Thread.Closure OBJECT
    arg, result: INTEGER
  OVERRIDES
    apply := ApplyF
  END;
```

```
PROCEDURE ApplyF(self: FClosure): REFANY =
  BEGIN self.result := F(self.arg); RETURN NIL END ApplyF;
```

Then we fork the computation of F(0) while computing F(1) concurrently in the main thread:

```
VAR
  cl := NEW(FClosure, arg := 0);
  t := Thread.Fork(cl);
  f1 := F(1);
EVAL Thread.Join(t);
RETURN f1 + cl.result
```

In practice, Join is not called very much. Most forked threads are permanent dæmon threads, or have no results, or communicate their results by some synchronization arrangement other than Join. If a thread finishes and no handles on it are accessible, then the thread disappears and its storage is garbage-collected. If the result of a thread is an exception, then a checked runtime error occurs—the exception is not propagated to calls of Thread.Join.

4.3.1 Mutual exclusion

The simplest way that Modula-3 threads interact is through access to shared global variables. Since threads are running concurrently, you must explicitly arrange to avoid errors that arise when more than one thread is accessing the shared variables. The simplest tool for doing this is a primitive that offers mutual exclusion (sometimes called critical sections), specifying for a particular region of code that only one thread can execute there at any time. In Modula-3, this is achieved with the data type MUTEX and the language's LOCK construct.

```
VAR m := NEW(MUTEX);
LOCK m DO ... statements ... END;
```

A mutex has two states: locked and unlocked, initially unlocked. The LOCK clause locks the mutex, then executes the contained statements, then unlocks the mutex. A thread executing inside the LOCK clause is said to *hold* the mutex. If another thread attempts to lock the mutex when it is already locked, the second thread blocks (enqueued on the mutex) until the mutex is unlocked.

The programmer can achieve mutual exclusion on a set of variables by associating them with a mutex, and accessing the variables only from a thread that holds the mutex (i.e., from a thread executing inside a LOCK clause that has locked the mutex). This is the basis of the notion of monitors, first described by Tony Hoare [12]. For example, in the following fragment the mutex m is associated with the global variable head; the LOCK clause provides mutual exclusion for adding the local variable newElement to a linked list whose head is head.

```
TYPE List = OBJECT ch: CHAR; next: List END;
VAR head: List;

LOCK m DO
  newElement.next := head;
  head := newElement
END;
```

The simplest sort of mutex is a global variable (as in the fragment above); in this case at most one thread is executing inside the LOCK clause at any instant.

A mutex can also be used to protect specific parts of a data structure instead of a group of global variables. In this case it is common to declare the mutex as a field of the data structure, near the fields that it protects. For example, a mutex field in an object is often used to protect the remaining data fields of the object. This allows at most one thread to access the fields of any particular object, but multiple threads can access different objects concurrently. A convenient way to arrange this is to declare the object type as a subtype of MUTEX, which places the mutex first, and saves a level of indirection.

4.3.2 Condition variables

A mutex is a simple resource scheduling mechanism. The resource being scheduled is the shared memory accessed inside the LOCK clause, and the scheduling policy is "one thread at a time". But more complicated scheduling policies are often needed, which require a mechanism that blocks a thread until some event happens. In Modula-3, this is achieved with the following declarations in the Thread interface:

```
TYPE Condition <: ROOT;
PROCEDURE Wait(m: MUTEX; c: Condition);
PROCEDURE Signal(c: Condition);
PROCEDURE Broadcast(c: Condition);
```

A *monitor* consists of some data, a mutex, and zero or more condition variables. A particular condition variable is always used in conjunction with the same mutex and its data. The Wait operation atomically unlocks the mutex and blocks the thread (enqueued on the condition variable). (This atomicity guarantee avoids the problem known in the literature as the "wake-up waiting" race [26].) The Signal operation does nothing unless there is a thread blocked on the condition variable, in which case it awakens at least one such blocked thread. The Broadcast operation is like Signal, except that it awakens all the threads currently blocked on the condition variable. When a thread is awakened from a call toWait, it re-locks the mutex and returns. If the mutex is not available, the thread will block until it is.

A condition variable's mutex protects the shared data that is used for the scheduling decision. If a thread wants the resource, it locks the mutex and examines the shared data. If the resource is available, the thread continues. If not, the thread unlocks the mutex and blocks, by calling Wait. Later, when some other thread makes the resource available it awakens the first thread by calling Signal or Broadcast. For example, the following fragment allows a thread to block until a linked list is non-empty, then remove the top element of the list. The linked list's first element is head, and the protecting mutex is m:

```
VAR nonEmpty := NEW(Thread.Condition);

LOCK m DO
  WHILE head = NIL DO Thread.Wait(m, nonEmpty) END;
  topElement := head;
  head := head.next;
END;
```

The following fragment could be used by a thread adding an element to the list:

```
LOCK m DO
  newElement.next := head;
  head := newElement;
  Thread.Signal(nonEmpty);
END;
```

4.3.3 Alerts

The final aspect of the Thread interface is a mechanism for interrupting a particular thread, causing it to back out of some long-term wait or computation. Here are the relevant declarations from the interface:

```
EXCEPTION Alerted;
PROCEDURE Alert(t: T);
PROCEDURE AlertWait(m: MUTEX, c: Condition) RAISES Alerted;
PROCEDURE TestAlert(): BOOLEAN;
```

The state of a thread includes a boolean known as alert-pending, initially false. A call to AlertWait behaves the same as Wait, except that if the thread's alert-pending flag is true, then instead of blocking on c the call sets alert-pending to false, re-locks m, and raises the exception Alerted. If you call Alert(t) when t is currently blocked on a condition variable inside a call of AlertWait then t is awakened, t re-locks the mutex m and then it raises the exception Alerted. A call to Alert(t) when t is not blocked in AlertWait, merely sets the alert-pending flag to true. The call TestAlert atomically tests and clears the thread's alert-pending boolean.

For example, consider a GetChar routine that blocks until a character is available on an interactive keyboard input stream. If some other thread determines that the input is no longer interesting (for example, because the user has clicked CANCEL with his mouse), then the first thread should return from GetChar. If you knew the condition variable on which GetChar blocks you could just signal it, but often that condition variable is hidden under one or more layers of abstraction. In this situation, you can achieve your goal by calling Thread.Alert(t), where t is the thread calling GetChar. For this to work, GetChar must contain something like the following fragment.

```
TRY
  WHILE empty DO Thread.AlertWait(m, nonEmpty) END;
  RETURN NextChar()
EXCEPT
  Thread.Alerted => RETURN EndOfFile
END;
```

Alerts are complicated, and their use produces complicated programs. We will discuss them in more detail later.

4.4 Using a mutex: accessing shared data

The basic rule for using mutual exclusion is straightforward: in a multi-threaded program all shared mutable data must be protected by associating it with some mutex, and you must access the data only from a thread that is holding the associated mutex (i.e., from a thread executing within a LOCK clause that locked the mutex).

4.4.1 Unprotected data

The simplest bug related to mutexes occurs when you fail to protect some mutable data and access it without the benefits of synchronization. For example, consider the following code fragment. The global variable table represents a table that can be filled with REFANY values by calling Insert. The procedure works by inserting a non-NIL argument at index i of table, then incrementing i. The table is initially empty (all NIL).

```
VAR table := ARRAY [0..999] OF REFANY {NIL, ..};
VAR i: [0..1000] := 0;

PROCEDURE Insert(r: REFANY) =
  BEGIN
    IF r # NIL THEN
    ①  table[i] := r;
    ②  i := i+1;
    END;
  END Insert;
```

Now consider what might happen if thread A calls Insert(x) concurrently with thread B calling Insert(y). If the order of execution happens to be that thread A executes ①, then thread B executes ①, then thread A executes ②, then thread B executes ②, confusion will result. Instead of the intended effect (that x and y are inserted into table, at separate indexes), the final state would be that y is correctly in the table, but x has been lost. Further, since ② has been executed twice, an empty (NIL) slot has been left orphaned in the table. Such errors would be prevented by enclosing ① and ② in a LOCK clause, as follows.

```
PROCEDURE Insert(r: REFANY) =
  BEGIN
    IF r # NIL THEN
      LOCK m DO
        table[i] := r;
        i := i+1;
      END;
    END;
  END Insert;
```

The LOCK clause enforces serialization of the threads' actions, so that one thread executes the statements inside the LOCK clause, then the other thread executes them.

The effects of unsynchronized access to mutable data can be bizarre, since they will depend on the precise timing relationship between your threads. Also, in most environments the timing relationship is non-deterministic (because of real-time effects like page faults, or the use of timer facilities, or because of actual asynchrony in a multiprocessor system).

The rule against accessing shared data without the protection of a lock is not enforced by Modula-3, since in some programs the association between a variable and the mutex that protects it can be hard to capture by a simple static declaration. For example, if a mutex in the root node of a tree structure protects data fields in all the internal nodes of the tree, there is no way to check statically whether the correct root is locked when an internal node is accessed.

In some situations, you might protect different parts of a record with different mutexes. You might also have some immutable fields that need no protection at all. But either of these techniques can make your program implementation-dependent. You must be careful about how the record is laid out in memory. If you pack fields into records sufficiently tightly that they cannot be accessed by atomic operations on your computer's memory, and if you protect such packed fields with different mutexes, you might get the wrong answer. This is because the generated instructions for modifying such fields involve reading them, modifying them in a register (or on-stack), then writing them back. If two threads are doing this concurrently for two fields that occupy the same memory word, you might get the wrong result.

You need to be especially conscious of this potential bug if you use packed types for laying out fields of records. You can preserve portability by using the constant Thread.AtomicSize to lay out the record so that fields protected by different mutexes are in different memory coherency units.

4.4.2 Invariants

When the data protected by a mutex is at all complicated, many programmers find it convenient to think of the mutex as protecting the invariant of the associated data. An invariant is a boolean function of the data that is true whenever the mutex is not held. So any thread that locks the mutex knows that it starts out with the invariant true. Each thread has the responsibility to restore the invariant before releasing the mutex. This includes restoring the invariant before calling Wait, since that unlocks the mutex.

For example, in the code fragment above (for inserting an element into a table), the invariant is that i is the index of the first NIL element in table, and all elements beyond index i are NIL. Note that the variables mentioned in the invariant are accessed only with this mutex held. Note also that the invariant is not true after the first assignment statement but before the second one—it is only guaranteed when the mutex is not being held.

Invariants are frequently simple enough that you barely think about them, but your program will often benefit if you write them down explicitly. And if they are too complicated to write down, you're probably doing something wrong. You might find it best to write down your invariants informally, as in the previous paragraph, or you might prefer to use some formal specification language such as Larch [9], the language used to specify the synchronization primitives of the Thread interface in Chapter 5. It is also generally a good idea to make it clear (by writing it down in the program) which mutex protects which data items.

4.4.3 Cheating

The rule that you must use a mutex to protect every access to global variables is based on a concurrency model where the actions of the threads are arbitrarily interleaved. If the data being protected by a mutex is particularly simple (for example just one integer, or even just one boolean), programmers are often tempted to skip using the mutex, since it introduces significant overhead and they "know" that the variables will be accessed with atomic instructions and that instructions are not interleaved. Before you succumb to this temptation, consider carefully the hardware on which your program will run. If your single integer variable is word aligned, and if you are running on a uni-processor, and if your compiler generates the obvious instruction sequences and doesn't slave variables into registers, then you will probably get the correct answer. In other circumstances you might not get the correct answer; or worse, you might usually get the correct answer but very occasionally get the wrong answer. Remember, too, that if your code is worth anything it is likely to be ported to machines that haven't even been designed yet. For machine independent correct code, you absolutely must use the synchronization primitives in the Thread interface.[2]

---

[2]There is indeed a strong argument that there should be a way for the programmer to take advantage of the atomicity of instructions, and so avoid the cost of a LOCK clause. However, it seems to be difficult to define such a feature in an efficient but machine-independent fashion.

One cheating technique I have found helpful is to use an unsynchronized access as a hint, that is, a cheap way of getting information that is either correct or causes you to invoke a more expensive, correct, way of getting the information. For example, if you want to call an initialization procedure exactly once you might use code like the following.

```
IF NOT initDone THEN
  LOCK m DO
    IF NOT initDone THEN
      Initialize();
      initDone := TRUE;
    END;
  END;
END;
```

This code relies on the fact that if a boolean variable is written and read concurrently, the read returns either TRUE or FALSE without error.

4.4.4   Deadlocks involving only mutexes

The simplest cases of deadlock occur when a thread tries to lock a mutex that it already holds. There are numerous more elaborate cases of deadlock involving mutexes, for example:

> Thread A locks mutex M1;
> Thread B locks mutex M2;
> Thread A blocks trying to lock M2;
> Thread B blocks trying to lock M1.

The most effective rule for avoiding such deadlocks is to apply a partial order to the acquisition of mutexes in your program. In other words, arrange that for any pair of mutexes M1, M2, each thread that ever locks both M1 and M2 does so in the same order (for example, M1 is always locked before M2), and that this order is free of cycles. This rule completely avoids deadlocks involving only mutexes (though as we will see later, there are other potential deadlocks when your program uses condition variables).

There is a technique that sometimes makes it easier to achieve this partial order. In the example above, thread A probably wasn't trying to modify exactly the same set of data as thread B. Frequently, if you examine the algorithm carefully you can partition the data into smaller pieces protected by separate mutexes. For example, when thread B wanted to lock M1, it might actually be wanting access to data disjoint from the data that thread A was accessing under M1. In such a case you might protect this disjoint data with a separate mutex, M3, and avoid the deadlock. This is just a technique to enable you to have a partial order on the mutexes (M1 before M2 before M3, in this example). But remember that the more you pursue this hint, the more complicated your locking becomes, and the more likely you are to have some unsynchronized access to shared data. The risk of deadlock is almost always preferable to the risk having your program give the wrong answer.

4.4.5 Poor performance through lock conflicts

Assuming that you have arranged your program to have enough mutexes that all the data is protected, and that it does not deadlock, the remaining mutex problems to worry about are all performance problems.

Whenever a thread is holding a mutex, it is potentially stopping other threads from making progress—if they block on the mutex. If the first thread can use all the machine's resources, that is probably fine. But if the first thread, while holding the mutex, ceases to make progress (for example by blocking on another mutex, or by taking a page fault, or by waiting for an i/o device), then the total throughput of your program is degraded. The problem is worse on a multiprocessor, where no single thread can utilize the entire machine; here if you cause another thread to block, it might mean that a processor goes idle. In general, to get good performance you must arrange that lock conflicts are rare events. The best way to reduce lock conflicts is to lock at a finer granularity; but this introduces complexity. There is no way out of this dilemma— it is a trade-off inherent in concurrent computation.

The most typical example where locking granularity is important is in a module that manages a set of objects, for example a set of open buffered files. The simplest strategy is to use a single mutex for all the operations: open, close, read, write, and so forth. But this would prevent multiple writes on separate files proceeding in parallel, for no good reason. So a better strategy is to use one lock for operations on the global list of open files, and one lock per open file for operations affecting only that file. This can be achieved by associating a mutex with the record representing each open file. The code might look something like the following:

```
TYPE File = MUTEX OBJECT ... END;
     globalTable = MUTEX OBJECT ... END;
VAR globalTable := NEW(GlobalTable);

PROCEDURE Open(name: String): File =
  BEGIN
    LOCK globalTable DO ... (* access globalTable *) ... END;
  END Open;
PROCEDURE Write(f: File, ...) =
  BEGIN
    LOCK f DO ... (* access f *) ... END;
  END Write;
```

Notice the use of subtyping: for example, since File is a subtype of MUTEX, "LOCK f" works just fine. If the mutex had been placed in one of the explicitly declared fields of the File object (say, the mu field) then it would have been necessary to write "LOCK f.mu" instead.

There is an interaction between mutexes and the thread scheduler that can produce particularly insidious performance problems. The scheduler is the part of the thread implementation (often part of the operating system) that decides which of the non-blocked threads should actually be given a processor to run on. Generally the scheduler makes its decision based on a priority associated with each thread. (Depending on the details of your system the priority might be fixed or dynamic, programmer-assigned or computed by the scheduler. Often the algorithm for deciding which thread to run is not documented.) Lock conflicts can lead to a situation where some high priority thread never makes progress at all, despite the fact that its high priority indicates that it is more urgent than the threads actually running. This can happen, for example, in the following scenario on a uni-processor. Thread A is high priority, thread B is medium priority and thread C is low priority. The sequence of events is:

> C is running (e.g., because A and B are blocked);
> C locks mutex m;
> B wakes up and preempts C
>   (i.e., B runs instead of C since B has higher priority);
> B embarks on some very long computation;
> A wakes up and preempts B (since A has higher priority);
> A tries to lock m;
> A blocks, and so the processor is given back to B;
> B continues its very long computation.

The net effect is that a high priority thread (A) is unable to make progress even though the processor is being used by a medium priority thread (B). This state is stable until there is processor time available for the low priority thread C to complete its work and unlock m.

You can avoid this problem by arranging for C to raise its priority before locking M. But this can be quite inconvenient, since it involves considering for each mutex which other thread priorities might be involved. The real solution of this problem lies with the implementer of your threads facility. He must somehow communicate to the scheduler that since A is blocked on m, the thread holding m should be viewed as having at least as high a priority as A. Unfortunately, your implementer has probably failed to do this—we don't do it in the SRC implementation.

4.4.6   Releasing the mutex within a lock clause

There are times when you want to unlock the mutex in some region of program nested inside a LOCK clause. For example, you might want to unlock the mutex before calling down to a lower level abstraction that will block or execute for a long time (in order to avoid provoking delays for other threads that want to lock the mutex). The Thread interface provides for this usage by offering the raw operations Acquire(m) and Release(m). You must exercise extra care if you take advantage of this. First, you must be sure that the operations are correctly bracketed, even in the presence of exceptions. Second, you must be prepared for the fact that the state of the monitor's data might have changed while you had the mutex unlocked. This can be tricky if you called Release explicitly (instead of just ending the LOCK clause) because you were imbedded in some flow control construct such as a conditional clause. Your program counter might now depend on the previous state of the monitor's data, implicitly making a decision that might no longer be valid. I recommend that you avoid this paradigm, to reduce the tendency to introduce quite subtle bugs.

4.5 Using a condition variable: scheduling shared resources

A condition variable is used when the simple one-at-a-time mutual exclusion provided by mutexes is not sufficient. Consider the following example, where one or more producer threads are passing data to one or more consumers. The data is transferred through an unbounded buffer formed by a linked list whose head is the global variable head. If the linked list is empty, the consumer blocks on the condition variable nonEmpty until the producer generates some more data. The list and the condition variable are protected by the mutex m.

```
VAR m := NEW(MUTEX);
VAR head: List;
VAR nonEmpty := NEW(Thread.Condition);

PROCEDURE Consume(): List =
  VAR topElement: List;
  BEGIN
    LOCK m DO
      WHILE head = NIL DO Thread.Wait(m, nonEmpty) END;
      topElement := head;
      head := head.next;
    END;
    RETURN topElement
  END Consume;

PROCEDURE Produce(newElement: List) =
  BEGIN
    LOCK m DO
      newElement.next := head;
      head := newElement;
      Thread.Signal(nonEmpty);
    END;
  END Produce;
```

This is fairly straightforward, but there are still some subtleties. Notice that when the consumer returns from the call of Wait its first action after re-locking the mutex is to check once more whether the linked list is empty. This is an example of the following general pattern, which I strongly recommend for all your uses of condition variables.

```
WHILE NOT expression DO Thread.Wait(m, c) END;
```

You might think that re-testing the expression is redundant: in the example above, the producer made the list non-empty before calling `Signal`. But the semantics of `Signal` do not guarantee that the awakened thread will be the next to lock the mutex. It is possible that some other consumer thread will intervene, lock the mutex, remove the list element and unlock the mutex, before the newly awakened thread can lock the mutex. (The condition variables described here are not the same as those originally described by Hoare [12]. Hoare's design would indeed provide a sufficient guarantee to make this re-testing redundant. But the design given here appears to be preferable, since it permits a much simpler implementation, and the extra check is not usually expensive.) A second reason for re-checking is that `Signal` is allowed to awaken more than one thread; this allows more efficient code to be generated for the `Wait` and `Signal` primitives.

In any case, use of this pattern makes your program more obviously, and more robustly, correct. With this style it is immediately clear that the expression is true before the following statements are executed. Without it, this fact could be verified only by looking at all the places that might signal the condition variable. In other words, this programming convention allows you to verify correctness by local inspection, which is always preferable to global inspection.

A final advantage of this convention is that it allows for simple programming of calls to `Signal` or `Broadcast`—extra wake-ups are benign. Carefully coding to ensure that only the correct threads are unblocked is now only a performance question, not a correctness one (but of course you must ensure that at least the correct threads are unblocked).

4.5.1   Using Broadcast

The `Signal` primitive is useful if you know that at most one thread can usefully be awakened. `Broadcast` awakens all threads that have called `Wait`. If you always program in the recommended style of re-checking an expression after return from `Wait`, then the correctness of your program will be unaffected if you replace calls of `Signal` with calls of `Broadcast`.

One use of `Broadcast` is when you want to simplify your program by awakening multiple threads, even though you know that not all of them can make progress. This allows you to be less careful about separating different wait reasons into different condition variables. This use trades slightly poorer performance for greater simplicity. Another use of `Broadcast` is when you really need to awaken multiple threads, because the resource you have just made available can be used by multiple threads.

A simple example where `Broadcast` is useful is in the scheduling policy known as shared/exclusive locking (or readers/writers locking). Most commonly this is used when you have some shared data being read and written by various threads: your algorithm will be correct (and perform better) if you allow multiple threads to read the data concurrently, but a thread modifying the data must do so when no other thread is accessing it.

The following procedures implement this scheduling policy. Any thread wanting to read your data calls AcquireShared, then reads the data, then calls ReleaseShared. Similarly any thread wanting to modify the data calls AcquireExclusive, then modifies the data, then calls ReleaseExclusive. When the variable i is greater than zero, it counts the number of active readers. When it is negative there is an active writer. When it is zero, no thread is using the data. If a potential reader inside AcquireShared finds that i is less than zero, it must block until the writer calls ReleaseExclusive.

```
VAR i := 0; m := NEW(MUTEX); c := NEW(Thread.Condition);

PROCEDURE AcquireExclusive() =
  BEGIN
    LOCK m DO
      WHILE i # 0 DO Thread.Wait(m, c) END;
      i := -1
    END;
  END AcquireExclusive;

PROCEDURE AcquireShared() =
  BEGIN
    LOCK m DO
      WHILE i < 0 DO Thread.Wait(m, c) END;
      i := i+1
    END;
  END AcquireShared;

PROCEDURE ReleaseExclusive() =
  BEGIN
    LOCK m DO i := 0; Thread.Broadcast(c) END;
  END ReleaseExclusive;

PROCEDURE ReleaseShared() =
  BEGIN
    LOCK m DO i := i-1; IF i = 0 THEN Thread.Signal(c) END END;
  END ReleaseShared;
```

Using Broadcast is convenient in ReleaseExclusive, because a terminating writer does not need to know how many readers are now able to proceed. But notice that you could re-code this example using just Signal, by adding a counter of how many readers are waiting, and calling Signal that many times in ReleaseExclusive. The Broadcast facility is just a convenience, taking advantage of information already available to the threads implementation. Notice that there is no reason to use Broadcast in ReleaseShared, because we know that at most one blocked writer can usefully make progress, and that at that point only writers can be blocked.

This particular encoding of shared/exclusive locking exemplifies many of the problems that can occur when using condition variables, as we will see in the following sections. As we discuss these problems, I will present revised encodings of this locking paradigm.

4.5.2   Spurious wake-ups

If you keep your use of condition variables very simple, you might introduce the possibility of awakening threads that cannot make useful progress. This can happen if you use Broadcast when Signal would be sufficient, or if you have threads waiting on a single condition variable for multiple reasons. For example, the shared/exclusive locking procedures shown earlier use just one condition variable for readers as well as writers. This means that when we call Broadcast in ReleaseExclusive, the effect will be to awaken both readers and writers. But if a reader is first to lock the mutex, it will increment i and prevent an awakened writer from making progress until the reader later calls ReleaseShared. This costs extra time spent in the thread scheduler, which is typically an expensive place to be. If your problem is such that these spurious wake-ups will be common, and unless your scheduler is unusually efficient, you should probably separate the blocked threads onto two condition variables—one for readers and one for writers. A terminating reader need only signal the writers' condition variable; a terminating writer would signal one of them, depending on which was non-empty. With this change, the procedures would look as follows.

```
VAR i, readWaiters := 0;
VAR m := NEW(MUTEX);
VAR cR, cW := NEW(Thread.Condition);

PROCEDURE AcquireExclusive() =
  BEGIN
    LOCK m DO
      WHILE i # 0 DO Thread.Wait(m, cW) END;
      i := -1
    END
  END AcquireExclusive;

PROCEDURE AcquireShared() =
  BEGIN
    LOCK m DO
      readWaiters := readWaiters+1;
      WHILE i < 0 DO Thread.Wait(m, cR) END;
      readWaiters := readWaiters-1;
      i := i+1
    END
  END AcquireShared;
```

```
PROCEDURE ReleaseExclusive() =
  BEGIN
    LOCK m DO
      i := 0;
      IF readWaiters > 0 THEN
        Thread.Broadcast(cR);
      ELSE
        Thread.Signal(cW);
      END
    END
  END ReleaseExclusive;

PROCEDURE ReleaseShared() =
  BEGIN
    LOCK m DO
      i := i-1;
      IF i = 0 THEN Thread.Signal(cW) END
    END
  END ReleaseShared;
```

4.5.3 Spurious lock conflicts

The straightforward use of condition variables can lead to excessive scheduling overhead. In the reader/writer example, when a terminating reader inside `ReleaseShared` calls `Signal`, it still has the mutex locked. On a uni-processor this would often not be a problem, but on a multiprocessor the effect is liable to be that a potential writer is awakened inside `Wait`, executes a few instructions, and then blocks trying to lock the mutex—because it is still held by the terminating reader, executing concurrently. A few microseconds later the terminating reader unlocks the mutex, allowing the writer to continue. This has cost us two extra re-schedule operations, which is a significant expense.

This is a common situation, and it has a simple solution. Since the terminating reader does not access the data protected by the mutex after the call of `Signal`, we can move that call to after the end of the lock clause, as follows. Notice that accessing `i` is still protected by the mutex.

```
PROCEDURE ReleaseShared() =
  VAR doSignal: BOOLEAN;
  BEGIN
    LOCK m DO
      i := i-1;
      doSignal := (i=0)
    END
    IF doSignal THEN Thread.Signal(cW) END
  END ReleaseShared;
```

There is a more complicated case of spurious lock conflicts when a terminating writer calls Broadcast. First, it does so with the mutex held. But also, only one of the waiting readers at a time can lock the mutex to re-check and increment i, so on a multiprocessor other awakened readers are liable to block trying to lock the mutex (this is quite unlikely on a uni-processor). If necessary, we can correct this by awakening just one reader in ReleaseExclusive (by calling Signal instead of Broadcast), and having each reader in turn awaken the next, as follows.

```
PROCEDURE AcquireShared() =
  BEGIN
    LOCK m DO
      readWaiters := readWaiters+1;
      WHILE i < 0 DO Thread.Wait(m, cR) END;
      readWaiters := readWaiters-1;
      i := i+1
    END;
    Thread.Signal(cR)
  END AcquireShared;
```

4.5.4 Starvation

Whenever you have a program that is making scheduling decisions, you must worry about how fair these decisions are; in other words, are all threads equal or are some more favored? Usually the scheduling policy of your implementation will be good enough that you don't need to worry about fairness, but sometimes you will need to become involved. The most extreme form of unfairness is *starvation*, where some thread will never make progress. This can arise in our reader-writer locking example (of course). If the system is heavily loaded, so that there is always at least one thread wanting to be a reader, the existing code will starve writers. This would occur with the following pattern.

```
Thread A calls AcquireShared; i := 1;
Thread B calls AcquireShared; i := 2;
Thread A calls ReleaseShared; i := 1;
Thread C calls AcquireShared; i := 2;
Thread B calls ReleaseShared; i := 1;
etc.
```

Since there is always an active reader, there is never a moment when a writer can proceed; potential writers will always remain blocked, waiting for i to reduce to 0. If the load is such that this is really a problem, we need to make the code yet more complicated. For example, we could arrange that a new reader would defer inside AcquireShared if there was a blocked potential writer. We could do this by adding a counter for blocked writers, as follows.

```
VAR writeWaiters := 0;

PROCEDURE AcquireShared() =
  BEGIN
    LOCK m DO
      readWaiters := readWaiters+1;
      IF writeWaiters > 0 THEN
        Thread.Wait(m, cR);
      END;
      WHILE i < 0 DO Thread.Wait(m, cR) END;
      readWaiters := readWaiters-1;
      i := i+1
    END;
    Thread.Signal(cR)
  END AcquireShared;

PROCEDURE AcquireExclusive() =
  BEGIN
    LOCK m DO
      writeWaiters := writeWaiters+1;
      WHILE i # 0 DO Thread.Wait(m, cW) END;
      writeWaiters := writeWaiters-1;
      i := -1
    END
  END AcquireExclusive;
```

There is no limit to how complicated this can become, implementing ever more elaborate scheduling policies. You must exercise restraint, and only add such features if they are really required by the actual load on the resource.

4.5.5 Complexity

As you can see, worrying about these spurious wake-ups, lock conflicts and starvation makes the program more complicated. The first solution of the reader/writer problem that I showed you had 15 lines inside the procedure bodies; the final version had 30 lines, and some quite subtle reasoning about its correctness. You need to consider, for each case, whether the potential cost of ignoring the problem is enough to merit writing a more complex program. This decision will depend on the performance characteristics of your threads implementation, on whether you are using a multiprocessor, and on the expected load on your resource. In particular, if your resource is mostly not in use then the performance effects will not be a problem, and you should adopt the simplest coding style.

Usually, I find that moving the call of Signal to beyond the end of the LOCK clause is easy and worth the trouble, and that the other performance enhancements are not worth making. But sometimes they are important, and you should only ignore them after explicitly considering whether they are required in your particular situation.

4.5.6   Deadlock

You can introduce deadlocks by using condition variables. For example, if you have two resources (call them ① and ②), the following sequence of actions produces a deadlock.

> Thread A acquires resource ①;
> Thread B acquires resource ②;
> Thread A wants ②, so it waits on ②'s condition variable;
> Thread B wants ①, so it waits on ①'s condition variable.

Deadlocks such as this are not significantly different from the ones we discussed in connection with mutexes. You should arrange that there is a partial order on the resources managed with condition variables, and that each thread wishing to acquire multiple resources does so according to this order. So, for example, you might decide that ① is ordered before ②. Then thread B would not be permitted to try to acquire ① while holding ②, so the deadlock would not occur.

One interaction between condition variables and mutexes is a subtle source of deadlock. Consider the following two procedures.

```
VAR a, b := NEW(MUTEX);
VAR c := NEW(Thread.Condition);
VAR ready: BOOLEAN;

PROCEDURE Get() =
  BEGIN
    LOCK a DO
      LOCK b DO
        WHILE NOT ready DO Thread.Wait(b, c) END;
        ready := FALSE
      END
    END
  END Get;

PROCEDURE Give() =
  BEGIN
    LOCK a DO
      LOCK b DO
        ready := TRUE; Thread.Signal(c);
      END
    END
  END Give;
```

If ready is FALSE and thread A calls Get, it will block on a call of Wait(b, c). This unlocks b, but leaves a locked. So if thread B calls Give, intending to cause a call of Signal(c), it will instead block trying to lock a, and your program will have deadlocked. Clearly, this example is trivial, since mutex a does not protect any data (and the potential for deadlock is quite apparent anyway), but the overall pattern does occur.

Most often this problem occurs when you lock a mutex at one abstraction level of your program then call down to a lower level, which (unknown to the higher level) blocks. If this block can be freed only by a thread that is holding the higher level mutex, you will deadlock. It is generally risky to call into a lower level abstraction while holding one of your mutexes, unless you understand fully the circumstances under which the called procedure might block. One solution here is to explicitly unlock the mutex before calling the lower level abstraction, as we discussed earlier; but as we discussed, this solution has its own dangers. A better solution is to arrange to end the LOCK clause before calling down. You can find further discussions of this problem, known as the *nested monitor problem*, in the literature [10].

4.6 Using Fork: working in parallel

As we discussed earlier, there are several classes of situations where you will want to fork a thread: to utilize a multiprocessor; to do useful work while waiting for a slow device; to satisfy human users by working on several actions at once; to provide network service to multiple clients simultaneously; and to defer work until a less busy time.

It is quite common to find straightforward application programs using several threads. For example, you might have one thread doing your main computation, a second thread writing some output to a file, a third thread waiting for (or responding to) interactive user input, and a fourth thread running in background to clean up your data structures (for example, re-balancing a tree). In the programs we build at SRC, several of our library packages fork threads internally.

When you are programming with threads, you usually drive slow devices through synchronous library calls that suspend the calling thread until the device action completes, but allow other threads in your address space to continue. You will find no need to use older schemes for asynchronous operation (such as interrupts, Unix signals or VMS AST's). If you don't want to wait for the result of a device interaction, invoke it in a separate thread. If you want to have multiple device requests outstanding simultaneously, invoke them in multiple threads. If your operating system still delivers some asynchronous events through these older mechanisms, the runtime library supporting your threads facility should convert them into more appropriate mechanisms. See, for example, the design of the Topaz system calls [22] or the exception and trapping machinery included with Sun's lightweight process library [14, 13].

If your program is interacting with a human user, you will usually want it to be responsive even while it is working on some request. This is particularly true of window-oriented interfaces. It is particularly infuriating to the user if the interactive display goes dumb just because the database query is taking a long time. You can achieve responsiveness by using extra threads. Often, the designer of your window system will have already done this for you, and will always call your program in a separate thread. At other times, the window system will call your program in a single thread synchronously with the user input event. In this latter case, you must decide whether the requested action is short enough to do it synchronously, or whether you should fork a thread. The complexity introduced by using forked threads here is that you need to exercise a lot of care in accessing data from the interactive interface (for example, the value of the current selection, or the contents of editable text areas) since these values might change once you start executing asynchronously. This is a difficult design issue, and each window system tackles it differently. I have not yet seen a totally satisfactory design.

Network servers are usually required to service multiple clients concurrently. If your network communication is based on RPC [2], this will happen without any work on your part, since the server side of your RPC system will invoke each concurrent incoming call in a separate thread, by forking a suitable number of threads internally to its implementation. But you can use multiple threads even with other communication paradigms. For example, in a traditional connection-oriented protocol (such as file transfer layered on top of TCP), you should probably fork one thread for each incoming connection. Conversely, if you are writing a client program and you don't want to wait for the reply from a network server, invoke the server from a separate thread.

The technique of adding threads in order to defer work is quite valuable. There are several variants of the scheme. The simplest is that as soon as your procedure has done enough work to compute its result, you fork a thread to do the remainder of the work, and then return to your caller in the original thread. This reduces the latency of your procedure (the elapsed time from being called to returning), in the hope that the deferred work can be done more cheaply later (for example, because a processor goes idle). The disadvantage of this simplest approach is that it might create large numbers of threads, and it incurs the cost of calling Fork each time. Often, it is preferable to keep a single housekeeping thread and feed requests to it. It's even better when the housekeeper doesn't need any information from the main threads, beyond the fact that there is work to be done. For example, this will be true when the housekeeper is responsible for maintaining a data structure in an optimal form, although the main threads will still get the correct answer without this optimization. An additional technique here is to program the housekeeper either to merge similar requests into a single action, or to restrict itself to run not more often than a chosen periodic interval.

On a multiprocessor you will want to use Fork to utilize as many processors as you can. There isn't much general advice I can give here—mostly, the decisions about when and what to fork are too problem-specific. One general technique is pipelining, which I discuss in the next section.

4.6.1 Pipelining

On a multiprocessor, there is one specialized use of additional threads that is particularly valuable. You can build a chain of producer-consumer relationships, known as a pipeline. For example, when thread A initiates an action, all it does is enqueue a request in a buffer. Thread B takes the action from the buffer, performs part of the work, then enqueues it in a second buffer. Thread C takes it from there and does the rest of the work. This forms a three-stage pipeline. The three threads operate concurrently except when they synchronize to access the buffers, so this pipeline is capable of utilizing up to three processors.

At its best, pipelining can achieve almost linear speed-up and can fully utilize a multiprocessor. A pipeline can also be useful on a uniprocessor if each thread will encounter some real-time delays (such as page faults, device handling or network communication).

For example, the following program fragment implements a simple three stage pipeline. An action is initiated by calling PaintChar. One auxiliary thread executes in Rasterize and another in Painter. The pipeline stages communicate through unbounded buffers implemented as linked lists whose last elements are rasterTail and paintTail. The initial values of the tails are dummy elements, to make the program simpler.

```
TYPE
   CharList = OBJECT ch: CHAR; next: CharList END;
   BitList = OBJECT bits: Bitmap; next: BitList END;
   CharClosure = Thread.Closure OBJECT init: CharList END;
   BitClosure = Thread.Closure OBJECT init: BitList END;

VAR
   charTail: CharList;
   bitTail: BitList;
   charClosure: CharClosure;
   bitClosure: BitClosure;
   m := NEW(MUTEX);
   c1, c2 := NEW(Thread.Condition);

PROCEDURE PaintChar(arg: CHAR) =
   VAR this: CharList;
   BEGIN
     NEW(this, ch := arg, next := NIL);
     (* Enqueue request for Rasterize thread *)
     LOCK m DO
       charTail.next := this;
       charTail := this
     END;
     Thread.Signal(c1)
   END PaintChar;
```

```
PROCEDURE Rasterize(self: CharClosure) =
  VAR last: CharList; this: PaintList;
  BEGIN
    last := self.init;
    LOOP
      LOCK m DO
        WHILE last.next = NIL DO Thread.Wait(m, c1) END;
        last := last.next
      END;
      NEW(this, bits := Font.Map(last.ch), next := NIL);
      LOCK m DO
        bitTail.next := this; bitTail := this
      END;
      Thread.Signal(c2)
    END
  END Rasterize;

PROCEDURE Painter(self: BitClosure) =
  VAR last: BitList;
  BEGIN
    last := self.init;
    LOOP
      LOCK m DO
        WHILE last.next = NIL DO Thread.Wait(m, c2) END;
        last := last.next
      END;
      Display.PaintBitmap(last.bits)
    END
  END Painter;

charTail := NEW(CharList, next := NIL);
bitTail := NEW(BitList, next := NIL);
charClosure :=
  NEW(CharClosure, init := charTail, apply := Rasterize);
bitClosure :=
  NEW(BitClosure, init := bitTail, apply := Painter);
EVAL Thread.Fork(charClosure);
EVAL Thread.Fork(bitClosure);
```

There are two problems with pipelining. First, you need to be careful about how much of the work gets done in each stage. The ideal is that the stages are equal: this will provide maximum throughput, by utilizing all your processors fully. Achieving this ideal requires hand tuning, and re- tuning as the program changes. Second, the number of stages in your pipeline determines statically the amount of concurrency. If you know how many processors you have, and exactly where the real-time delays occur, this will be fine.

For more flexible or portable environments it can be a problem. Despite these problems, pipelining is a powerful technique that has wide applicability.

4.6.2 The impact of your environment

The design of your operating system and runtime libraries will affect the extent to which it is desirable or useful to fork threads. Your operating system should not suspend the entire address space just because one thread is blocked for an i/o request (or for a page fault). Your operating system and your libraries must accept concurrent calls from multiple threads. Generally, in a well-designed environment for supporting multi-threaded programs you will find that the facilities of your operating system and libraries are available as synchronous calls that block only the calling thread [22].

You will need to know some of the performance parameters of your threads implementation. What is the cost of creating a thread? What is the cost of keeping a blocked thread in existence? What is the cost of a context switch? What is the cost of a LOCK clause when the mutex is not locked? Knowing these, you will be able to decide to what extent it is feasible or useful to add extra threads to your program.

4.6.3 Potential problems with adding threads

You need to exercise a little care in adding threads, or you will find that your program runs slower instead of faster.

If you have significantly more threads ready to run than there are processors, you will usually find that your performance degrades. This is partly because most thread schedulers are quite slow at making general re-scheduling decisions. If there is a processor idle waiting for your thread, the scheduler can probably get it there quite quickly. But if your thread has to be put on a queue, and later swapped into a processor in place of some other thread, it will be more expensive. A second effect is that if you have lots of threads running they are more likely to conflict over mutexes or over the resources managed by your condition variables.

Mostly, when you add threads just to improve your program's structure (for example driving slow devices, or responding to mouse clicks speedily, or for RPC invocations) you will not encounter this problem; but when you add threads for performance purposes (such as performing multiple actions in parallel, or deferring work, or utilizing multiprocessors), you will need to worry about whether you are overloading the system.

But let me stress that this warning applies only to the threads that are ready to run. The expense of having threads blocked on condition variables is usually less significant, being just the memory used for scheduler data structures and the thread stack. The programs at SRC often have quite a large number of blocked threads. (50 is not uncommon in application programs; there are usually hundreds blocked inside the operating system—even on a personal workstation.)

Thread creation and termination facilities are not usually cheap. A good implementation will cache a few terminated thread carcasses, to avoid the cost of creating a stack on each Fork, but Fork will still probably cost a much as several re-scheduling decisions. You shouldn't fork too small a computation. One useful measure of a threads implementation on a multiprocessor is the smallest computation for which it is profitable to fork a thread.

Nevertheless, our experience at SRC with a 5-way multiprocessor has been that programmers are about as likely to err by creating too few threads as by creating too many.

4.7   Using Alert: Diverting the flow of control

The purpose of alerts is to cause termination of a long running computation or a long-term wait. For example, on a multiprocessor it might be useful to fork multiple competing algorithms to solve the same problem, and when the first of them completes you abort the others. Or you might embark on a long computation (e.g., a database query), but abort it if the user clicks a CANCEL button.

The programming convention we use at SRC is that any procedure in a public interface that might incur a long computation or a long-term wait should be alertable. In other words, a long computation should occasionally call TestAlert and long-term waits should be calls of AlertWait instead of Wait. In this context "long" means long enough to upset a human user. The attraction of this convention is that you can be sure that the user can always regain control of the application program. The disadvantage is that programs calling these procedures must be prepared for the Alerted exception to come out of them. This convention is less rigorously applied when an entry point only occasionally causes a long-term wait.

Another programming convention we have is that you should only alert a thread if you forked the thread. For example, a package should not alert a caller's thread that happens to be executing inside the package. This convention allows you to view any alert as a request to terminate completely.

The problem with alerts (or any other form of asynchronous interrupt mechanism, such as Apollo's task_$signal) is that they are, by their very nature, intrusive. Using them will tend to make your program less well structured. A straightforward-looking flow of control in one thread can suddenly be diverted because of an action initiated by another thread. This is another example of a facility that makes it harder to verify the correctness of a piece of program by local inspection. Unless alerts are used with great restraint, they will make your program unreadable, unmaintainable, and perhaps incorrect.

There are alternatives to using alerts. If you know which condition variable a thread is blocked on, you can prod it more simply by setting a boolean flag and signalling the condition variable. A package can provide additional entry points whose purpose is to prod a thread blocked inside the package on a long-term wait.

Alerts are most useful when you don't know exactly what is going on. For example, the target thread might be blocked in any of several packages, or within a single package it might be blocked on any of several condition variables. In these cases an alert is certainly the best solution. Even when other alternatives are available, it might be best to use alerts just because they are a uniform scheme for provoking thread termination.

Notice that if t is computing rather than blocked, Alert(t) does not cause an exception to be raised in t. It is t's responsibility to periodically call TestAlert in long-running computations. The reason for this is that if t could be alerted asynchronously, it would be essentially impossible for it to maintain the invariants of its critical sections. Some extensions to the Thread interface allow a thread to enable asynchronous interrupts. Such facilities should be used with great care.

4.8 Additional Techniques

Most of the programming paradigms for using threads are quite simple. I've described several of them earlier; you will discover many others as you gain experience. A few useful techniques are much less obvious. This section describes some of them.

4.8.1 Up-calls

Most of the time most programmers build their programs using layered abstractions. Higher level abstractions call only lower level ones, and abstractions at the same level do not call each other. All actions are initiated at the top level.

This methodology carries over quite well to a world with concurrency. You can arrange that each thread will honor the abstraction boundaries. Permanent dæmon threads within an abstraction initiate calls to lower levels, but not to higher levels. The abstraction layering has the added benefit that it forms a partial order, and this order is sufficient to prevent deadlocks when locking mutexes, without any additional care from the programmer.

This purely top-down layering is not satisfactory when actions that affect high-level abstractions can be initiated at a low layer in your system. One frequently encountered example of this is on the receiving side of network communications. Other examples are user input and spontaneous state changes in peripheral devices such as disks and tapes.

Consider the example of a communications package dealing with incoming packets from a network. Here there are typically three or more layers of dispatch (corresponding to the data link, network, and transport layers in OSI terminology). If you try to maintain a top-down calling hierarchy, you will find that you incur a context switch in each of these layers. The thread that wishes to receive data from its transport layer connection cannot be the thread that dispatches an incoming Ethernet packet, since the Ethernet packet might belong to a different connection, or a different protocol (for example, UDP instead of TCP), or a different protocol family altogether (for example, DECnet instead of IP). Many implementers have tried to maintain this layering for packet reception, and the effect has been uniformly bad performance—dominated by the cost of context switches.

The alternative technique is known as *up-calls* [4]. In this methodology, you maintain a pool of threads willing to receive incoming data link layer (e.g. Ethernet) packets. The receiving thread dispatches on Ethernet protocol type and calls up to the network layer (e.g., DECnet or IP), where it dispatches again and calls up to the transport layer (e.g. TCP), where there is a final dispatch to the appropriate connection. In some systems, this up-call paradigm extends into the application. The attraction here is high performance: there are no unnecessary context switches. All the top-performing network implementations are structured this way.

You do pay for this performance. As usual, the programmer's task has been made more complicated. Partly this is because each layer now has an up-call interface as well as the traditional down-call interface. But also the synchronization problem has become more delicate. In a purely top-down system it is fine to hold one layer's mutex while calling a lower layer (unless the lower layer might block on a condition variable and cause the sort of nested monitor deadlock we discussed earlier). But in the presence of up-calls this can easily provoke a deadlock involving just the mutexes—if an up-calling thread holding a lower level mutex needs to lock the higher level one. In other words, the presence of up-calls makes it more likely that you will violate the partial order rule for locking mutexes. To avoid this, you should generally avoid holding a mutex while making an up-call (but this is easier said than done).

4.8.2   Version stamps

Sometimes concurrency can make it more difficult to use cached information. This can happen when a thread executing at a low level in your system invalidates information known to a thread currently executing at a higher level. For example, information about a disk volume might change—either because of hardware problems or because the volume has been removed and replaced. You can use up-calls to invalidate cache structures at the higher level, but this will not invalidate state held locally by a thread. In the most extreme example, a thread might obtain information from a cache, and be about to call an operation at the lower level. Between the time the information comes from the cache and the time that the call actually occurs, the information might have become invalid.

A technique known as *version stamps* can be useful here. In the low level abstraction you maintain a counter associated with the true data. Whenever the data changes, you increment the counter. (Assume the counter is large enough to never overflow.) Whenever a copy of some of the data is issued to a higher level, it is accompanied by the current value of the counter. If higher level code is caching the data, it caches the associated counter value too. Whenever you make a call back down to the lower level, and the call or its parameters depend on previously obtained data, you include the associated value of the counter. When the low level receives such a call, it compares the incoming value with the current value of the counter. If they are different it returns an exception to the higher level, which then knows to re-consider its call. (Sometimes, you can provide the new data with the exception). Incidentally, this technique is also useful when maintaining cached data across a distributed system.

4.8.3 Work crews

There are situations that are best described as "an embarrassment of parallelism", when a natural structure for your program has vastly more concurrency than can be efficiently accommodated on your machine. For example, a compiler implemented using concurrency might be willing to use a separate thread to compile each procedure, or even each statement. In such situations, if you fork one thread for each action you will create so many threads that the scheduler becomes quite inefficient, or so many that you have numerous lock conflicts, or so many that you run out of memory for the stacks.

Your choice here is either to be more restrained in your forking, or to use an abstraction that will control your forking for you. Such an abstraction is described in Vandevoorde and Roberts' paper [23]. The basic idea is to enqueue requests for asynchronous activity and have a fixed pool of threads that perform the requests. The complexity comes in managing the requests, synchronizing between them, and co-ordinating the results. See the paper for a full description.

An alternative proposal is to implement Fork in such a way that it defers actually creating a new thread until there is a processor available to run it. We call this proposal *lazy forking*, but we have not yet pursued it at SRC.

4.9 Building your program

A successful program must be useful, correct, live (as defined below) and efficient. Your use of concurrency can impact each of these. I have discussed quite a few techniques in the previous sections that will help you. But how will you know if you have succeeded? The answer is not clear, but this section might help you towards discovering it.

The place where concurrency can affect usefulness is in the design of the interfaces to library packages. You must design your interfaces with the assumption that your callers will be using multiple threads. This means that you must ensure that all the entry points are thread re-entrant (i.e. they can be called by multiple threads concurrently), even if this means that each procedure immediately locks a central mutex. You must not return results in shared global variables, nor in global statically allocated storage. Your calls should be synchronous, not returning until their results are available—if your caller wants to do other work meanwhile, he can do it in other threads. Even if you don't presently have any multi-threaded clients of the interface, I strongly recommend that you follow these guidelines so that you will avoid problems in the future.

By *correct* I mean that if your program eventually produces an answer, it will be the one defined by its specification. Your programming environment is unlikely to provide much help here beyond what it already provides for sequential programs. Mostly, you must be fastidious about associating each piece of data with a mutex. If you don't pay constant attention to this, your task will be hopeless. If you use mutexes correctly, and you always use condition variables in the recommended style (re-testing the boolean expression after returning from `Wait`), then you are unlikely to go wrong.

By *live*, I mean that your program will eventually produce an answer. The alternatives are infinite loops or deadlock. I can't help you with infinite loops. I believe that the hints of the preceding sections will help you to avoid deadlocks. But if you fail and produce a deadlock, it should be quite easy to detect. Your major help in analyzing a deadlock will come from a symbolic debugger. The debugger must provide at least minimal support for threads—enumerating the existing threads and looking at each thread's stack. Hopefully, your debugger will also provide some filtering in the thread enumeration, for example finding all threads that have a stack frame in a particular module, or finding all threads that are blocked on a particular mutex or condition variable. A very nice feature would be a facility to determine which thread is holding a particular mutex.

By *efficient*, I mean that your program will make good use of the available computer resources, and therefore will produce its answer quickly. Again, the hints in the previous sections should help you to keep concurrency from adversely affecting your performance. And again, your programming environment needs to give you some help. Performance bugs are the most insidious of problems, since you might not even notice that you have them. The sort of information you need to obtain includes statistics on lock conflicts (for example, how often threads have had to block on this mutex, and how long they then had to wait) and on concurrency levels (for example, what was the average number of threads ready to execute in your program, or what percentage of the time were n threads ready).

One final warning: don't emphasize efficiency at the expense of correctness. It is much easier to start with a correct program and work on making it efficient, than to start with an efficient program and work on making it correct.

Writing concurrent programs has a reputation for being exotic and difficult. I believe it is neither. You need a system that provides you with good primitives and suitable libraries, you need basic caution and carefulness, you need an armory of useful techniques, and you need to know of the common pitfalls. I hope that this chapter has helped you towards sharing my belief.

Chapter 5

Thread Synchronization: A Formal Specification

A.D. Birrell, J.V. Guttag, J. J. Horning, R. Levin

5.1 Introduction

The careful documentation of interfaces is an important step in the production of software upon which other software is to be built. If people are to use software without having to understand its implementation, documentation must convey semantic as well as syntactic information. When the software involves concurrency, adequate documentation is particularly hard to produce, since the range of possible behaviors is likely to be large and difficult to characterize [15].

We believe that documentation containing formal specifications can be significantly better than documentation restricted to informal or semi-formal descriptions. It can be made more precise and complete, and is more likely to be interpreted consistently by various readers. Our experience in specifying and documenting the synchronization facilities of the Modula-3 Thread interface supports this view.

The specification has evolved over several years of use at SRC by programmers of the Taos operating system [22] for the Firefly multiprocessor workstation [28].

The synchronization primitives of the Thread interface are similar to those in many other systems, but their use on a multiprocessor raises questions about their precise semantics that are difficult to answer using even careful informal descriptions, such as those in Chapter 4.

We briefly describe the formal language we use to specify interfaces involving concurrency, and then present the specification itself. We intend to give the reader a complete and precise understanding of the properties that client programmers may rely on when using the synchronization primitives. The specification should answer any questions about how the Modula-3 Thread primitives differ from others with which the reader is familiar. Finally, we discuss our experience with the use of the specification.

5.1.1 Semaphores: P, V

The Topaz Thread interface extends the Modula-3 required Thread interface by providing binary semaphores with their traditional P and V operations. The implementation of semaphores is identical to mutexes, but they are used differently. ("We used the semaphores in two completely different ways. The difference is so marked that, looking back, one wonders whether it was really fair to present the two ways as uses of the very same primitives. On the one hand, we have the semaphores used for mutual exclusion, on the other hand, the private semaphores."—Dijkstra, 1968 [5].) There is no notion of a thread "holding" a semaphore, and no precondition on executing V, so calls of P and V need not be textually linked.

We discourage programmers from using semaphores directly, since we prefer the additional structure that comes with the use of mutexes and condition variables. However semaphores are needed to synchronize with interrupt routines. This is because an interrupt routine cannot protect shared data with a mutex—because the interrupt might have pre-empted a thread in a critical section protected by that mutex—and using Wait and Signal to synchronize requires use of an associated mutex. Instead, a thread waits for an interrupt routine action by calling P(sem), and the interrupt routine unblocks it by calling V(sem).

5.2 Specification Approach

We use the Larch two-tiered approach to specification [30, 29, 8, 9]. The *Larch Shared Language* tier [7] uses a subset of first-order logic to define mathematical abstractions that can be used in the *interface language* tier to specify program interfaces. As it happens, all the abstractions needed for the Thread specification are well known (e.g., booleans, enumerations, and sets) and appear in the *Larch Shared Language Handbook* [6] or are obvious extensions of something there, so we do not discuss them here. The Larch interface language for Modula-3, LM3, consists of definition modules augmented with special pragmas giving precise specifications for the interface items they define.

The logical basis for our treatment of concurrency is very similar to the one discussed in [16, 17]. However, our specification deals only with safety properties and termination, not with general liveness properties.

Our specifications of procedures for concurrent programs are similar to our specifications of procedures for sequential programs. In both cases, the specifications prescribe the observable effects of procedures, without saying how they are to be achieved. In a sequential program, the states between a procedure call and its return cannot be observed in the calling environment. Thus we can specify a procedure by giving a predicate relating just the state when the procedure is called and the state when it returns [11]. Similarly, an *atomic action* in a concurrent program has no visible internal structure; its observable effects can also be specified by a predicate on just two states.

Our method is based on the observation that any behavior of a concurrent system can be described as the execution of a sequence of atomic actions. A key property of atomic actions is *serializability*, which means that each concurrent execution of a group of atomic actions has the same observable effects as some sequential execution of the same actions. Serializability allows us to ignore concurrency in reasoning about the effects of an atomic action. Each atomic action appears indivisible, both to the thread invoking it and to all other threads.

In specifying atomic actions, we don't specify how atomicity is to be achieved, only that it must be. In an implementation, atomic actions may proceed concurrently as long as the concurrency isn't observable. Atomicity is intimately related to abstraction; at each level of abstraction atomicity is ensured by using sequences of lower-level actions, some of which are known to be atomic relative to each other. For example, the atomicity of the synchronization primitives is ensured by the atomicity of the underlying hardware's test-and-set instruction.

Atomicity requirements constrain both the thread executing the atomic action and all other threads that share variables with the action. For such a set of actions to be atomic relative to each other, their implementations must all adhere to some synchronization protocol. It is necessary to consider them all when verifying atomicity, just as it is necessary to consider all the operations of an abstract data type when verifying its implementation [19].

Atomic procedures execute just one atomic action per call. Each can be specified in terms of just two states: the state immediately preceding and the state immediately following the action. They are particularly easy to specify and to understand, since they behave so much like procedures in a sequential environment. Thus we would prefer for most procedures to appear atomic to their callers. However, most concurrent programs contain a few procedures that do not appear atomic; these present a more difficult specification challenge.

The observable effects of a *non-atomic procedure* cannot be described in terms of just two states. Its effects may span more states, and actions of other threads may be interleaved with its atomic actions. However, each execution of a non-atomic procedure can be viewed as a sequence of atomic actions. We specify a non-atomic procedure by giving a predicate that defines the allowable sequences of atomic actions (i.e., sequences of pre-post state pairs). Each execution of the procedure must be equivalent to such a sequence. Although it is sometimes necessary to specify constraints on the sequence as a whole, for the Thread interface it suffices to specify the atomic actions separately.

The Thread interface contains two non-atomic synchronization procedures (Wait and AlertWait), each executing a fixed sequence of visible atomic actions per call. Such procedures are nearly as easy to specify as atomic procedures. We specify that (the visible effect of) executing the procedure must be equivalent to executing named actions in a stated order (possibly separated by actions of other threads), and then write a predicate specifying each of the named actions.

All procedures in this interface that are not explicitly compositions are atomic.

5.3   Formal Specification

Now we present the formal specification without much commentary about the interface itself. This specification should be used in conjunction with informal material, such as that in Chapter 4, that provides intuition and says how the primitives are intended to be used. We omit the Larch Shared Language tier, and some of the connective references, since the theories used are all well-known. The constant none of type Thread.T, the type TSet (set of Thread.T), and the set operators are defined in the LSL tier.

- Rather than giving a separate tutorial on the LM3 language used in this specification, we will use notes of this form to briefly discuss the meaning of LM3 constructs following their first uses.

5.3.1   Mutex, Acquire, Release

```
TYPE Mutex <: ROOT;

<* PRIVATE VAR holder: ARRAY Mutex OF T
   INITIALLY FOR ALL m: Mutex holder[m] = none *>
```

- A variable declared PRIVATE is purely an auxiliary for use in the specification. It is not accessible to client programs, and need not appear explicitly in the implementation.

- An INITIALLY clause defines a condition that holds prior to the first action of any of the procedures in the interface.

```
PROCEDURE Acquire(m: Mutex);
<* MODIFIES holder[m]
   WHEN holder[m] = none
   ENSURES holder'[m] = CURRENT *>
```

- A MODIFIES clause identifies the variables that a procedure is permitted to change.

- A WHEN clause states a condition that must be satisfied for an atomic action (in this case, the execution of the procedure body) to take place. It is not a precondition of the call. The implementation is responsible for ensuring that the condition holds before it makes any externally visible change to the state. A WHEN clause may thus impose a delay until actions of other threads make its predicate true. An omitted WHEN clause is equivalent to WHEN TRUE, that is, no delay is required.

- An ENSURES clause states a postcondition that an atomic action must establish.

- An unprimed variable in a predicate stands for its value in the *pre state*—the state in which the atomic action begins. A variable marked with a ' stands for its value in the *post state*—the state at the conclusion of the atomic action.

- The keyword CURRENT stands for the identity of the thread executing the specified action.

```
PROCEDURE Release(m: Mutex);
<* REQUIRES holder[m] = CURRENT
   MODIFIES holder[m]
   ENSURES holder'[m] = none *>
```

- A REQUIRES clause states a precondition that the implementation may rely on; the caller must ensure that the condition holds at the start of the procedure's first (and in this case, only) atomic action. The specification does not constrain the implementation to any particular behavior if the precondition is not satisfied. An omitted REQUIRES clause is equivalent to REQUIRES TRUE, that is, nothing is required.

If Release(m) is executed when there are several threads waiting to perform Acquire(m), the WHEN clause of each of them will be satisfied. Only one thread will hold m next, because—by atomicity of Acquire—it must appear that one of the Acquires is executed first; its ENSURES clause falsifies the WHEN clauses of all the others. Our specification does not say which of the blocked threads will be unblocked first, nor when this will happen.

5.3.2 Semaphore, P, V

```
TYPE Semaphore <: ROOT;

<* PRIVATE VAR locked: ARRAY Semaphore OF BOOLEAN
   INITIALLY FOR ALL s: Semaphore NOT locked[s] *>

PROCEDURE P(s: Semaphore);
<* MODIFIES locked[s]
   WHEN NOT locked[s]
   ENSURES locked'[s] *>
```

```
PROCEDURE V(s: Semaphore);
<* MODIFIES locked[s]
   ENSURES NOT locked'[s] *>
```

5.3.3 Blocking and unblocking on condition variables

```
TYPE Condition <: ROOT;

<* PRIVATE VAR waiting: ARRAY Condition OF TSet
   INITIALLY FOR ALL c: Condition waiting[c] = {} *>

PROCEDURE Wait(m: Mutex; c: Condition);
<* REQUIRES holder[m] = CURRENT
   MODIFIES holder[m], waiting[c]
   COMPOSITION OF Enqueue; Resume END
   ACTION Enqueue
     ENSURES holder'[m] = none
       AND waiting'[c] = waiting[c] ∪ {CURRENT}
   ACTION Resume
     WHEN holder[m] = none AND NOT (CURRENT ∈ waiting[c])
     ENSURES holder'[m] = CURRENT AND UNCHANGED(waiting) *>
```

- A COMPOSITION OF clause indicates that any execution of the procedure must be equivalent to execution of the named actions in the given order, possibly interleaved with actions of other threads. All actions, and all procedures not specified as composite, must appear atomic to clients of the interface.

- An ACTION clause specifies a named action in much the same way as a PROCEDURE specification does. It is within the scope of the procedure header, and may refer to its formal parameters.

- The keyword UNCHANGED applied to a variable is shorthand for equating its pre and post values.

```
PROCEDURE Signal(c: Condition);
<* MODIFIES waiting[c]
   ENSURES waiting'[c] = {} OR waiting'[c] ⊂ waiting[c] *>

PROCEDURE Broadcast(c: Condition);
<* MODIFIES waiting[c]
   ENSURES waiting'[c] = {} *>
```

Any implementation that satisfies Broadcast's specification also satisfies Signal's. We cannot strengthen Signal's postcondition: as discussed in Chapter 4, our implementation of Signal usually unblocks just one waiting thread, but may unblock more.

5.3.4 Alerts

```
EXCEPTION Alerted;

<* PRIVATE VAR alerted: ARRAY T OF BOOLEAN
   INITIALLY FOR ALL t: T NOT alerted[t] *>

PROCEDURE Alert(t: T);
<* MODIFIES alerted[t]
   ENSURES alerted'[t] *>

PROCEDURE TestAlert(): BOOLEAN;
<* MODIFIES alerted[CURRENT]
   ENSURES
      (RESULT ⇒ alerted[CURRENT]) AND
      (alerted'[CURRENT] = (alerted[CURRENT] AND NOT RESULT)) *>
```

- The keyword RESULT in a predicate stands for the value that is returned by the procedure.

A key issue in the design of a threads package with alerts is the amount of nondeterminism allowed in TestAlert. If a thread executes Alert(t) before the thread t executes TestAlert, will TestAlert return TRUE? Clients would prefer an unqualified "yes." However, in a distributed system with remote procedure calls, t may migrate from node to node and Alert may have to "chase" it. Guaranteeing that TestAlert will always return TRUE may be unacceptably inefficient, and clients may have to settle for "usually." In a non-distributed system, the ENSURES clause could be strengthened to ENSURES RESULT = alert[CURRENT] AND NOT alert'[CURRENT].

```
PROCEDURE AlertP(s: Semaphore) RAISES {Alerted};
<* MODIFIES locked[s], alerted[CURRENT]
   WHEN NOT locked[s] OR alerted[CURRENT]
   ENSURES (RAISE = RETURN AND NOT locked[s] AND locked'[s]
      AND UNCHANGED(alerted))
    OR (RAISE = Alerted AND alerted[CURRENT]
      AND NOT alerted'[CURRENT] AND UNCHANGED(locked)) *>
```

- RAISE in a predicate stands for the exception raised by the procedure. RAISE = RETURN is true if the procedure returns without raising an exception. Each procedure specification with an empty RAISES clause has an implicit RAISE = RETURN conjoined to its ENSURES clause.

AlertP's ENSURES clause allows non-determinism that will be discussed in the next section.

```
    PROCEDURE AlertWait(m: Mutex; c: Condition) RAISES {Alerted};
<* REQUIRES holder[m] = CURRENT
    MODIFIES holder[m], waiting[c], alerted[CURRENT]
    PRIVATE VAR alertChosen: BOOLEAN
    COMPOSITION OF Enqueue; ChooseOutcome; GetMutex END
    ACTION Enqueue
      ENSURES holder'[m] = none
        AND waiting'[c] = waiting[c] ∪ {CURRENT}
        AND UNCHANGED(alerted)
    ACTION ChooseOutcome
      WHEN NOT (CURRENT ∈ waiting[c]) OR alerted[CURRENT]
      ENSURES alertChosen' = NOT (CURRENT ∈ waiting[c])
        AND waiting'[c] = delete(CURRENT, waiting[c])
        AND alerted'[CURRENT]
          = (alerted[CURRENT] AND NOT alertChosen')
        AND UNCHANGED(holder)
    ACTION GetMutex
      WHEN holder[m] = none
      ENSURES RAISE = (IF alertChosen THEN Alerted ELSE RETURN)
        AND holder'[m] = CURRENT
        AND UNCHANGED(waiting, alerted) *>
```

5.4 Discussion

A prose description of the Thread synchronization primitives was written when the interface was first designed [25, 24]. While it gave an indication of how the primitives were intended to be used, it left too many questions about the guaranteed behavior of the interface unanswered.

To provide more precise information for programmers who were starting to use the interface, a semi-formal operational specification was written. This description was both precise and (for the most part) accurate. The main problems with it were that it was too subtle and that important information was rather widely distributed. For example, to discover that Signal might unblock more than one thread involved looking at several procedures and observing that a race condition existed. If one failed to notice this race condition—and most readers seemed to—one was misled about the behavior of Signal. This is not a criticism of the particular specification, but rather an indication that it is difficult to write straightforward operational specifications of concurrent programs. In our specification, the weakness of the guarantee is explicit in Signal's ENSURES clause.

The operational specification was the starting point for our formal specification, and served us well. The two of us who wrote the formal specification still had questions for the two involved in the implementation, but never resorted to studying the actual code.

The specification presented here is part of the standard documentation for programmers using the Thread interface and for those responsible for its implementation. They seem to be able to read our specification and understand its implications. Two incidents illustrate this; both relate to places where the version of the specification we first released did not conform to the implementation:

- The original specification of AlertWait did not contain the WHEN clause in GetMutex. That this presented a problem was discovered in less than an hour by someone with no prior knowledge of either the interface or the specification technique.

- The second problem was more subtle. In the specification of AlertP, the ENSURES clause allows non-determinacy. If the semaphore is unlocked and CURRENT has been alerted, the specification allows the implementation to make an arbitrary choice between returning and raising Alerted. The original specification required AlertP to raise the exception in this case. This was consistent with the operational specification. After our specification was released, a programmer pointed out that the implementation was non-deterministic: sometimes it raised the exception and sometimes it returned. The implementors decided that the efficiency advantages gained by allowing non-determinism made it desirable to weaken the specification.

We must also report two more worrisome incidents:

- An error in the specification that had not been noticed during more than a year of use was discovered[1] while the original version of this chapter was being prepared for publication. The problem was again in the specification of AlertWait. The specification incorrectly required that when ChooseOutcome made alertChosen' TRUE it left the value of waiting[c] unchanged. This would leave a thread in waiting[c] that was no longer blocked on the condition variable; this could affect the results of subsequent calls to Signal.

- More recently, yet another problem was found.[2] We had specified AlertWait as the combination of just two actions, Enqueue and AlertResume, with the latter being nondeterministic:

```
ACTION AlertResume
  WHEN holder[m] = none
    AND (NOT (CURRENT ∈ waiting[c]) OR alerted[CURRENT])
  ENSURES holder'[m] = CURRENT
    AND ((RAISE = RETURN AND NOT (CURRENT ∈ waiting[c])
        AND UNCHANGED(waiting, alerted))
      OR (RAISE = Alerted AND alerted[CURRENT]
        AND waiting'[c] = delete(CURRENT, waiting[c])
        AND NOT alerted'[CURRENT]))
```

---

[1] by Greg Nelson, in the course of preparing a review.
[2] by Garret Swart, studying the original version of this chapter.

Unfortunately, it is not possible to deduce from this specification that a thread unblocked by Signal won't leave AlertWait by raising Alerted, rather than returning. Thus it is not guaranteed that Signal will cause at least one blocked thread to return from a Wait or AlertWait (if there are any), even though the implementation carefully ensures this.[3]

We are vexed that it took so long for anyone to notice these errors. We can think of several possible contributing factors:

- AlertWait is the most complicated procedure in this interface, and also the least familiar. The specifiers had less experience to fall back on. Disentangling the essential properties of the interface from the incidental properties of the implementation proved harder than we had anticipated.

- AlertWait involves a complex interaction between two potentially conflicting guarantees that are separately straightforward: signals never get lost (if there are blocked threads to receive them) and alerts never get lost.

- Semaphores and condition variables are similar in many ways. After studying the specification of AlertP (where these complications do not arise), it may be too easy to overlook the consequences of using different abstractions to specify semaphores and condition variables.

- Even after the first problem was discovered, it was difficult to convince ourselves (one at a time) that it was indeed a bug. The most effective argument was operational: suppose a thread, t, raises Alerted, then a thread invokes Signal, which chooses to remove t from waiting[c], which means that no blocked thread is awakened by that Signal.

A more encouraging aspect of our experience is the role played by the specification in insulating clients from the implementation of the Thread interface:

- In the Topaz system at SRC, mutexes are implemented using queues of blocked threads, without recording which thread currently holds the mutex; this is quite different from what one might guess after reading our specification. The client programmer, however, need not know this. The specification abstracts from details of the implementation to provide a simpler model. (In fact, some programmers have complained because SRC's debugger doesn't provide a simple way to determine which thread holds a locked mutex.)

- Although the underlying implementation has been reworked several times, both to improve efficiency and to make it easy to collect statistics on contention, the specification of the synchronization primitives (other than AlertWait) has been unchanged for several years. Client programmers have not needed to respond to, or even know about, the implementation changes.

---

[3]Mark Manasse showed us how to construct a program that could detect that AlertWait consisted of more than two actions, proving that no two-action composition could be an adequate specification.

- Although semaphores and mutexes have identical implementations, the interface provides distinct types with different specifications. Mutexes have holders and semaphores don't; Release has a REQUIRES clause and V doesn't. The choice to have two types for the two different ways of using the underlying mechanism had already been made by the designers when the formal specification was started. Client programs that rely only on the specified properties of these types would continue to work even if their implementations were different.

Our experience with the Thread specification indicates that formal specifications of concurrent programs can be used productively by systems programmers, but it says little about the ease with which they can be produced. The specification was written by two of us who have many years of experience in writing formal specifications.

Writing good specifications is difficult and time consuming. In our experience, the bulk of the time goes first to understanding the object to be specified and then to choosing abstractions to help structure the presentation of that understanding. We spend relatively little time translating our understanding into the specification language itself.

Understanding systems with a high degree of concurrency is particularly difficult. When studying the designs of such systems, it is often hard to disentangle the behavior implied by a particular implementation from the behavior that all implementations should be required to exhibit. At the very least, specifiers must have ready access to the designers of the system to answer such questions.

In summary, formal specifications can be useful in documenting interfaces. A formal specification is not a replacement for careful prose documentation, but it can help to improve documentation by providing precision and completeness where needed. It can contribute structure and regularity, enforce precision, and encourage accuracy and completeness. However, specifications are themselves prone to error and must be carefully checked.

5.5 Acknowledgments

Leslie Lamport and Jeannette Wing were both involved in the discussions leading to this specification, and helped us to understand the issues involved.

Chapter 6

I/O Streams: Abstract Types, Real Programs

Mark R. Brown and Greg Nelson

Where the stream runneth smoothest, the water is deepest.
—*John Lyly*

6.1 Introduction

Our first goal is to define Modula-3 interfaces for text input and output. The interfaces define two types of objects, *readers* and *writers*, collectively called *streams*. Streams come in a potentially unlimited number of classes, such as streams to and from terminals, disk files, etc. We hope these interfaces will become standards.

Our second goal is to illustrate the *partially opaque type*, a Modula-3 feature that allows flexible data abstraction. A quick survey of the literature will show that there are hundreds of language features to support abstract data types, but only one example—the stack. To give a realistic example of the partially opaque type in action, we will describe the Modula-3 streams package in detail, from top to bottom.

Our final goal is to illustrate the explicit isolation of unsafe code. Reading and writing characters must be fast, and on some systems this will require unsafe, machine-dependent code. The program described in this chapter contains two modules that can be re-programmed in a machine-dependent way. (Of course, reprogramming them does not affect the abstract properties of streams.) We present versions of the modules that are suitable for byte-addressable machines. They use pointer arithmetic, and are therefore unsafe.

As a general rule, the upper layers of a system are safer than the lower layers. In Modula-3, where safety has a precise technical meaning, the transition between the safe and the unsafe is not gradual: it occurs where an unsafe module exports a safe interface. Programming this layer is very error-prone; the streams package provides a realistic example of the dangers.

We will view streams at three levels of detail. At the highest level, the client interfaces Rd and Wr define streams as abstract types. In this view the types are completely opaque. At the intermediate level, the class interfaces RdClass and WrClass reveal the buffer structure that is needed to implement new classes of streams. Here the types are partially opaque. At the lowest level, the modules RdRep and WrRep reveal the complete representation, and contain the potentially machine-dependent code.

The client and class interfaces are safe; the low-level modules are unsafe. There are also two interfaces, UnsafeWr and UnsafeRd, which reveal the semaphores that make operations on readers and writers atomic.

Perhaps the first object-oriented I/O package was part of the Simula system [3]. The first to use class-independent buffering seems to be the I/O system for the OS6 described by J. E. Stoy and C. Strachey in 1972 [27]. The package described in this chapter is closely based on the Modula-2+ streams package used in the Topaz System at Digital's Systems Research Center.

6.2 The Wr interface

A Wr.T (or "writer") is a character output stream. The basic operation on a writer is PutChar, which extends a writer's character sequence by one character. Some writers (called "seekable writers") also allow overwriting in the middle of the sequence. For example, writers to random access files are seekable, but writers to terminals and sequential files are not.

Writers can be (and usually are) buffered. This means that operations on the writer don't immediately affect the underlying target of the writer, but are saved up and performed later. For example, a writer to a disk file is not likely to update the disk after each character.

Abstractly, a writer `wr` consists of:

`len(wr)`	a non-negative integer
`c(wr)`	a character sequence of length `len(wr)`
`cur(wr)`	an integer in the range $[0..len(wr)]$
`target(wr)`	a character sequence
`closed(wr)`	a boolean
`seekable(wr)`	a boolean
`buffered(wr)`	a boolean

These values are generally not directly represented in the data fields of a writer object, but in principle they determine the state of the writer.

The sequence `c(wr)` is zero-based: `c(wr)[i]` is valid for i from 0 through `len(wr)-1`. The value of `cur(wr)` is the index of the character in `c(wr)` that will be replaced or appended by the next call to PutChar. If `wr` is not seekable, then `cur(wr)` is always equal to `len(wr)`, since in this case all writing happens at the end.

The difference between `c(wr)` and `target(wr)` reflects the buffering: if `wr` is not buffered, then `target(wr)` is updated to equal `c(wr)` after every operation; if `wr` is buffered, then updates to `target(wr)` can be delayed. For example, in a writer to a file, `target(wr)` is the actual sequence of characters on the disk; in a writer to a terminal, `target(wr)` is the sequence of characters that have actually been transmitted (this sequence may not exist in any data structure, but it still exists abstractly).

If `wr` is buffered, then the assignment `target(wr) := c(wr)` can happen asynchronously at any time, although the procedures in this interface are atomic with respect to such assignments.

Every writer is a monitor; that is, it contains an internal lock that is acquired and held for each operation in this interface, so that concurrent operations will appear atomic. For faster, unmonitored access, see the `UnsafeWr` interface (Section 6.7).

The rest of this section is a listing of the `Wr` interface, together with comments specifying the effect of each procedure. It is convenient to define the action PutC(`wr`, `ch`), which outputs the character `ch` to the writer `wr`:

```
PutC(wr, ch) =
  IF closed(wr) THEN RAISE Error(Code.Closed) END;
  IF cur(wr) = len(wr) THEN
    "Extend c(wr) by one character, incrementing len(wr)"
  END;
  c(wr)[cur(wr)] := ch;
  INC(cur(wr))
```

PutC is only used in specifying the interface; it is not a real procedure.

```
INTERFACE Wr;
FROM Thread IMPORT Alerted;

TYPE
  T <: ROOT;
  Code = {Closed, Unseekable};
EXCEPTION Failure(REFANY); Error(Code);
```

Since there are many classes of writers, there are many ways that a writer can break—for example, the network can go down, the disk can fill up, etc. All problems of this sort are reported by raising the exception Failure. The documentation of each writer class should specify what failures the class can raise and how they are encoded in the argument to Wr.Failure (which has type REFANY).

Illegal operations (for example, writing to a closed writer) raise the exception Error.

```
PROCEDURE PutChar(wr: T; ch: CHAR)
  RAISES {Failure, Alerted, Error};
```

> Output ch to wr. More precisely, this is equivalent to:
>
> ```
> PutC(wr, ch); IF NOT buffered(wr) THEN Flush(wr) END
> ```

Many operations on a writer can wait indefinitely. For example, PutChar can wait if the user has suspended output to his terminal. These waits can be alertable, so each procedure that might wait includes Thread.Alerted in its raises clause.

```
PROCEDURE PutText(wr: T; t: TEXT)
  RAISES {Failure, Alerted, Error};
```

> Output t to wr. More precisely, this is equivalent to:
>
> ```
> FOR i := 0 TO Text.Length(t) - 1 DO
>   PutC(wr, Text.GetChar(t, i))
> END;
> IF NOT buffered(wr) THEN Flush(wr) END
> ```
>
> except that, like all operations in this interface, it is atomic with respect to other operations in the interface. (It would be wrong to write PutChar instead of PutC, since PutChar always flushes if the writer is unbuffered.)

```
PROCEDURE PutString(wr: T; a: ARRAY OF CHAR)
  RAISES {Failure, Alerted, Error};
```

> Output a to wr. More precisely, this is equivalent to:
>
> ```
> FOR i := FIRST(a) TO LAST(a) DO PutC(wr, a[i]) END;
> IF NOT buffered(wr) THEN Flush(wr) END
> ```
>
> except that it is atomic.

```
PROCEDURE Seek(wr: T; n: CARDINAL)
  RAISES {Failure, Alerted, Error};
```

> Set the current position of wr to n. This is an error if wr is closed. More precisely, this is equivalent to:

```
IF closed(wr) THEN RAISE Error(Code.Closed) END;
IF NOT seekable(wr) THEN RAISE Error(Code.Unseekable) END;
cur(wr) := MIN(n, len(wr));
```

```
PROCEDURE Flush(wr: T) RAISES {Failure, Alerted, Error};
```

> Perform all buffered operations. That is, set target(wr) := c(wr), unless wr is closed, in which case raise Error(Code.Closed).

```
PROCEDURE Close(wr: T) RAISES {Failure, Alerted, Error};
```

> Flush wr, release any resources associated with wr, and set closed(wr) := true. The documentation for a procedure that creates a writer should specify what resources are released when the writer is closed. This leaves closed(wr) equal to TRUE even if it raises an exception, and is a no-op if wr is closed.

```
PROCEDURE Length(wr: T): CARDINAL
  RAISES {Failure, Alerted, Error};
```

```
PROCEDURE Index(wr: T): CARDINAL RAISES {Error};
```

```
PROCEDURE Seekable(wr: T): BOOLEAN RAISES {};
```

```
PROCEDURE Closed(wr: T): BOOLEAN RAISES {};
```

```
PROCEDURE Buffered(wr: T): BOOLEAN RAISES {};
```

> These procedures return len(wr), cur(wr), seekable(wr), closed(wr), and buffered(wr), respectively. Length and Index raise Error(Code.Closed) if wr is closed; the other three procedures do not.

```
END Wr.
```

6.3   The Rd interface

An Rd.T (or "reader") is a character input stream. The basic operation on a reader is GetChar, which returns the source character at the "current position" and advances the current position by one. Some readers are "seekable", which means that they also allow setting the current position anywhere in the source. For example, readers from random access files are seekable; readers from terminals and sequential files are not.

Some readers are "intermittent", which means that the source of the reader trickles in rather than being available to the implementation all at once. For example, the input stream from an interactive terminal is intermittent. An intermittent reader is never seekable.

Abstractly, a reader `rd` consists of

`len(rd)`	the number of source characters
`src(rd)`	a sequence of length `len(rd)+1`
`cur(rd)`	an integer in the range `[0..len(rd)]`
`avail(rd)`	an integer in the range `[cur(rd)..len(rd)+1]`
`closed(rd)`	a boolean
`seekable(rd)`	a boolean
`intermittent(rd)`	a boolean

These values are not necessarily directly represented in the data fields of a reader object. In particular, for an intermittent reader, `len(rd)` may be unknown to the implementation. But in principle the values determine the state of the reader.

The sequence `src(rd)` is zero-based: `src(rd)[i]` is valid for i from 0 to `len(rd)`. The first `len(rd)` elements of `src` are the characters that are the source of the reader. The final element is a special value eof used to represent end-of-file. The value eof is not a character.

The value of `cur(rd)` is the index in `src(rd)` of the next character to be returned by GetChar, unless `cur(rd) = len(rd)`, in which case a call to GetChar will raise the exception EndOfFile.

The value of `avail(rd)` is important for intermittent readers: the elements whose indexes in `src(rd)` are in the range `[cur(rd)..avail(rd)-1]` are available to the implementation and can be read by clients without blocking. If the client tries to read further, the implementation will block waiting for the other characters. If rd is not intermittent, then `avail(rd)` is equal to `len(rd)+1`. If rd is intermittent, then `avail(rd)` can increase asynchronously, although the procedures in this interface are atomic with respect to such increases.

The definitions above encompass readers with infinite sources. If rd is such a reader, then `len(rd)` and `len(rd)+1` are both infinity, and there is no final eof value.

Every reader is a monitor; that is, it contains an internal lock that is acquired and held for each operation in this interface, so that concurrent operations will appear atomic. For faster, unmonitored access, see the UnsafeRd interface (Section 6.7).

The remainder of this section is a listing of the Rd interface, together with comments specifying the effect of each procedure.

```
INTERFACE Rd;
FROM Thread IMPORT Alerted;

TYPE
  T <: ROOT;
  Code = {Closed, Unseekable, Intermittent, CantUnget};
EXCEPTION EndOfFile; Failure(REFANY); Error(Code);
```

Since there are many classes of readers, there are many ways that a reader can break—for example, the connection to a terminal can be broken, the disk can signal a read error, etc. All problems of this sort are reported by raising the exception Failure. The documentation of reader class should specify what failures the class can raise and how they are encoded in the argument to Failure (which has type REFANY).

Illegal operations raise the exception Error.

```
PROCEDURE GetChar(rd: T): CHAR
  RAISES {EndOfFile, Failure, Alerted, Error};
```

> Return the next character from rd. More precisely, this is equivalent to the following, in which res is a local variable of type CHAR:

```
IF closed(rd) THEN RAISE Error(Code.Closed) END;
Block until avail(rd) > cur(rd);
IF cur(rd) = len(rd) THEN
  RAISE EndOfFile
ELSE
  res := src(rd)[cur(rd)];
  INC(cur(rd));
  RETURN res
END
```

Many operations on a reader can wait indefinitely. For example, GetChar can wait if the user is not typing. In general these waits are alertable, so each procedure that might wait includes Thread.Alerted in its RAISES clause.

```
PROCEDURE EOF(rd: T): BOOLEAN RAISES {Failure, Alerted, Error};
```

> Return TRUE iff rd is at end-of-file. More precisely, this is equivalent to:

```
IF closed(rd) THEN RAISE Error(Code.Closed) END;
Block until avail(rd) > cur(rd);
RETURN cur(rd) = len(rd)
```

> Notice that on an intermittent reader, EOF can block. For example, if there are no characters buffered in a terminal reader, EOF must wait to see if the user types the end-of-file escape. If you are using EOF in an interactive input loop, the right sequence of operations is:

1. prompt the user;

2. call EOF, which probably waits on user input;

3. presuming that EOF returned FALSE, read the user's input.

PROCEDURE UnGetChar(rd: T) RAISES {Error}

"Pushes back" the last character read from rd, so that the next call to GetChar will read it again. More precisely, this is equivalent to the following

```
IF closed(rd) THEN
  RAISE Error(Code.Closed)
END;
IF cur(rd) > 0 THEN
  DEC(cur(rd))
END
```

except there is a special rule: UnGetChar(rd) is only guaranteed to work if GetChar(rd) was the last operation on rd. Thus UnGetChar cannot be called twice in a row, or after Seek or EOF. If this rule is violated, the implementation is allowed (but not required) to raise Error(CantUnget).

PROCEDURE CharsReady(rd: T): CARDINAL RAISES {Failure}

Return some number of characters that can be read without indefinite waiting. The "end of file marker" counts as one character for this purpose, so CharsReady will return 1, not 0, if EOF(rd) is true. More precisely, this is equivalent to the following:

```
IF closed(rd) THEN RAISE Error(Code.Closed) END;
IF avail(rd) = cur(rd) THEN
  RETURN 0
ELSE
  RETURN some number in the range [1 .. avail(rd) - cur(rd)]
END;
```

Warning: CharsReady can return a result less than avail(rd) - cur(rd); so the code to flush buffered input without blocking requires a loop:

```
LOOP
  n := Rd.CharsReady(rd);
  IF n = 0 THEN EXIT END;
  FOR i := 1 TO n DO
    EVAL Rd.GetChar(rd)
  END
END;
```

```
PROCEDURE GetSub(
    rd: T;
    VAR (*out*) str: ARRAY OF CHAR)
    : CARDINAL
  RAISES {Failure, Alerted, Error};
```

Read from `rd` into `str` until `rd` is exhausted or `str` is filled. More precisely, this is equivalent to the following, in which `i` is a local variable:

```
i := 0;
WHILE NOT EOF(rd) AND i # NUMBER(str) DO
  str[i] := GetChar(rd); INC(i)
END;
RETURN i
```

```
PROCEDURE GetSubLine(
    rd: T;
    VAR (*out*) str: ARRAY OF CHAR): CARDINAL
  RAISES {Failure, Alerted, Error};
```

Read from `rd` into `str` until a newline is read, `rd` is exhausted, or `sub` is filled. More precisely, this is equivalent to the following, in which `i` is a local variable:

```
i := 0;
WHILE
  NOT EOF(rd) AND
  i # NUMBER(str) AND
  (i = 0 OR str[i-1] # '\n')
DO
  str[i] := GetChar(rd); INC(i)
END;
RETURN i
```

```
PROCEDURE GetText(
    rd: T;
    len: INTEGER)
    : TEXT
  RAISES {Failure, Alerted, Error};
```

Read from `rd` until it is exhausted or `len` characters have been read, and return the result as a TEXT. More precisely, this is equivalent to the following, in which `i` and `res` are local variables:

```
res := ""; i := 0;
WHILE NOT EOF(rd) AND i # len DO
  res := res & Text.FromChar(GetChar(rd));
  INC(i)
END;
RETURN res
```

```
PROCEDURE GetLine(rd: T): TEXT
  RAISES {EndOfFile, Failure, Alerted, Error};
```

> If EOF(rd) then raise EndOfFile. Otherwise, read characters until a newline is read or rd is exhausted, and return the result as a TEXT—but discard the final newline if it is present. More precisely, this is equivalent to the following, in which ch and res are local variables:

```
IF EOF(rd) THEN
  RAISE EndOfFile
ELSE
  res := "";
  ch := '\000'; (* any char but newline *)
  WHILE NOT EOF(rd) AND ch # '\n' DO
    ch := GetChar(rd);
    IF ch # '\n' THEN res := res & Text.FromChar(ch) END
  END;
  RETURN res
END
```

```
PROCEDURE Seek(rd: T; n: CARDINAL) RAISES {Failure, Alerted, Error};
```

> This is equivalent to:

```
IF closed(rd) THEN
  RAISE Error(Code.Closed)
ELSIF NOT seekable(rd) THEN
  RAISE Error(Code.Unseekable)
ELSE
  cur(rd) := MIN(n, len(rd))
END
```

```
PROCEDURE Close(rd: T) RAISES {Failure, Alerted};
```

> Release any resources associated with rd and set closed(rd) := TRUE. The documentation of a procedure that creates a reader should specify what resources are released when the reader is closed. This leaves rd closed even if it raises an exception, and is a no-op if rd is closed.

```
PROCEDURE Index(rd: T): CARDINAL RAISES {};
```

> This is equivalent to:

```
IF closed(rd) THEN
  RAISE Error(Code.Closed)
ELSE
  RETURN cur(rd)
END
```

```
PROCEDURE Length(rd: T): CARDINAL
  RAISES {Failure, Alerted, Error};
```

This is equivalent to:

```
IF closed(rd) THEN
  RAISE Error(Code.Closed)
ELSIF intermittent(rd) THEN
  RAISE Error(Code.Intermittent)
ELSE
  RETURN len(rd)
END
```

```
PROCEDURE Intermittent(rd: T): BOOLEAN RAISES {};
```

```
PROCEDURE Seekable(rd: T): BOOLEAN RAISES {};
```

```
PROCEDURE Closed(rd: T): BOOLEAN RAISES {};
```

Return intermittent(rd), seekable(rd), and closed(rd), respectively. These can be applied to closed readers.

```
END Rd.
```

6.4   The Stdio and FileStream interfaces

The interface Stdio provides streams for standard input, standard output, and standard error:

```
INTERFACE Stdio;
IMPORT Rd, Wr;

VAR
  stdin: Rd.T;
  stdout: Wr.T;
  stderr: Wr.T;

END Stdio.
```

The initialization of these streams depends on the underlying operating system. If the output streams are directed to terminals, they should be unbuffered, so that explicit Wr.Flush calls are unnecessary for interactive programs. If the streams are directed to or from random-access files, they should be seekable. It is possible that stderr is equal to stdout; therefore, programs that perform seek operations on stdout should take care not to destroy output data when writing error messages.

The `FileStream` interface provides simple routines for opening files. The detailed semantics of the file system vary greatly from operating system to operating system, so it is to be expected that this interface will grow in different directions in different systems. But all systems should be able to implement the following weakly-specified interface, and thereby provide a measure of portability for simple clients.

The interface doesn't specify whether the readers and writers returned by the procedures are seekable or buffered. Probably readers and writers to disk files are seekable and buffered, but in general this depends on the system. Closing a file reader or writer closes the underlying file.

```
INTERFACE FileStream;
IMPORT Rd, Wr;

PROCEDURE OpenRead(n: TEXT): Rd.T;
```

> Return a reader whose source is the contents of the file named n, or NIL if there is no such file.

```
PROCEDURE OpenWrite(n: TEXT): Wr.T;
```

> Return a writer whose target is the contents of the file named n. If the file does not exist it will be created; if it does exist it will be truncated to length zero. Return NIL if the file cannot be created or truncated.

```
PROCEDURE OpenAppend(n: TEXT): Wr.T;
```

> Return a writer whose target is the contents of the file named n. If the file does not exist it will be created; if it does exist then the writer will be positioned to append to the existing contents of the file. Return NIL if the file cannot be created or extended.

```
END FileStream.
```

6.5 The WrClass interface

There is no end to the number of useful classes of readers and writers. Here are a few examples from SRC's standard libraries:

- Tee writers, which write copies of their stream to each of two other writers; for example, to a terminal and a log file. The name comes from the Unix program "tee", which performs a similar function in the realm of pipes.

- Various ways to make new readers from old readers: for example, by concatenation, subsequencing, duplication, and filtering.

- Split writers, which are intended for use by applications that use parallel threads writing to a single writer. Split writers keep the output from each thread separate; this creates the illusion that one thread writes all of its output before the next thread starts writing its output.

- Local pipes, in which a reader is connected to a writer so that its source is the writer's target.

- Formatted writers, in which the client can mark the start and end of logical objects and specify desirable places to break the objects into lines. Formatted writers are basic tools for building pretty-printers.

It is beyond the scope of this chapter to describe these classes in detail. Instead we will describe the interfaces that allow you to define new classes.

The basic idea is that readers and writers are objects whose method suites are determined by their class. In the most obvious version of this idea, a writer class's putChar method would determine the effect of Wr.PutChar for writers of the class:

```
PutChar(wr, ch) = wr.putChar(ch)
```

The putChar method for a terminal writer would send characters to the terminal; while the method for a disk file writer would send characters to the disk, etc.

There are two reasons for rejecting this obvious version. The first reason is that it is inefficient to call a method for every PutChar. The second and more important reason is that most writers are buffered, and it is undesirable to force every client to reimplement buffering.

Instead, the streams system provides *class-independent buffering*. That is, PutChar and GetChar are implemented by class-independent code that operates on a buffer; class-dependent code is invoked only when the buffer fills up (in the case of a writer) or empties (in the case of a reader). Thus the cost of invoking a class method is amortized over a large number stream operations. There are those who argue against this design, claiming that if PutChar and GetChar are procedures instead of methods, then the stream system is "not object-oriented". Perhaps, but the system is nonetheless efficient and flexible.

In this section we define the WrClass interface, which reveals the buffer structure in a writer object and the specifications for the methods that operate on the buffer. To define a new writer class, you import WrClass and define a subtype with method overrides appropriate to the new class.

In addition to the buffer structure, a writer contains fields that are used by the class-independent code implementing PutChar and GetChar. These fields are irrelevant to class implementations, which deal with entire buffers, not with individual characters. Because Modula-3 has partial revelations, the WrClass interface can reveal the buffer structure while concealing the fields needed only by the class-independent code.

The remainder of this section is a commented listing of the `WrClass` interface.

```
INTERFACE WrClass;
IMPORT Wr;
FROM Thread IMPORT Alerted;
FROM Wr IMPORT Failure, Error;

TYPE
  Private <: ROOT;

REVEAL
  Wr.T = Private BRANDED OBJECT
    buff: REF ARRAY OF CHAR;
    st: CARDINAL; (* index into buff *)
    lo, hi, cur: CARDINAL; (* indexes into c(wr) *)
    closed, seekable, buffered: BOOLEAN
  METHODS
    seek (n: CARDINAL) RAISES {Failure, Alerted, Error};
    length(): CARDINAL
        RAISES {Failure, Alerted, Error} := LengthDefault;
    flush () RAISES {Failure, Alerted, Error} := FlushDefault;
    close () RAISES {Failure, Alerted, Error} := CloseDefault
  END;
```

The private fields that are needed by the class-independent code but are irrelevant to the buffer structure are lumped together into the opaque type `Private`.

There are several ways of hiding a group of fields of an object type. The common opaque type declaration `TYPE T <: U` reveals that the U fields are a prefix of T but leaves room for additional fields to be revealed later in T's suffix. `WrClass` uses another common idiom: `TYPE Private <: ROOT; T = Private OBJECT ... END`, which leaves room for additional fields in T's prefix. It is also possible to leave room in both the prefix and the suffix: `TYPE Private <: ROOT; T <: Private OBJECT ... END`.

The reason `WrClass` leaves room in `Wr.T`'s prefix is to allow a later revelation that `Wr.T <: Thread.Mutex`, that is, that every writer is a mutex. If instead the mutex were placed in the suffix of `Wr.T`, then every writer would *contain* a mutex, which would cost an extra allocation.

The next step is to relate the concrete representation of the buffer structure to the abstract definition of a writer that was presented in the `Wr` interface. In some methodologies, this would be done by defining an *abstraction function* from the concrete representation to the abstract type. But the `WrClass` interface does not specify the representation of the target of a writer, so it is not possible to define an abstraction function at this point. But we can define the relation between the abstract type and the buffer structure, and leave it to class implementations to define the rest of the abstraction function.

Let `wr` be a writer, which abstractly is given by `c(wr)`, `target(wr)`, `cur(wr)`, `closed(wr)`, `seekable(wr)`, `buffered(wr)`. The actual representation of `wr` is an object of type `Wr.T`. The `wr.cur`, `wr.closed`, `wr.seekable`, and `wr.buffered` fields in the object represent the corresponding abstract attributes of `wr`. The `wr.buff`, `wr.st`, `wr.lo`, and `wr.hi` fields in the object represent a buffer containing the unflushed part of `c(wr)`. The target of the writer is represented in some class-specific way, which is not specified by this interface.

More precisely, we say that the state of the writer object `wr` is *valid* if the following conditions V1 through V4 hold:

V1. the cur field and the booleans are correct:

```
wr.cur = cur(wr) AND
wr.closed = closed(wr) AND
wr.buffered = buffered(wr) AND
wr.seekable = seekable(wr)
```

V2. the indexes of any unflushed characters are in the range `[lo..cur-1]`. That is, for all i in `[0..len(wr)-1]` but not in `[wr.lo..wr.cur-1]`,

```
c(wr)[i] = target(wr)[i]
```

V3. the (possibly) unflushed characters are stored in `buff` starting with `buff[st]`. That is, for all i in `[wr.lo..wr.cur-1]`,

```
c(wr)[i] = wr.buff[wr.st + i - wr.lo]
```

(Usually `st` is zero. Non-zero values may be useful to satisfy buffer alignment constraints.)

V4. the current position is either contained in the buffer, or just past the buffer:

```
wr.lo <= wr.cur <= wr.hi
```

It is possible that `buff = NIL` in a valid state, since the range of i's in V3 can be empty; for example, in case `lo = cur`.

We say that the state is *ready* if the buffer contains the current position; that is, if

```
        NOT wr.closed
AND wr.buff # NIL
AND wr.lo <= cur(wr) < wr.hi
```

If the state is ready, then `Wr.PutChar` can be implemented by storing into the buffer. The class-independent code in `WrRep` does exactly this, until the buffer is full, at which point it calls a class method to consume the buffer and provide a new one.

In general, the class-independent code modifies `cur` and `buff[i]` for i in the range `[st..st+(hi-1)-lo]`, but not `st`, `lo`, `hi`, or the `buff` reference itself. The class-independent code locks the writer before calling any methods; therefore, no two method activations initiated by the class-independent code will be concurrent. If a writer method applies one of the operations from the Wr interface to the writer itself, deadlock will result.

In general, the class-independent implementation of an operation in the Wr interface must call one of the writer's methods whenever the operation cannot be carried out using the current buffer. The most important method is the seek method, which positions the writer so that a given position is contained in the current buffer. That is, the method call wr.seek(n) treats n as a position to seek to, and moves the buffer to contain this position. More precisely:

> Given a valid state, wr.seek(n) must produce a valid ready state in which cur(wr) = MIN(n, len(wr)) and c(wr) is unchanged.

That is, wr.seek(n) sets cur(wr) to n, as expected, or to len(wr) if n > len(wr). Furthermore it must produce a ready state; that is, it must set the buff, lo, and hi fields so that the new current position is represented in the buffer. The seek method is required to preserve validity; in particular, if it changes buffers, it must update the target with the contents of the old buffer.

An important special case is when n = wr.cur = wr.hi; that is, when the buffer has overflowed and the effect of the seek is simply to advance from the last character of a buffer to the first character of a new buffer. Every writer class (seekable or not) must provide a seek method that supports this special case. The method must support the general case only if the writer is seekable.

The flush method updates the underlying target of the writer. That is:

> Given a valid state, wr.flush() must produce a valid state in which c(wr) and cur(wr) are unchanged and target(wr) = c(wr).

If a writer is unbuffered, the class-independent code will call the flush method after every modification to the buffer.

The close method releases all resources associated with a writer. That is:

> Given a valid state in which target(wr) = c(wr), the call wr.close() must release all resources associated with wr.

The exact meaning is class-specific. After the method returns, the class-independent code will set the closed bit in the writer.

The length method returns the length of the writer. That is:

> Given a valid state, wr.length() must return len(wr), leaving a valid state in which c(wr) and cur(wr) are unchanged.

The next two procedures are needed to code class-specific operations.

```
PROCEDURE Lock(wr: Wr.T);
```

> The writer `wr` must be unlocked; lock it and make its state valid.

```
PROCEDURE Unlock(wr: Wr.T);
```

> The writer `wr` must be locked and valid; unlock it and restore the private invariant of the class-independent writer implementation.

A class-specific operation on a writer `wr` should use the following template:

```
Lock(wr); TRY ... FINALLY Unlock(wr) END
```

The methods don't have to do this, since the class-independent code automatically locks and unlocks the writer around method calls. The next section provides examples of the use of `Lock` and `Unlock`.

The last declarations in the interface are for the default methods:

```
PROCEDURE LengthDefault(wr: Wr.T): CARDINAL;
```

```
PROCEDURE CloseDefault(wr: Wr.T);
```

```
PROCEDURE FlushDefault(wr: Wr.T);
```

> `LengthDefault` returns `wr.cur`, while `CloseDefault` sets `wr.buff` to `NIL` and `FlushDefault` is a no-op.

```
END WrClass.
```

6.6   Text writers

As an example of a writer class implementation, this section describes a simple version of text writers.

The target of a text writer is an internal buffer whose contents can be retrieved as a TEXT. Retrieving the buffer resets the target to be empty.

Text writers are buffered and unseekable, and never raise `Failure` or `Alerted`. The fact that they are buffered is essentially unobservable, since there is no way for the client to access the target except through the text writer. The interface is:

```
INTERFACE TextWr;
IMPORT Wr;

TYPE T <: Wr.T;
```

```
PROCEDURE New(): T;
```

>   Return a new text writer with c = "" and cur = 0.

```
PROCEDURE ToText(wr: T): TEXT;
```

>   Return c(wr), resetting c(wr) to "" and cur(wr) to 0.

```
END TextWr.
```

Next we describe a simple implementation. A fast implementation would probably import the private representation of the Text interface.

```
MODULE TextWr;
IMPORT Wr, WrClass, Text;
FROM Wr IMPORT Failure;
EXCEPTION FatalError;

REVEAL T = Wr.T BRANDED OBJECT
    text: TEXT
  OVERRIDES
    seek := Seek;
    close := Close
  END;
```

```
CONST BuffSize = 500;
```

A single buffer of the given size is used; each time it fills up, its characters are appended to text. That is, the representation invariant for a text writer wr is

$$\text{target}(wr) = wr.text \ \& \ \text{SUBARRAY}(wr.buff\hat{\ }, \ 0, \ wr.cur-wr.lo)$$

This constraint, together with the definition of a valid writer in WrClass, determine the abstract writer value as a function of its concrete representation.

Since wr is unseekable, len(wr) is always equal to wr.cur, and therefore text writers can inherit the length method from Wr.T. Since the client cannot access the target of a text writer, the flush method (which is a no-op) can also be inherited.

```
PROCEDURE New(): T =
  BEGIN
    RETURN
      NEW(T,
        st := 0,
        lo := 0,
        cur := 0,
        hi := BuffSize,
        buff := NEW(REF ARRAY OF CHAR, BuffSize),
```

```
        closed := FALSE,
        seekable := FALSE,
        buffered := TRUE,
        text := "")
  END New;
PROCEDURE Seek(wr: T; n: CARDINAL) RAISES {Failure} =
  BEGIN
    IF wr.cur # n THEN
      RAISE FatalError (* Bug in WrRep *)
    END;
    wr.text := wr.text &
      Text.FromStr(SUBARRAY(wr.buff^, 0, wr.cur - wr.lo));
    wr.lo := wr.cur;
    wr.hi := wr.lo + NUMBER(wr.buff^)
  END Seek;
```

Since text writers are not seekable, the `seek` method won't be asked to do anything more than advance to the next buffer—unless there is a bug in WrRep. There is no excuse for such a bug, so if this happens the method causes a checked runtime error, by the simple technique of raising an exception that is not present in the procedure's raises set.

```
PROCEDURE Close(wr: T) =
  BEGIN
    wr.buff := NIL;
    wr.text := NIL
  END Close;

PROCEDURE ToText(wr: T): TEXT =
  VAR result: Text.T;
  BEGIN
    WrClass.Lock(wr);
    TRY
      wr.seek(wr.cur);
      result := wr.text;
      wr.text := "";
      wr.cur := 0;
      wr.lo := 0;
      wr.hi := NUMBER(wr.buff^)
    FINALLY
      WrClass.Unlock(wr)
    END;
    RETURN result
  END ToText;


BEGIN END TextWr.
```

6.7 The unsafe interfaces

The routines in the UnsafeWr and UnsafeRd interfaces are like the corresponding routines in the Wr and Rd interfaces, but it is the client's responsibility to lock the stream before calling them. The lock can be acquired once and held for several operations, which is faster than acquiring the lock for each operation, and also makes the whole group atomic. Danger is the price of speed: it is an unchecked runtime error to call one of these operations without locking the stream.

The UnsafeWr interface also provides routines for formatted printing of integers and reals. Using them is more efficient but less convenient than using the Fmt interface from Section 3.5. For example, the statement

```
Wr.PutText(wr, "Line " & Fmt.Int(n) & " of file " & f)
```

can be replaced with the following faster code:

```
LOCK wr DO
  FastPutText(wr, "Line ");
  FastPutInt (wr, n);
  FastPutText(wr, " of file ");
  FastPutText(wr, f)
END
```

If several threads are writing characters concurrently to the same writer, treating each PutChar as an atomic action is likely to produce inscrutable output—it is usually preferable if the units of interleaving are whole lines, or even larger. It is therefore convenient as well as efficient to import UnsafeWr and use LOCK clauses like the one above to make small groups of output atomic. But don't forget to acquire the lock! If you call one of the routines in this interface without it, then the unsafe code in WrRep might crash your program in a rubble of bits. A historical note: the main public interface to Modula-2+ writers used the unsafe, unmonitored routines. Errors were more frequent than expected, mostly because of concurrent calls to Wr.Flush or Wr.Close, which often occur as implicit finalization actions when the programmer doesn't expect them. In the Modula-3 design we have therefore made the main interfaces safe.

Here is the interface:

```
UNSAFE INTERFACE UnsafeWr;

IMPORT Wr, Thread;
FROM Thread IMPORT Alerted;
FROM Wr IMPORT Failure, Error;
FROM Fmt IMPORT Base, Style;
```

```
REVEAL
  Wr.T <: Thread.Mutex;
```

Thus an importer of UnsafeWr can write code like LOCK wr DO ... END.

```
PROCEDURE FastPutChar(wr: Wr.T; ch: CHAR)
  RAISES {Failure, Alerted, Error};
```

> Like Wr.PutChar, but wr must be locked (as in all routines in the interface).

```
PROCEDURE FastPutText(wr: Wr.T; t: TEXT)
  RAISES {Failure, Alerted, Error};
```

> Like Wr.PutText.

```
PROCEDURE FastPutString(wr: Wr.T; a: ARRAY OF CHAR)
  RAISES {Failure, Alerted, Error};
```

> Like Wr.PutString.

```
PROCEDURE FastPutInt(wr: Wr.T; n: INTEGER; base := 10)
  RAISES {Failure, Alerted, Error};
```

> Like Wr.PutText(wr, Fmt.Int(n, base)).

```
PROCEDURE FastPutReal(
  wr: Wr.T;
  r: REAL;
  precision: CARDINAL := 6;
  style := Style.Mix)
  RAISES {Failure, Alerted, Error};
```

> Like Wr.PutText(wr, Fmt.Real(wr, precision, style)).

```
PROCEDURE FastPutLongReal(
  wr: Wr.T;
  r: LONGREAL;
  precision: CARDINAL := 6;
  style := Style.Mix)
  RAISES {Failure, Alerted, Error};
```

> Like Wr.PutText(wr, Fmt.LongReal(wr, precision, style)).

```
END UnsafeWr.
```

The UnsafeRd interface is similar, but GetChar and Eof are the only operations that are sufficiently performance-critical to be included:

```
UNSAFE INTERFACE UnsafeRd;
IMPORT Rd, Thread;
FROM Thread IMPORT Alerted;
FROM Rd IMPORT Failure, Error, EndOfFile;

REVEAL
  Rd.T <: Thread.Mutex;

PROCEDURE FastGetChar(rd: Rd.T): CHAR
  RAISES {EndOfFile, Failure, Alerted, Error};
```

Like Rd.GetChar, but rd must be locked.

```
PROCEDURE FastEOF(rd: Rd.T): BOOLEAN
  RAISES {Failure, Alerted, Error};
```

Like Rd.EOF, but rd must be locked.

```
END UnsafeRd.
```

6.8 The WrRep module

Finally we come to the machine-dependent part of the design: the unsafe modules that make the common operations fast. These modules can be reprogrammed to take advantage of the character manipulation instructions available on a particular machine. The versions of the modules presented here require that bytes be addressable, and achieve efficiency by arithmetic on byte pointers. They also require that the garbage collector is not relocating, that concurrent assignments to references are atomic, and that character arrays are packed.

This section and the rest of this chapter deal in low-level details that should be skipped if they become wearisome. But if you are planning to use the freedom of UNSAFE modules, this section illustrates the responsibilities that go with it.

```
UNSAFE MODULE WrRep EXPORTS Wr, WrClass, UnsafeWr;
IMPORT Thread, Fmt, Text;
FROM Thread IMPORT Alerted;
EXCEPTION FatalError;

REVEAL
  Private =.
    Thread.Mutex BRANDED OBJECT
      next, stop: UNTRACED REF CHAR := NIL;
      buffP: REF ARRAY OF CHAR
    END;
```

Recall that a Wr.T was defined in WrClass to consist of the Private fields followed by the buffer structure. The Private fields start with a Thread.Mutex, which is as expected, since UnsafeWr revealed that Wr.T is a subtype of Thread.Mutex.

The idea is that wr.next points at the character of wr.buff that will be written by the next call to PutChar. The fast path writes this character and advances wr.next, until wr.next = wr.stop, at which point the code takes a slower path:

```
<*INLINE*> PROCEDURE FastPutChar(wr: T; ch: CHAR)
  RAISES {Failure, Alerted, Error} =
  (* wr is clean (see below) and locked. *)
  BEGIN
    IF wr.next # wr.stop THEN
      wr.next^:= ch;
      INC(wr.next, ADRSIZE(CHAR))
    ELSE
      SlowPutChar(wr, ch)
    END
  END FastPutChar; (* wr is clean and locked *)
```

Notice that FastPutChar does not update wr.cur, and therefore does not maintain the validity of wr. This saves time, and the correct value for wr.cur can be computed from wr.next whenever a valid state is required.

We call a writer "clean" if it satisfies the invariant of FastPutChar; we will derive the precise definition of this invariant bit by bit. First, since the fast path through FastPutChar implements PutChar by storing into the buffer and not flushing afterwards, we conclude that a clean writer wr must satisfy the following condition:

C1. If wr.next $\neq$ wr.stop, then wr is buffered and ready, and

$$\text{wr.next} = \text{ADR(wr.buff[wr.st + cur(wr) - wr.lo]))}$$

Notice the use of cur(wr) instead of wr.cur, since the latter value may be invalid.

A noteworthy consequence of C1 is that in a clean writer, wr.next = NIL implies wr.stop = NIL. (If wr.next were NIL but wr.stop were not, then C1 would imply that NIL was a buffer address, which is nonsense.) Because both fields default to NIL, a newly-allocated writer will satisfy C1. The first call to FastPutChar on a new writer will take the slow path, which can set up the pointers so that subsequent calls will be fast.

Next, consider that when the fast path of FastPutChar fills the buffer it must preserve C1; therefore it must make next = stop if it fills the buffer. Thus a clean writer wr must satisfy

C2. If wr.next $\neq$ wr.stop, then

$$\text{wr.stop} =$$
$$\text{ADR(wr.buff[wr.st + (wr.hi - 1) - wr.lo]) + ADRSIZE(CHAR)}$$

You might think that this equation could be simplified by removing the "- 1" from inside the subscript and the "+ ADRSIZE(CHAR)" from outside, but this would access a non-existent array element if stop points just past the end of buff. The fast path through FastPutChar maintains C2, since it doesn't affect the consequent, and it can only change the antecedent by making it false.

Next, consider that it must be possible to make a clean writer valid, for example, in order to call its methods. We will do this by updating the cur field. It follows that the lagging cur field must be the only violation of validity; that is, a clean writer wr satisfies

> C3. All the validity conditions V1 through V4 defined in WrClass hold for wr, except that the equation for wr.cur in V1 may fail.

Inspection shows that the fast path through FastPutChar maintains C3.

To make a clean writer valid we will compute the correct value for wr.cur from wr.next using the equation in C1. Unfortunately, C1 only requires that this equation hold when wr.next $\neq$ wr.stop, but we will often need to make a clean writer valid when these pointers are equal; for example, when the buffer fills. We therefore add a condition that says that the equation holds whenever wr.next is not NIL:

> C4. If wr.next $\neq$ NIL, then
>
> $$(wr.next = ADR(wr.buff[wr.st + cur(wr) - wr.lo])))$$

The fast path maintains C4, since it increments both sides of the equality by one.

Finally, we must deal with the case wr.next = NIL, which is the case in a writer that is newly allocated by the runtime system. Such a writer will be valid, since it was given to us by a class implementation, and we have not yet invalidated it by any calls to FastPutChar. Thus we conclude that a clean writer wr satisfies:

> C5. If wr.next = NIL, then wr is valid.

The fast path maintains C5, since it maintains the stronger invariant wr.next $\neq$ NIL.

We define a writer to be *clean* if it satisfies C1–C5.

Conditions C3, C4, and C5 justify the following procedure for making a clean writer valid:

```
<*INLINE*> PROCEDURE MakeValid(wr: T) =
  BEGIN (* wr is locked and clean. *)
    IF wr.next # NIL THEN
      wr.cur :=
        wr.lo + (wr.next - ADR(wr.buff[wr.st])) DIV ADRSIZE(CHAR)
    END
  END MakeValid; (* wr is locked, clean, and valid *)
```

The reverse operation, MakeClean, sets the next and stop pointers to produce a clean state. It also returns a boolean indicating whether the writer is ready. Here is its spec:

```
PROCEDURE MakeClean(wr: T): BOOLEAN
```

> Assuming `wr` is valid and locked, set `wr.next` and `wr.stop` to produce a valid
> clean state; furthermore if `wr` is ready and buffered, make `wr.next` different from
> `wr.stop`. Return TRUE if and only if the state is ready.

`MakeClean` has two uses: to reset the `next` and `stop` pointers after a class method has
accessed the buffers, and to reset the pointers from their initial NIL values the first time a
writer is encountered by this module. (In the second case, `MakeClean` is being applied to
a writer that is already clean, in spite of its name.)

Before giving the implementation of `MakeClean`, we will show how it is used in the code
for `SlowPutChar`, which is a long but straightforward case analysis, as is usual for a slow
path that takes care of all the cases that are ignored in a fast path:

```
PROCEDURE SlowPutChar(wr: T; ch: CHAR)
  RAISES {Failure, Alerted, Error} =
  BEGIN (* wr is clean and locked; wr.next = wr.stop. *)
    IF wr.closed THEN RAISE Error(Code.Closed) END;
    IF wr.next # NIL THEN
      MakeValid(wr)
    ELSE
      (* wr is already valid; but might be newly allocated. *)
      EVAL MakeClean(wr)
    END;
    (* wr is valid and clean *)
    IF wr.cur = wr.hi THEN
      wr.seek(wr.cur);
      (* wr is valid and ready *)
      IF NOT MakeClean(wr) THEN
        RAISE FatalError (* Seek method erred *)
      END
    END;
    (* wr is valid, clean, and ready *)
    IF wr.next # wr.stop THEN
      wr.next^ := ch;
      INC(wr.next, ADRSIZE(CHAR))
    ELSE
      (* wr is unbuffered *)
      wr.buff[wr.st + wr.cur - wr.lo] := ch;
      INC(wr.cur);
      wr.flush()
    END
  END SlowPutChar;
```

Here is the implementation of `MakeClean`, which is short but tricky:

```
VAR mu := NEW(Thread.Mutex);

PROCEDURE MakeClean(wr: T): BOOLEAN =
  BEGIN
    LOCK mu DO
      wr.buffP := wr.buff;
      IF (wr.lo <= wr.cur) AND (wr.cur < wr.hi)
          AND (wr.buffP # NIL) AND (NOT wr.closed)
      THEN
        (* wr is ready *)
        wr.next := ADR(wr.buffP[wr.st + wr.cur - wr.lo]);
        wr.stop :=
          ADR(wr.buffP[wr.st + wr.hi - wr.lo - 1]) + ADRSIZE(CHAR);
        IF wr.stop < wr.next  THEN
          RAISE FatalError (* Who changes wr without the lock? *)
        END;
        IF NOT wr.buffered THEN wr.stop := wr.next END;
        RETURN TRUE
      ELSE
        (* wr is not ready *)
        wr.stop := NIL;
        wr.next := NIL;
        RETURN FALSE
      END
    END
  END MakeClean;
```

The language requires that this procedure avoid unchecked runtime errors even if a buggy class implementation is modifying the writer without holding the lock. The unsafe operations in this module are the computations of `wr.next` and `wr.stop`, together with the increment to `wr.next`. The danger is that errors in the address arithmetic could make `wr.next` point somewhere outside of `wr.buff`, causing PutChar to spray characters randomly into memory. To prevent this, it suffices to ensure that these two pointers both point into the array `wr.buff^` (or immediately after the array) and that they are in the proper order. MakeClean guarantees this, since

1. After copying `wr.buff` into `wr.buffP`, it uses `wr.buffP` for the rest of the computation, so it won't matter if `wr.buff` changes concurrently. (Recall that we are assuming that reads and writes of references are atomic.)

2. In the computation of `wr.next` and `wr.stop`, the subscripts into `wr.buffP` will be checked, and a runtime error will occur if they are out of range, even if `wr.st`, `wr.cur`, `wr.hi`, and `wr.lo` are changing concurrently.

3. The program checks that `wr.next` precedes `wr.stop` after computing them.

4. The program maintains `wr.buffP` equal to `wr.buff`, which guarantees that `wr.buff^` will not be collected, even if a buggy class implementation changes `wr.buff` without locking the writer.

5. The program uses a local mutex to guarantee that at most one instance of `MakeClean` is applied to a writer at once, which could otherwise happen if a buggy class implementation uses `Lock` and `Unlock` incorrectly.

All of this may seem like paranoia, but the rule is that a module exporting a safe interface must guarantee that *no programing error* by a safe client of that interface can lead to an unchecked runtime error. Changing the buffer structure without locking the writer is a possible programming error by a client of `WrClass`. We therefore must program `WrRep` in such a way that this error cannot lead to an unchecked runtime error. Otherwise we would be obliged to add the word "UNSAFE" to the `WrClass` interface.

A client of `UnsafeWr` could call `FastPutChar` concurrently from two threads, which could advance next past stop and clobber memory. We have no defense against this, which is why `UnsafeWr` is unsafe.

The remainder of the program is straightforward, and will be listed with few comments. We won't present the code for the procedures `PutText`, `FastPutText`, `FastPutString`, `FastPutInt`, `FastPutReal`, or `FastPutLongReal`, since they don't illustrate any interesting new points.

```
PROCEDURE Lock(wr: T) =
  BEGIN Thread.Acquire(wr); MakeValid(wr) END Lock;

PROCEDURE Unlock(wr: T) =
  BEGIN EVAL MakeClean(wr); Thread.Release(wr) END Unlock;

<*INLINE*> PROCEDURE PutChar(wr: T; ch: CHAR)
  RAISES {Failure, Alerted, Error} =
    (* wr must be unlocked. *)
  BEGIN
    LOCK wr DO FastPutChar(wr, ch) END
  END PutChar;

PROCEDURE Index(wr: T): CARDINAL RAISES {Error} =
  BEGIN
    LOCK wr DO
      IF wr.closed THEN RAISE Error(Code.Closed) END;
      MakeValid(wr);
      RETURN wr.cur
    END
  END Index;
```

```
PROCEDURE PutString (wr: T; a: ARRAY OF CHAR)
  RAISES {Failure, Alerted, Error} =
  VAR
    n := 0;
  BEGIN
    Lock(wr);
    TRY
      WHILE n # NUMBER(a) DO
        WITH m = MIN(NUMBER(a) - n, wr.hi - wr.cur) DO
          SUBARRAY(wr.buff^, wr.cur - wr.lo, m)
            := SUBARRAY(a, n, m);
          INC(n, m);
          INC(wr.cur, m);
          IF wr.cur = wr.hi THEN wr.seek(wr.cur) END
        END
      END
    FINALLY
      Unlock(wr)
    END
  END PutString;

PROCEDURE Seek(wr: T; n: CARDINAL) RAISES {Failure, Alerted, Error} =
  BEGIN
    LOCK wr DO
      IF wr.closed THEN RAISE Error(Code.Closed) END;
      IF NOT wr.seekable THEN RAISE Error(Code.Unseekable) END;
      MakeValid(wr);
      TRY wr.seek(n) FINALLY EVAL MakeClean(wr) END
    END
  END Seek;

PROCEDURE Length(wr: T): CARDINAL RAISES {Failure, Alerted, Error} =
  BEGIN
    LOCK wr DO
      IF wr.closed THEN RAISE Error(Code.Closed) END;
      MakeValid(wr);
      TRY RETURN wr.length() FINALLY EVAL MakeClean(wr) END
    END
  END Length;
```

Notice that the FINALLY clause in Length will be evaluated as the RETURN happens, without losing track of the value returned. It is important for implementations to generate efficient code for this situation, since it happens every time a RETURN statement is executed within a LOCK clause. (In fact, in the above code, both the explicit FINALLY and the LOCK clause's implicit FINALLY are executed as the RETURN happens.)

```
PROCEDURE Flush(wr: T) RAISES {Failure, Alerted, Error} =
  BEGIN
    LOCK wr DO
      IF wr.closed THEN RAISE ERROR(Code.Closed) END;
      MakeValid(wr);
      TRY wr.flush() FINALLY EVAL MakeClean(wr) END
    END
  END Flush;

PROCEDURE Close(wr: T) RAISES {Failure, Alerted} =
  BEGIN
    LOCK wr DO
      IF NOT wr.closed THEN
        MakeValid(wr);
        TRY
          wr.flush();
          wr.close()
        FINALLY
          wr.closed := TRUE;
          wr.next := wr.stop;
          wr.buffP := NIL
        END
      END
    END
  END Close;

PROCEDURE Seekable(wr: T): BOOLEAN =
  BEGIN
    LOCK wr DO RETURN wr.seekable END
  END Seekable;

PROCEDURE Closed(wr: T): BOOLEAN =
  BEGIN LOCK wr DO RETURN wr.closed END END Closed;

PROCEDURE Buffered(wr: T): BOOLEAN =
  BEGIN
    LOCK wr DO RETURN wr.buffered END
  END Buffered;

PROCEDURE CloseDefault(wr: T) =
  BEGIN wr.buff := NIL END CloseDefault;

PROCEDURE FlushDefault(wr: T) =
  BEGIN END FlushDefault;

PROCEDURE LengthDefault(wr: T): CARDINAL =
  BEGIN RETURN wr.cur END LengthDefault;

BEGIN END WrRep.
```

The reader may feel that our uncompromising pursuit of safety and efficiency has led to a design that is too complex. The program would be much simpler if WrRep kept the writer valid at all times, and the cost would be only a few instructions per operation. The point is that our design allows a range of implementations of WrRep. We have presented one that illustrates the issues that arise at the boundary between safe and unsafe code. Substituting a simpler WrRep would not affect clients of Wr or of WrClass.

6.9 The RdClass interface

The RdClass interface is analogous to the WrClass interface. It reveals that every reader contains a buffer of characters together with methods for managing the buffer. New reader classes are created by importing RdClass (to gain access to the buffer and the methods) and then defining a subclass of Rd.T whose methods provide the new class's behavior. The opaque type Private hides irrelevant details of the class-independent code.

```
INTERFACE RdClass;
IMPORT Rd;
FROM Thread IMPORT Alerted;
FROM Rd IMPORT Failure, Error;

TYPE
  Private <: ROOT;
  SeekResult = {Ready, WouldBlock, Eof};

REVEAL
  Rd.T = Private BRANDED OBJECT
    buff: REF ARRAY OF CHAR;
    st: CARDINAL; (* index into buff *)
    lo, hi, cur: CARDINAL; (* indexes into src(rd) *)
    closed, seekable, intermittent: BOOLEAN;
  METHODS
    seek(dontBlock: BOOLEAN): SeekResult
      RAISES {Failure, Alerted, Error};
    length(): CARDINAL RAISES {Failure, Alerted, Error}
      := LengthDefault;
    close() RAISES {Failure, Alerted, Error}
      := CloseDefault;
  END;
```

Let rd be a reader, abstractly given by len(rd), src(rd), cur(rd), avail(rd), closed(rd), seekable(rd), and intermittent(rd). The data fields cur, closed, seekable, and intermittent in the object represent the corresponding abstract attributes of rd. The buff, st, lo, and hi fields represent a buffer that contains part of src(rd), the rest of which is represented in some class-specific way.

More precisely, we say that a reader `rd` is *valid* if V1 through V3 hold:

V1. the characters of `buff` starting with `st` accurately reflect `src`. That is, for all `i` in [rd.lo .. rd.hi-1],

    rd.buff[rd.st + i - rd.lo] = src(rd)[i]

V2. if the `cur` field is in range, it is up-to-date:

    cur(rd) = MIN(rd.cur, len(rd))

(This equation implies that `rd.cur > len(rd)` has exactly the same meaning as `rd.cur = len(rd)`. This convention allows the implementation to use "lazy seeking"; that is, `Rd.Seek` can simply update `rd.cur`, without calling any class methods.)

V3. the reader does not claim to be both intermittent and seekable:

    NOT (rd.intermittent AND rd.seekable)

It is possible that `buff` = NIL in a valid state, since the range of `i`'s in V1 may be empty; for example, in case `lo` = `hi`.

There is no requirement that `cur(rd)` be anywhere near `rd.lo` or `rd.hi` in a valid state. If in fact `cur(rd)` lies between these values, we say the reader is *ready*. More precisely, `rd` is ready if:

    NOT rd.closed AND
    rd.buff # NIL AND
    rd.lo <= rd.cur < rd.hi

If the state is ready, then `Rd.GetChar` can be implemented by fetching from the buffer.

The class-independent code modifies `rd.cur`, but no other variables revealed in this interface. The class-independent code locks the reader before calling any methods.

Here are the specifications for the methods:

The basic purpose of the `seek` method is to make the reader ready. To seek to a position `n`, the class-independent code sets `rd.cur := n`; then if it is necessary to make the reader ready, it calls `rd.seek`. As in the case of writers, the `seek` method can be called even for an unseekable reader in the special case of advancing to the next buffer.

There is a wrinkle to support the implementation of `CharsReady`. If `rd` is ready, the class-independent code can handle the call to `CharsReady(rd)` without calling any methods (since there is at least one character ready in the buffer), but if `rd.cur` = `rd.hi`, then the class independent code needs to find out from the class implementation whether any characters are ready in the next buffer. Using the `seek` method to advance to the next buffer won't do, since this could block, and `CharsReady` isn't supposed to block. Therefore, the `seek` method takes a boolean argument saying whether blocking is allowed.

If blocking is forbidden and the next buffer isn't ready, the method returns the special value WouldBlock; this allows the class-independent code to return zero from CharsReady.

More precisely,

> Given a valid state with rd.seekable or rd.cur = rd.hi, the effect of the call res := rd.seek(dontBlock) is to leave rd valid without changing the abstract state of rd. Furthermore, if res = Ready then rd is ready and cur(rd) = rd.cur; while if res = Eof, then cur(rd) = rd.cur = len(rd); and finally if res = WouldBlock then dontBlock was TRUE and avail(rd) = cur(rd).

The length method returns the length of a non-intermittent reader. That is:

> Given a valid state in which rd.intermittent is FALSE, the call rd.length() returns len(rd) without changing the state of rd.

Finally,

> Given a valid state, the call rd.close() releases all resources associated with wr.

The exact meaning is class-specific. Validity is not required when the method returns (since after it returns, the class-independent code will set the closed bit in the reader, which makes the rest of the state irrelevant).

The remainder of the interface is similar to the corresponding part of the WrClass interface:

```
PROCEDURE Lock(rd: Rd.T) ;
```

> The reader rd must be unlocked; lock it and make its state valid.

```
PROCEDURE Unlock(rd: Rd.T) ;
```

> The reader rd must be locked and valid; unlock it and restore the private invariant of the reader implementation.

```
PROCEDURE LengthDefault(rd: Rd.T): CARDINAL
  RAISES {Failure, Alerted, Error};

PROCEDURE CloseDefault(rd: Rd.T) RAISES
  {Failure, Alerted, Error};
```

> The procedure LengthDefault causes a checked runtime error, representing the failure to supply a length method for a non-intermittent reader. The procedure CloseDefault sets rd.buff to NIL.

```
END RdClass.
```

6.10   The RdRep module

This module is very similar to the WrRep module, so we will list its code with only a few comments. We omit the straightforward implementations of the procedures GetSubLine, GetText, GetLine, Intermittent, Seekable, and Closed from the Rd interface, and of all the procedures in the RdClass interface.

```
UNSAFE MODULE RdRep EXPORTS Rd, RdClass, UnsafeRd;
IMPORT Thread, Text;
FROM Thread IMPORT Alerted;
EXCEPTION FatalError;

REVEAL
  Private =
    Thread.Mutex BRANDED OBJECT
      next, stop: UNTRACED REF CHAR := NIL;
      buffP: REF ARRAY OF CHAR;
  END;
```

The implementation of Rd.Seek is lazy. When a client calls Rd.Seek with an index that does not lie within the buffer, Rd.Seek simply records the destination index in rd.cur and sets both rd.next and rd.stop to NIL. When rd.next ≠ NIL, the Rd implementation ignores the value of rd.cur in determining cur(rd), but when rd.next = NIL the Rd implementation uses the value of rd.cur.

A reader rd is "clean" if the following conditions hold (see the WrRep module for more explanation):

C1. If rd.next # rd.stop, then

    Ready(rd) AND
        (rd.next = ADR(rd.buff[rd.st + cur(rd) - rd.lo]))

C2. If rd.next # rd.stop, then

    rd.stop =
        ADR(rd.buff[rd.st + (rd.hi - 1) - rd.lo]) + ADRSIZE(CHAR)

C3. The validity conditions V1 and V3 hold for rd.

C4. If rd.next # NIL then

    (rd.next = ADR(rd.buff[rd.st + cur(rd) - rd.lo]))

C5. If rd.next = NIL, then rd is valid.

```
<*INLINE*> PROCEDURE MakeValid(rd: T) =
  (* rd locked and clean *)
  BEGIN
    IF rd.next # NIL THEN
      rd.cur :=
        rd.lo + (rd.next - ADR(rd.buff[rd.st])) DIV ADRSIZE(CHAR)
    END
  END MakeValid;
  (* rd is locked, clean, and valid.  Furthermore, if rd.next#NIL,
  then rd.cur=cur(rd); this is important for the implementation
  of Index. *)

PROCEDURE MakeClean(rd: T) =
  BEGIN
    rd.buffP := rd.buff;
    IF (rd.lo <= rd.cur) AND
       (rd.cur < rd.hi)  AND
       (rd.buffP # NIL)
    THEN
      rd.next := ADR(rd.buffP[rd.st + rd.cur - rd.lo]);
      rd.stop :=
        ADR(rd.buffP[rd.st + rd.hi - rd.lo - 1]) + ADRSIZE(CHAR);
      IF rd.stop < rd.next THEN
        RAISE FatalError (* Who's changing rd without the lock? *)
      END
    ELSE
      rd.stop := NIL;
      rd.next := NIL
    END
  END MakeClean;

PROCEDURE SlowGetChar(rd: T): CHAR
    RAISES {EndOfFile, Failure, Alerted, Error} =
    (* rd is locked and clean; rd.next = rd.stop *)
  VAR res: CHAR;
  BEGIN
    IF rd.closed THEN RAISE Error(Code.Closed) END;
    TRY
      MakeValid(rd);
      IF rd.seek(dontBlock := FALSE) = SeekResult.Eof THEN
        RAISE EndOfFile
      END
    FINALLY
      MakeClean(rd)
    END;
```

```
    IF rd.next = rd.stop THEN
      RAISE FatalError (* Seek method didn't make reader ready *)
    END;
    res := rd.next^;
    INC(rd.next, ADRSIZE(CHAR));
    RETURN res
  END SlowGetChar;

<*INLINE*> PROCEDURE GetChar(rd: T): CHAR
    RAISES {EndOfFile, Failure, Alerted, Error} =
  BEGIN (* rd is unlocked *)
    LOCK rd DO
      RETURN FastGetChar(rd)
    END
  END GetChar;

<*INLINE*> PROCEDURE FastGetChar(rd: T): CHAR
    RAISES {EndOfFile, Failure, Alerted, Error} =
    (* rd is locked *)
  VAR res: CHAR;
  BEGIN
    IF rd.next # rd.stop THEN
      res := rd.next^;
      INC(rd.next, ADRSIZE(CHAR))
    ELSE
      res := SlowGetChar(rd)
    END;
    RETURN res
  END FastGetChar;

<*INLINE*> PROCEDURE EOF(rd: T): BOOLEAN
    RAISES {Failure, Alerted, Error} =
    (* rd is unlocked *)
  BEGIN
    LOCK rd DO RETURN FastEOF(rd) END
  END EOF;

<*INLINE*> PROCEDURE FastEOF(rd: T): BOOLEAN
    RAISES {Failure, Alerted, Error} =
    (* rd is locked *)
  BEGIN
    IF rd.next # rd.stop THEN RETURN FALSE
    ELSE RETURN SlowEOF(rd)
    END
  END FastEOF;
```

```
PROCEDURE SlowEOF(rd: T): BOOLEAN RAISES {Failure, Alerted} =
  (* rd is locked; rd.next = rd.stop *)
  VAR res: CHAR;
  BEGIN
    IF rd.closed THEN
      RAISE Error(Code.Closed)
    ELSE
      MakeValid(rd);
      TRY
        RETURN rd.seek(dontBlock := FALSE) = SeekResult.Eof
      FINALLY
        MakeClean(rd)
      END
    END
  END SlowEOF;

PROCEDURE UnGetChar(rd: T) RAISES {Error} =
  BEGIN
    LOCK rd DO
      IF rd.closed THEN RAISE Error(Code.Closed) END;
      IF (rd.next = NIL) OR (rd.next = ADR(rd.buff[rd.st])) THEN
        RAISE Error(Code.CantUnget)
      END;
      DEC(rd.next)
    END
  END UnGetChar;

PROCEDURE Length(rd: T): CARDINAL
  RAISES {Failure, Alerted, Error} =
  BEGIN
    LOCK rd DO
      IF rd.closed THEN
        RAISE Error(Code.Closed)
      ELSIF rd.intermittent THEN
        RAISE Error(Code.Intermittent)
      ELSE
        TRY
          MakeValid(rd);
          RETURN rd.length()
        FINALLY
          MakeClean(rd)
        END
      END
    END
  END Length;
```

```
PROCEDURE Seek(rd: T; n: CARDINAL)
  RAISES {Failure, Alerted, Error} =
  BEGIN
    LOCK rd DO
      IF rd.closed THEN RAISE Error(Code.Closed) END;
      IF NOT rd.seekable THEN RAISE Error(Code.Unseekable) END;
      rd.cur := n;
      MakeClean(rd)
    END
  END Seek;

PROCEDURE Index(rd: T): CARDINAL
  RAISES {Failure, Alerted, Error} =
  BEGIN
    LOCK rd DO
      IF rd.closed THEN RAISE Error(Code.Closed) END;
      MakeValid(rd);
      IF rd.seekable AND (rd.next = NIL) THEN
        rd.cur := MIN(rd.cur, rd.length())
      END;
      RETURN rd.cur
    END
  END Index;

PROCEDURE CharsReady(rd: T): CARDINAL
RAISES {Failure, Alerted, Error} =
  BEGIN
    LOCK rd DO
      IF rd.closed THEN RAISE Error(Code.Closed) END;
      MakeValid(rd);
      IF NOT (rd.lo <= rd.cur AND rd.cur < rd.hi) THEN
        TRY
          IF rd.seek(dontBlock := TRUE) = SeekResult.Eof
            THEN RETURN 1
          END
        FINALLY
          MakeClean(rd)
        END;
        IF rd.cur > rd.hi THEN
          RAISE FatalError (* Seek method erred *)
        END
      END;
      RETURN rd.hi - rd.cur
    END
  END CharsReady;
```

```
PROCEDURE GetSub (rd: T; VAR (*out*) str: ARRAY OF CHAR): CARDINAL
  RAISES {Failure, Alerted, Error} =
  VAR i := 0;
  BEGIN
    Lock(rd);
    TRY
      LOOP
        (* i chars have been read into str *)
        IF rd.cur < rd.lo OR rd.cur >= rd.hi THEN
          IF rd.seek(FALSE) = SeekResult.Eof THEN EXIT END
        END;
        (* rd.lo <= rd.cur = cur(rd) < rd.hi *)
        WITH n = MIN(rd.hi - rd.cur, NUMBER(str) - i) DO
          SUBARRAY(str, i, n) :=
            SUBARRAY(rd.buff^, rd.cur-rd.lo, n);
          INC(i, n);
          INC(rd.cur, n)
        END;
        IF i = NUMBER(str) THEN EXIT END
      END
    FINALLY
      Unlock(rd)
    END;
    RETURN i
  END GetSub;


PROCEDURE Close(rd: T) RAISES {Failure, Alerted, Error} =
  BEGIN
    LOCK rd DO
      IF NOT rd.closed THEN
        TRY
          MakeValid(rd);
          rd.close()
        FINALLY
          rd.closed := TRUE;
          rd.next := NIL;
          rd.stop := NIL;
          rd.buffP := NIL
        END
      END
    END
  END Close;


BEGIN END RdRep.
```

6.11   Concluding remarks

We have heard programmers say "there is no way to give a formal specification for an object-oriented interface, since the different subclass methods can do different things". We hope this chapter presents a less superficial view. To give a formal specification for an object-oriented interface, the key is to distinguish the abstraction represented by an object from the object itself, as we have distinguished cur(wr) from wr.cur, for example. The implementor of a subclass has considerable freedom to "instantiate" the abstraction (for example, by choosing the target of a class of writers), but no additional freedom to change the meaning of the operations, which are defined once and for all in terms of the abstraction. Admittedly there may be operations (like Close) that leave considerable freedom to the class implementor, but if all the operations are like this, the abstraction is not likely to be very useful.

Our treatment has been rigorous only in a very pragmatic way. The stream interfaces would surely benefit from being translated into Larch [8], or some equally formal specification language. Nevertheless, we feel that many programs being written today could be improved by a dose of specification of the pragmatic sort illustrated by this chapter.

It is interesting that the traditional technique of program development and verification via invariants was most useful in the lowest level of the system. The desire to optimize the fast path introduced a case analysis into the slow path, which was best managed by carefully writing invariants. The pattern of reasoning we used is somewhat different from the standard methods of deriving a loop invariant from a postcondition: we began by coding the fast path based on efficiency considerations; from this code we derived the global cleanliness invariant; from this we derived the case analysis on the slow path. This pattern can be used in many similar situations.

Specifying the interfaces was harder than coding the implementation. We used interfaces in layers to hide dangerous information from safe clients, while revealing it to unsafe clients. There are many views of a Wr.T: a client of Wr sees a pure opaque type, a client of WrClass sees only the buffer structure, a client of UnsafeWr sees the mutex, and the implementation sees everything. A client that defines a new class sees the class fields and the buffer fields, but not the mutex or the private fields.

To achieve this pattern of information-hiding without partially opaque object types, it would be necessary to allocate each group of fields separately and link them together with additional references. This would require several allocations per writer, which would be costly. Partial opacity makes it possible to achieve this information-hiding with essentially no runtime penalty. In our design, creating a writer requires allocating a single ten-word object (assuming one-word mutexes, references, and integers). The method suite does not have to be allocated dynamically, since its contents are known at compile time, and different instances of a class all point at the same statically allocated method suite.

The least methodical part of the design is the delicate code required to export a safe interface from an unsafe module. Writing this code is a little like writing a secure operating system without any help from the virtual memory system. At present, will power seems more useful than methodology for avoiding errors in this kind of code. We hope we managed to illustrate the pitfalls without falling into any.

Chapter 7

Trestle Window System Tutorial

Greg Nelson

You don't do windows? Learn how!
You learn as your windows are being cleaned!
—Leroy's Blazing Window Cleaners

Trestle is a Modula-3 toolkit for the X window system. Like the readers and writers described in Chapter 6, Trestle is a collection of interfaces structured around a central abstract type: a "virtual bitmap terminal" or VBT, which represents a share of the workstation's screen, keyboard, and mouse—a thing comparable to the viewers, windows, or widgets of other systems.

The layers of the VBT abstraction are structured like the layers of the stream abstractions: there is a basic interface for clients who just want to use windows, a more revealing interface for clients who want to implement new classes of windows, and a hidden representation that achieves speed by amortizing the cost of a class method invocation over a number of basic operations.

The treatment of I/O streams in Chapter 6 toured these layers from the top down. This treatment works well for a familiar abstraction like a stream, but not so well for an unfamiliar abstraction like a VBT. In this chapter we take a different approach, using example programs that introduce the properties of the VBT abstraction gradually. The programs are short and easy, and a number of exercises have been included. Programming with windows has a reputation for being difficult; we hope to show that it can be great fun.

For the precise specifications of the layers of the VBT abstraction, see the *Trestle Reference Manual* [21].

This chapter can also serve as an introduction to object-oriented programming. Objects and inheritance are used almost constantly in programming user interfaces, because there are so many windows that are similar to one another but not quite the same. Method overriding is the basic tool for creating new window classes that are slight variations on existing classes. For example, a ButtonVBT.T has more than two dozen methods, but only four of them are supplied by the ButtonVBT module. The others are inherited from ButtonVBT.T's supertype, Filter.T.

The last programs in this chapter supplement Chapter 4 by illustrating some fairly advanced techniques for dealing with concurrent threads. Trestle was originally designed as a research project by Mark Manasse and Greg Nelson. One of the goals of the project was to determine how much a multiprocessor could speed up a window system. As a result, Trestle's locking is aggressively fine-grained. (See "A performance analysis of a multiprocessor window system" [20].)

7.1 Hello Trestle

To use Trestle, you need a copy of SRC Modula-3 and an X server for your system. If you have these, you may want to compile and run the example programs as you read the tutorial; they are in the trestletutorial directory of the Modula-3 distribution.

The first example program is in the file Hello.m3:

```
MODULE Hello EXPORTS Main;
IMPORT Trestle, TextVBT;
VAR v := TextVBT.New("Hello Trestle");
BEGIN
  Trestle.Install(v);
  Trestle.AwaitDelete(v)
END Hello.
```

A TextVBT is a class of VBT that displays a text string. The example program creates a TextVBT, installs it on the screen, and waits for the user to delete the window. Figure 7.1 shows what the window looks like. When the user deletes the window with the window manager, Trestle.AwaitDelete will return and the program will exit. If the window manager provides no way to delete windows, the window will stay installed until the user kills or exits the program.

7.2 Split windows

VBTs are generally organized into a tree structure, with the root VBT representing the top-level application window. The internal nodes are called "split" VBTs or "parent"

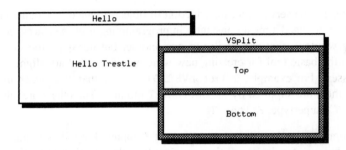

Figure 7.1: The first example program creates a window that displays the text Hello Trestle. The second shows how to split a window into two with an adjustable dividing bar. The title bars, outer borders, and black shadows are produced by the window manager, and will vary from system to system.

VBTs: they divide their screens between one or more child VBTs according to some layout depending on the class of split. At the leaves of the tree are VBTs that contain no subwindows.

A typical application consists of a number of leaf VBTs whose behavior is specific to that application, together with some more leaf VBTs that provide buttons, scrollbars, and other "interactors", all held together by a tree of splits that define the geometric layout.

An HVSplit is a split in which the children are stacked horizontally or vertically, as illustrated by the following program:

```
MODULE VSplit EXPORTS Main;

IMPORT Trestle, TextVBT, BorderedVBT, HVSplit, Axis, HVBar,
  Pixmap, PaintOp;

VAR v :=
  BorderedVBT.New(
    HVSplit.Cons(Axis.T.Ver,
      BorderedVBT.New(TextVBT.New("Top")),
      HVBar.New(size := 3.0, texture := Pixmap.Gray),
      BorderedVBT.New(TextVBT.New("Bottom"))),
    size := 3.0,
    texture := Pixmap.Gray)

BEGIN
  Trestle.Install(v);
  Trestle.AwaitDelete(v)
END VSplit.
```

The call HVSplit.Cons(Axis.T.Ver, ch1, ch2, ...) creates a vertical split with children ch1, ch2, ... in top-to-bottom order. (Axis.T.Ver and Axis.T.Hor are the Trestle names for the vertical and horizontal axes. HVSplit.Cons creates a horizontal split if its first argument is Axis.T.Hor.)

A "filter" is a split with one child. The call BorderedVBT.New(ch, size := s, texture := t) creates a filter in which the parent paints a border around the child ch; the border is s millimeters wide and is painted with the texture t. (A *pixmap* is a rectangular array of pixels; a *texture* is an infinite pattern of pixels obtained by tiling the plane with a pixmap.) In the VSplit program, the outer call to BorderedVBT.New produces a wide gray border the matches the adjusting bar; the two inner calls default the size and texture arguments, producing a thin solid border of the user's default foreground color. Figure 7.1 shows what the window looks like.

The call HVBar.New(size := s, texture := t) produces an adjusting bar for an HVSplit; the bar is s millimeters wide and is painted with the texture t. The user can drag the bar with the mouse to adjust the sizes of the other children.

To support users who have more than one type of display on their desks, the screentype of a VBT is not constant, but changes as the user moves the VBT from screen to screen. Trestle supplies resources like fonts, pixmaps, cursor shapes, and painting operation codes in both screen-dependent and screen-independent forms. The standard Trestle splits and interactors all use screen-independent resources and take dimensions specified in millimeters, so that they will look about the same when they move from screen to screen. For example, the value Pixmap.Gray in the program above is a screen-independent pixmap: it varies with the screentype to produce a uniform effect on all screens. Screen-dependent resources are provided for sophisticated applications that depend on features available only on a particular screen—for example, color map animation.

Exercise 1. The incomplete program Monster shown below creates a depth 8 tree of alternating adjustable horizontal and vertical splits (Figure 7.2). The 256 leaves of the tree are labeled with the numbers 0 through 255. The heart of the program is a recursive procedure that constructs a subtree of the monstrous split. The base case of the procedure just returns a bordered TextVBT. The recursive case of the procedure is left for you to write as an exercise. (If you have SRC Modula-3, you will find the incomplete program in the tutorial directory; just edit it and type "make Monster".)

Hint: The array Axis.Other[ ] exchanges Axis.T.Hor and Axis.T.Ver.

```
MODULE Monster EXPORTS Main;

IMPORT
  Trestle, VBT, Axis, BorderedVBT, HVSplit, HVBar, TextVBT, Font,
  Rect, Pixmap, Fmt;
```

```
PROCEDURE New(lo, hi: INTEGER; hv: Axis.T): VBT.T =
  (* Return a tree of splits whose leaves are labeled with the
     integers in [lo .. hi-1] and whose root split has axis hv. *)
  BEGIN
    IF hi - lo = 1 THEN
      RETURN
        BorderedVBT.New(TextVBT.New(Fmt.Int(lo)));
    ELSE
    (* You fill in this part *)
    END
  END New;

VAR v :=
  BorderedVBT.New(New(0, 256, Axis.T.Hor), 3.0, Pixmap.Gray);

BEGIN
  Trestle.Install(v, "Tiling Monster");
  Trestle.AwaitDelete(v)
END Monster.
```

7.3 Points, Rectangles, and Regions

The interfaces Point, Rect, and Region define dozens of useful operations on integer lattice points and sets thereof. We won't present complete listings of the interfaces, since they are long and consist mostly of procedures whose functions are obvious from their names, but we will briefly introduce the basic data types and most common routines.

A Point.T is a two-dimensional point with integer coordinates; the horizontal and vertical coordinates of a point pt are named pt.h and pt.v. The procedures Point.Add and Point.Sub provide component-wise addition and subtraction on points.

A Rect.T is a set of points lying in a rectangle whose sides are parallel to the coordinate axes. The directions on the screen are named after the compass points, with north at the top. A point pt lies in a rectangle rect if

- pt.h is in [rect.west .. rect.east - 1]
- pt.v is in [rect.north .. rect.south - 1]

Notice that h increases west to east; v increases north to south (for which we offer our apologies to Descartes).

Here are some useful operations on rectangles:

`Rect.NorthWest(rect), Rect.NorthEast(rect)`
`Rect.SouthWest(rect), Rect.SouthEast(rect)`

The four vertices of `rect`.

`Rect.Middle(rect)`

The center point of `rect`.

`Rect.IsEmpty(rect)`

Tests whether `rect` is empty.

`Rect.Member(pt, rect)`

Tests whether the point `pt` lies in the rectangle `rect`.

`Rect.Overlap(rect1, rect2)`

Tests whether the two rectangles have any point in common.

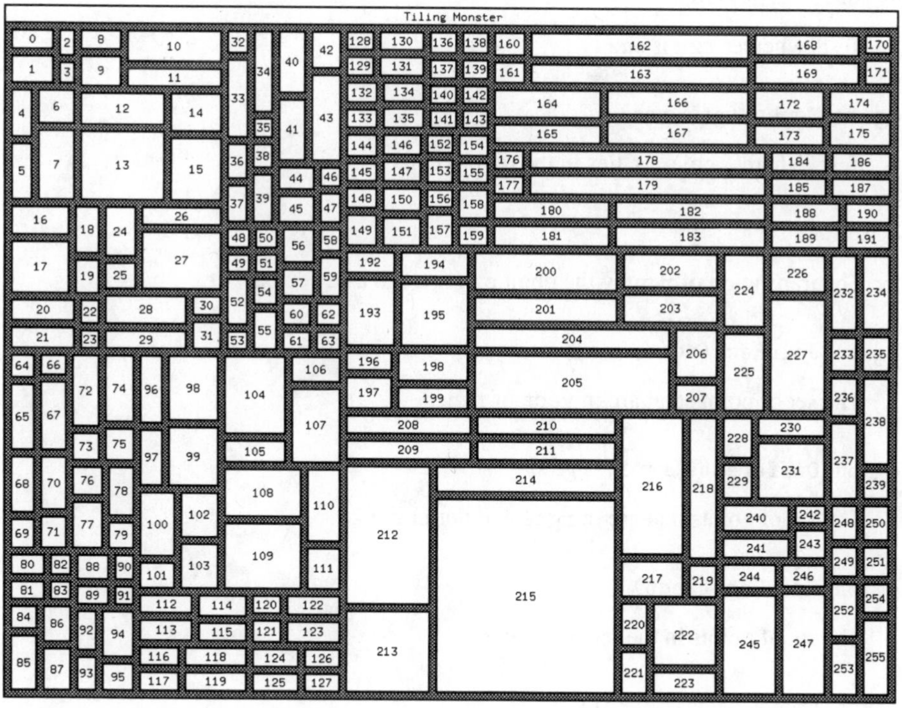

Figure 7.2: A nightmare if you don't like tiling windows (or even if you do). The Tiling Monster is a tree of adjustable binary splits eight levels deep.

`Rect.FromPoint(pt)`

> The rectangle containing only the point pt.

`Rect.Meet(rect1, rect2)`

> The intersection of the two rectangles.

`Rect.Add(rect, pt)`

> The translation of `rect` by the point pt regarded as a vector.

`Rect.Empty, Rect.Full`

> The empty rectangle and the largest representable rectangle.

A `Region.T` represents an arbitrary set of integer lattice points, compactly encoded as a set of disjoint rectangles. Here are some useful operations on regions:

`Region.IsEmpty(rgn)`

> Tests whether `rgn` is empty.

`Region.Member(pt, rgn)`

> Tests whether point pt lies in the region `rgn`.

`Region.Add(rgn, pt)`

> The translation of `rgn` by the point pt regarded as a vector.

`Region.JoinRect(rect, rgn)`

> The set of points that are in `rect` or `rgn`.

`Region.Difference(rgn1, rgn2)`

> The set of points that are in `rgn1` and not in `rgn2`.

`Region.FromRect(rect)`

> The set of points in the rectangle `rect`.

`Region.Empty, Region.Full`

> The empty region and the largest representable region.

For example, here is a procedure that we will find useful later: it creates a circular region:

```
PROCEDURE Circle(r: REAL): Region.T =
(* Return the circle of radius r centered at the origin *)
  VAR res := Region.Empty;
  BEGIN
    FOR h := FLOOR(-r) TO CEILING(r) DO
      FOR v := FLOOR(-r) TO CEILING(r) DO
        IF h * h + v * v <= FLOOR(r * r) THEN
          WITH rect = Rect.FromPoint(Point.T{h, v}) DO
            res := Region.JoinRect(rect, res)
          END
        END
      END
    END;
    RETURN res
  END Circle;
```

This loop simply tests each relevant integer lattice point for membership in the circle and adds it to the region if appropriate. The procedure won't win any prizes for efficiency, but it works. The final region is compactly represented, even though it was built up from singleton rectangles, because the operations in the Region interface always compact their results.

7.4 Painting

Changing the visible contents of a Trestle window's screen is called *painting*. In general, every VBT painting procedure is determined by

- a destination, which is a set of screen pixels;

- a source, which is conceptually an infinite array of pixels, together with a rule for associating source and destination pixels;

- an operation op, which is a map that takes a destination and source pixel and produces a destination pixel.

The effect of a painting procedure is to set d := op(d, s) for each destination pixel d and corresponding source pixel s.

Thus, in general, the final value of a destination pixel depends on its initial value and the value of the corresponding source pixel. But many painting operations ignore the source pixel; such an operation is called a *tint*. If op is a tint, we just write op(d) instead of op(d, s). For example, the two most basic painting operations are the tints PaintOp.Bg and PaintOp.Fg, defined by

```
PaintOp.Bg(d) = the screen's background pixel
PaintOp.Fg(d) = the screen's foreground pixel
```

They ignore both the source and the initial value of their destination: painting with Bg sets the destination pixels to the "background" pixel value, while painting with Fg sets them to the "foreground" pixel value. The background and foreground pixels vary from screentype to screentype; you can think of Bg as white and Fg as black (unless you prefer video-reversed screens).

Another useful tint is `PaintOp.Swap`, which exchanges the screen's foreground and background pixel. If it is applied to any other pixel the result depends on the screentype, but for any pixel d of any screentype it satisfies

```
Swap(Swap(d)) = d
Swap(d) # d
```

Swap can be used on general screens the way XOR is used on bitmap screens.

Trestle also supplies the tint `PaintOp.Transparent`, defined by

```
Transparent(d) = d
```

for any pixel d. Transparent may seem useless at first—but the number zero also seems useless until you need it.

There are an unlimited variety of other tints, of which we mention one:

`PaintOp.FromRGB(r, g, b)`

Returns a tint that sets a pixel to the color whose mixture of red, green and blue is given by (r, g, b). The tint will work on both color-mapped and true-color displays. On a black-and-white display, the result will be white or black depending on whether the intensity of (r, g, b) exceeds a certain threshold.

So much for tints. A useful paint operation that is not a tint is BgFg, defined by

```
PaintOp.BgFg(d, 0) = the screen's background pixel
PaintOp.BgFg(d, 1) = the screen's foreground pixel
```

BgFg should be used with sources that are one-bit deep, such as fonts, textures, and bitmaps; the effect is to copy the source to the destination, interpreting 0 as background and 1 as foreground.

Similarly, we have TransparentFg, defined by

```
PaintOp.TransparentFg(d, 0) = d
PaintOp.TransparentFg(d, 1) = the screen's foreground pixel
```

TransparentFg is also used with sources that are one-bit deep; the effect is to copy the source to the destination, leaving the bits that correspond to 0's unchanged and setting the bits that correspond to 1's to the foreground pixel.

BgFg and TransparentFg are examples of the following general rule: if X and Y are two of the tints Bg, Fg, Swap, and Transparent, then Trestle supplies the paint operation XY defined by XY(d, 0) = X(d) and XY(d, 1) = Y(d).

Finally, we mention one painting operation that is neither a tint nor formed from a pair of tints:

    PaintOp.Copy(d, s) = s

Copy should be used only when the source pixels are of the same type as the destination pixels; for example, when copying from one part of the screen to another.

Trestle has painting procedures that operate on rectangles, regions, stroked and filled paths, and other exotic shapes, but for now we will just describe the following three:

VBT.PaintTint(v, clip, op)

> Set d := op(d) for each pixel d in the screen of the VBT v that lies in the rectangle clip. The operation must be a tint. This is Trestle's fastest painting operation.

VBT.PaintRegion(v, rgn, op)

> Set d := op(d) for each pixel d in the screen of the VBT v that lies in the region rgn. The operation must be a tint.

VBT.Scroll(v, clip, delta, op := PaintOp.Copy)

> Set d := op(d, s) for each pair of pixels d, s such that d lies in the given clipping rectangle, d and s both lie in v's screen, and the displacement from s to d is the vector delta. If op is defaulted to Copy, the effect is to translate a rectangle of pixels from v's screen by delta, overwriting the contents of the clip rectangle. The operation must apply to source pixels and destination pixels of the same type.

7.5 Handling events: the Spot program

A VBT is an object whose methods define its response to user events. For example, if the user reshapes a window, the system will call the window's reshape method; if the user exposes some part of the window, the system will call the window's repaint method, and if the user clicks the mouse over the window, the system will call the window's mouse method.

As an example, we will write a program called Spot that displays a single spot on the screen (see Figure 7.3). The user can move the spot to a new position by clicking with the mouse. When the window is reshaped, the spot moves to the middle of the new screen.

A VBT.Leaf is a VBT that responds to events by ignoring them. The Spot program defines a subtype of VBT.Leaf in which the mouse, repaint, and reshape methods are overridden with procedures that behave as follows:

On an exposure, repaint the white background and the spot.

On a reshape, move the spot to the center of the new screen and repaint.

On a mouse click, move the spot to the position of the click.

The subtype also has a data field to record the position of the spot, as a region. In our first version of the program, the spot will be a circle 10.5 pixels in diameter. So far the program is:

```
MODULE Spot EXPORTS Main;

IMPORT VBT, Trestle, Region, Rect, Point, PaintOp;

TYPE
  SpotVBT = VBT.Leaf OBJECT
    spot: Region.T
  OVERRIDES
    mouse := Mouse;
    repaint := Repaint;
    reshape := Reshape
  END;
VAR
  v := NEW(SpotVBT, spot := Circle(10.5));

(* Definitions of Circle, Repaint, Reshape, and Mouse *)

BEGIN
  Trestle.Install(v);
  Trestle.AwaitDelete(v)
END Spot.
```

We have already described Circle, so all that remains is to describe the procedures Mouse, Repaint, and Reshape.

Trestle calls a window's repaint method whenever a region of the window has been exposed. The repaint method for the Spot window is:

```
PROCEDURE Repaint(v: SpotVBT; READONLY rgn: Region.T) =
  BEGIN
    VBT.PaintRegion(v, rgn, PaintOp.Bg);
    VBT.PaintRegion(v, v.spot, PaintOp.Fg)
  END Repaint;
```

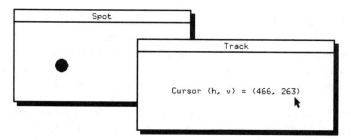

Figure 7.3: Clicking in the Spot window moves the spot; rolling the cursor in the Track window updates the displayed coordinates continuously.

The argument `rgn` is the region to be repainted. Often it is simpler and faster to repaint more than strictly necessary; this procedure repaints the whole spot whether it is needed or not, since computing region intersections is not cheap. But it would be an improvement to test if the bounding rectangles of the regions overlap, and if not, skip repainting the spot. The bounding rectangle of a region `rgn` is `rgn.r`; thus the better repaint method is:

```
PROCEDURE Repaint(v: SpotVBT.T; READONLY rgn: Region.T) =
  BEGIN
    VBT.PaintRegion(v, rgn, PaintOp.Bg);
    IF Rect.Overlap(rgn.r, v.spot.r) THEN
      VBT.PaintRegion(v, v.spot, PaintOp.Fg)
    END
  END Repaint;
```

The rectangular extent of a window is called its "domain". Trestle calls a window's reshape method whenever its domain changes. The reshape method for the Spot window is:

```
PROCEDURE Reshape(v: SpotVBT; READONLY cd: VBT.ReshapeRec) =
  VAR delta :=
    Point.Sub(Rect.Middle(cd.new), Rect.Middle(v.spot.r));
  BEGIN
    v.spot := Region.Add(v.spot, delta);
    Repaint(v, Region.Full)
  END Reshape;
```

The `cd` argument to the method contains several fields, but the only one that matters here is `cd.new`, which is the new domain of the window. To move the spot to the center of the new domain, the method simply translates the spot region by the vector `delta` from the current center of the spot to the center of the new domain. Then it repaints the entire window by passing `Region.Full` to the repaint method.

When a window moves it may be faster to copy the pixels from the old domain to the new domain instead of recomputing the new pixels from scratch. Therefore, the `cd` argument to the `reshape` method includes a rectangle `cd.saved`, which is the portion of the old domain of the window that Trestle has preserved. The `reshape` method can copy the pixels in this rectangle to the appropriate portion of the new domain, using `VBT.Scroll`. This optimization is important for large areas whose contents are expensive to recompute, but for the `Spot` program the saved pixels aren't worth bothering about.

Exercise 2. Change the `reshape` method to preserve the position of the spot relative to the northwest corner of the window, instead of moving it to the middle. (Hint: the record `cd` contains a field `cd.prev`, which is the previous domain of the `VBT`.)

Trestle calls the mouse method of a window whenever the user clicks the mouse over the window. The mouse method for the `Spot` window is:

```
PROCEDURE Mouse(v: SpotVBT; READONLY cd: VBT.MouseRec) =
  VAR delta: Point.T;
  BEGIN
    IF cd.clickType = VBT.ClickType.FirstDown THEN
      delta := Point.Sub(cd.cp.pt, Rect.Middle(v.spot.r));
      v.spot := Region.Add(v.spot, delta);
      Repaint(v, Region.Full)
    END
  END Mouse;
```

The `cd` argument to `Mouse` contains several fields. The field `cd.clickType` tells whether this is `FirstDown`—that is, a down transition from a state where all buttons were up, a `LastUp`—that is, an up transition that produces a state where all buttons are up, or an `OthersDown`—that is, a chording transition. The `Spot` program responds only to down clicks.

The field `cd.cp` is the cursor position where the mouse button went down. A cursor position is either "gone" (meaning somewhere outside the window) or contains a point representing a position inside the window. In the case of a `VBT.FirstDown`, the position is guaranteed not to be "gone", so the program simply accesses the point, which is `cd.cp.pt`.

Although we have not used it in the `Spot` program, every `VBT` v has a method `v.rescreen` that the system calls whenever v's screentype changes. The method is passed a record `cd` of type `VBT.RescreenRec` containing several fields; `cd.st` is the new screentype. Whenever v's screentype changes, v's domain is automatically reshaped to the empty rectangle `Rect.Empty`: the `rescreen` method implies an implicit reshape. Typically the next event will be a reshape to a non-empty rectangle on the new screen.

Exercise 3: Modify the program so that its spot will be about eight millimeters in diameter, regardless of the screen resolution. (Hint: `VBT.MMToPixels(v, mm, ax)` returns the number of pixels (as a REAL) that corresponds to `mm` millimeters on v's screentype in the axis `ax`. For the purpose of this exercise, you can assume that the screentype has the same resolution in the horizontal and vertical dimensions.)

7.6 Tracking the mouse

Our next example program is called `Track`, because it installs a window that tracks the cursor. When the cursor is anywhere over the window, the coordinates of the cursor are displayed in the center of the window. When the cursor is outside the window, the text "Cursor gone" is displayed.

The track window behaves exactly like a `TextVBT` with respect to repaints, reshapes, and mouse clicks; it behaves differently only when the system delivers a cursor position. Therefore it inherits most of its methods from `TextVBT`, overriding only the `position` method and declaring one new method of its own, for initialization:

```
TYPE
  TrackVBT = TextVBT.T OBJECT
    METHODS
      init(): TrackVBT := Init
    OVERRIDES
      position := Position
    END;


(* definitions of Position and Init *)

VAR
  v := NEW(TrackVBT).init();

BEGIN
  Trestle.Install(v);
  Trestle.AwaitDelete(v)
END Track.
```

The `TrackVBT` must initialize its supertype `TextVBT`, since a newly-allocated `TextVBT` must be initialized with some text string before it can be used. (In the previous example program, the `SpotVBT` did not initialize its supertype `VBT.Leaf`, since a newly-allocated `VBT.Leaf` is ready to use.)

Every VBT class that needs initialization after allocation provides an `init` method for doing so. The arguments to the method depend on the class. By convention, the `init` method also returns the VBT after initializing it. The `init` method for a subtype is responsible for calling the `init` method of its supertype, if this is necessary. Here is the `init` method for a `TrackVBT`:

```
PROCEDURE Init(v: TrackVBT): TrackVBT;
  BEGIN
    EVAL TextVBT.T.init(v, "Cursor Gone");
    RETURN v
  END Init;
```

The call `TextVBT.T.init(v, t)` will initialize a newly-allocated TextVBT v to display the text t. (It would not be incorrect to simply return the result from `TextVBT.T.init`, which will be v, but it would cost an unnecessary NARROW.)

In general, if a VBT class `Cl.T` has an associated procedure `Cl.New`, then by convention the call `Cl.New(args)` means the same thing as `NEW(Cl.T).init(args)`. So if you want to, you can write `NEW(BorderedVBT.T).init(ch)` instead of `BorderedVBT.New(ch)`, and similarly for TextVBT, HVBar, and all the other VBT classes.

All that remains is to specify TrackVBT's position method.

To track the cursor, you specify a region called a "cage". Generally the region should contain the current cursor position. Trestle waits for the cursor to leave the cage, and reports this event by calling your position method, which sets a new cage containing the new position, and so it goes.

If you're not interested in tracking the cursor at all, set the cage to the special value `VBT.EverywhereCage`.

If you want to know when the cursor leaves your window, set the cage to be the window's domain.

If you want to know when it comes back, set the cage to be the special cage `VBT.GoneCage`, which contains all positions outside the window, including the artificial position "gone".

If you're interested in any motion of the cursor, however tiny, set the cage to be the single point containing the current cursor position: then the next motion of the mouse will generate a position code.

Here is the position procedure for the Track program:

```
PROCEDURE Position(v: TrackVBT; READONLY cd: VBT.PositionRec) =
  BEGIN
    IF cd.cp.gone THEN
      TextVBT.Put(v, "Cursor gone");
    ELSE
      TextVBT.Put(v,
        Fmt.F("h = %s, v = %s",
          Fmt.Int(cd.cp.pt.h), Fmt.Int(cd.cp.pt.v)));
    END;
    VBT.SetCage(v, VBT.CageFromPosition(cd.cp))
  END Position;
```

The only field of cd that matters in this program is `cd.cp`, which is a cursor position. If `cd.cp.gone` is true, then the system is reporting that the cursor has left the window. In this case, the program changes the text of the TextVBT to be "Cursor gone", using the procedure `TextVBT.Put`, and waits for the cursor to return to the window by setting its cage to VBT.GoneCage. VBT.CageFromPosition(cp) returns a cage that contains only the position cp—that is, GoneCage if cp is gone, and a one-point rectangular cage otherwise.

If cd.cp.gone is false, then the system is reporting that the cursor is at position cd.cp.pt. In this case the program constructs the text string representing the position of the cursor (using procedures from the Fmt interface), uses TextVBT.Put to display the string, and sets a one-point cage around this cursor position, so that the system will report the next cursor motion.

Finally, here is an exercise to try your hand at.

Exercise 4. The incomplete program Draw listed below is a simple drawing program that allows you to draw line segments by pressing a mouse button at the start point, dragging the mouse, and releasing it at the end point. During dragging, the end point of the segment follows the cursor, pulling the line like a rubber band. The body of the position procedure is left blank for you to complete. Figure 7.4 shows what the window looks like.

In order to handle repaints, the program keeps track of the line segments in a variable path of type Path.T. All that you need to know about Path.T's for this exercise is that

```
Path.Empty(path)
```

sets path to be empty, that

```
Path.MoveTo(path, p); Path.LineTo(path, q)
```

adds the segment (p, q) to path, and that

```
Path.Translate(path, delta)
```

will return the result of adding delta to all vertices of all segments in path.

You should also know that

```
VBT.Stroke(v, clip, path, op)
```

applies the tint op to each pixel of v that lies in the given clipping rectangle and on some segment of the given path, and that

```
VBT.Line(v, clip, p, q, op)
```

is like VBT.Stroke for a path containing only the segment (p, q).

The program also uses buttons:

```
ButtonVBT.New(ch, p)
```

is a filter that looks like its child ch, but when the user clicks on it, the *action procedure* p will be called. The action procedure is passed the button itself and the MouseRec for the mouse click on the button. Finally,

Figure 7.4: A simple drawing program that illustrates mouse tracking, buttons, and drawing PostScript-like paths.

ButtonVBT.MenuBar(v_1, v_2, ..., v_n)

produces a horizontal split with children v_1, ..., v_n, left-justified and separated by small
horizontal gaps.

One of the buttons of the program exits the program. It uses the procedure

Trestle.Delete(v)

which deletes the installed window v.

```
MODULE Draw EXPORTS Main;

IMPORT VBT, Trestle, Point, Rect, Path, ButtonVBT, PaintOp, Path,
  Region, HVSplit, TextVBT, Axis;
FROM VBT IMPORT ClickType;

TYPE DrawVBT = VBT.Leaf OBJECT
  path: Path.T;
  drawing := FALSE;
  p, q: Point.T
  (* drawing => the user is rubber banding the segment (p,q) *)
  OVERRIDES
    repaint := Repaint;
    reshape := Reshape;
    mouse := Mouse;
    position := Position
  END;
```

```
PROCEDURE Repaint(v: DrawVBT; READONLY rgn: Region.T) =
  BEGIN
    VBT.PaintRegion(v, rgn, PaintOp.Bg);
    VBT.Stroke(v, rgn.r, v.path, PaintOp.Fg)
  END Repaint;

PROCEDURE Reshape(v: DrawVBT; READONLY cd: VBT.ReshapeRec) =
  BEGIN
    v.path :=
      Path.Translate(v.path,
        Point.Sub(Rect.Middle(cd.new), Rect.Middle(cd.prev)));
    v.drawing := FALSE;
    Repaint(v, Region.Full)
  END Reshape;

PROCEDURE XorPQ(v: DrawVBT) =
  (* Invert each pixel on the line from p to q. *)
  BEGIN
    VBT.Line(v, Rect.Full, v.p, v.q, PaintOp.Swap)
  END XorPQ;

PROCEDURE Mouse(v: DrawVBT; READONLY cd: VBT.MouseRec) =
  BEGIN
    IF cd.clickType = ClickType.FirstDown THEN
      v.drawing := TRUE;
      v.p := cd.cp.pt;
      v.q := v.p;
      XorPQ(v);
      VBT.SetCage(v, VBT.CageFromPosition(cd.cp))
    ELSIF v.drawing AND cd.clickType = ClickType.LastUp THEN
      Path.MoveTo(v.path, v.p);
      Path.LineTo(v.path, v.q);
      VBT.Line(v, Rect.Full, v.p, v.q, PaintOp.Fg)
      v.drawing := FALSE
    ELSIF v.drawing THEN (* Chord cancel *)
      XorPQ(v);
      v.drawing := FALSE
    END
  END Mouse;

PROCEDURE Position(v: DrawVBT; READONLY cd: VBT.PositionRec) =
  BEGIN
    (* You fill in this part *)
  END Position;
```

```
PROCEDURE DoErase(b: ButtonVBT.T; READONLY cd: VBT.MouseRec) =
  BEGIN
    Path.Empty(drawVBT.path);
    drawVBT.drawing := FALSE;
    Repaint(drawVBT, Region.Full)
  END DoErase;

PROCEDURE DoExit(b: ButtonVBT.T; READONLY cd: VBT.MouseRec) =
  BEGIN
    Trestle.Delete(main)
  END DoErase;

VAR
  drawVBT := NEW(DrawVBT, path := Path.New());
  menuBar :=
    ButtonVBT.MenuBar(
      ButtonVBT.New(TextVBT.New("Erase"), DoErase),
      ButtonVBT.New(TextVBT.New("Exit"), DoExit));
  main := HVSplit.Cons(Axis.T.Ver, menuBar, drawVBT);
BEGIN
  Trestle.Install(main);
  Trestle.AwaitDelete(main)
END Draw.
```

Notice that the mouse method implements the *chord cancel* convention: an unexpected chord on the mouse will cancel the drawing operation.

7.7 The Fifteen Puzzle

Trestle has dozens of splits. In addition to HVSplits, there are ZSplits (overlapping windows), PackSplits (in which the children are packed into rows like the words in a paragraph), and TSplits, in which the parent gives its screen to one child at a time. The Split interface provides operations that apply to splits in general, such as deleting, replacing, and enumerating children. To introduce the Split interface, we will program Sam Loyd's famous Fifteen Puzzle (see Figure 7.5).

The puzzle requires fifteen numbered cells to be sorted in order by sliding them around within a four by four frame. In our computerized version, clicking on a cell adjacent to the empty space will slide it into the space. There is also a button that scrambles the puzzle into a random solvable position.

Here is the type declaration for a Cell:

```
TYPE Cell = BorderedVBT.T OBJECT
  METHODS
    init(ch: VBT.T): Cell := Init
  OVERRIDES
    mouse := Mouse
  END;
```

NEW(Cell).init(ch) produces a VBT that looks like ch, but its shape is a rigid square and its mouse method moves the cell around in the puzzle. For the numbered cells, ch will be a black-bordered TextVBT; for the empty cell, ch will be a white TextureVBT child. (A TextureVBT is a VBT that displays a fixed texture.)

The cells are packed into rows using an HSplit, and the rows are stacked on top of one another using a VSplit:

```
VAR puzzle := HVSplit.Cons(Axis.T.Ver,
  HVSplit.Cons(Axis.T.Hor, New(1), New(2), New(3), New(4)),
  HVSplit.Cons(Axis.T.Hor, New(5), New(6), New(7), New(8)),
  HVSplit.Cons(Axis.T.Hor, New(9), New(10), New(11), New(12)),
  HVSplit.Cons(Axis.T.Hor, New(13), New(14), New(15), New(16)));


  space: Cell;  (* The cell representing the empty space *)
  cell: ARRAY [1..15] OF Cell;  (* cell[i] = cell numbered i *)


PROCEDURE New(n: INTEGER): Cell =
  BEGIN
    IF n = 16 THEN
      space := NEW(Cell).init(TextureVBT.New(PaintOp.Bg));
      RETURN space
    ELSE
      cell[n] :=
        NEW(Cell).init(BorderedVBT.New(TextVBT.New(Fmt.Int(n))));
      RETURN cell[n]
    END
  END New;
```

Here is the initialization procedure for creating a new cell:

```
PROCEDURE Init(c: Cell; ch: VBT.T): Cell =
  BEGIN
    EVAL BorderedVBT.T.init(c,
      RigidVBT.FromHV(ch, 20.0, 20.0),
      op := PaintOp.Bg);
    RETURN c
  END Init;
```

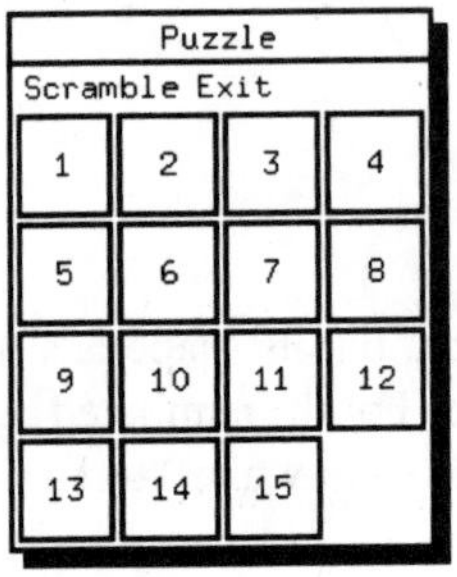

Figure 7.5: A computer version of the Fifteen Puzzle illustrates many operations on split windows, including "reparenting".

`BorderedVBT.T.init(c, ch, op := PaintOp.Bg)` initializes c to be a `BorderedVBT` with child ch and a thin border that will be painted with the background color. These thin white borders keep the cells from touching one another.

`RigidVBT.FromHV(ch, n, m)` returns a filter that looks and behaves like its child ch, except that its preferred size range is n by m millimeters. Here is how this works: Every VBT has a shape method that determines its preferred size range. For example, the shape method for a `BorderedVBT` calls its child's shape method and then adds the border size. The shape method for a `RigidVBT` returns values supplied when the filter is created, ignoring its child's preferred size range.

We could have saved a filter level by overriding the shape method of `Cell` instead of using `RigidVBT`, but such parsimony would be out of place in a program like this one.

Since the cells move around as the user works on the puzzle, we need a procedure for finding a cell's current row and column:

```
PROCEDURE GetRowCol(c: Cell; VAR (*out*) row, col: INTEGER) =
  VAR
    parent: HVSplit.T := VBT.Parent(c);
    grandparent: HVSplit.T := VBT.Parent(parent);
  BEGIN
    col := Split.Index(c, parent);
    row := Split.Index(parent, grandparent)
  END GetRowCol;
```

The children of any split are ordered; `Split.Index(p, ch)` returns the number of children of split p that precede its child ch. `HSplits` are ordered left-to-right; `VSplits` are ordered top-to-bottom. Therefore, in `Puzzle`, the column of a cell is its index in the parent `HSplit`, and the row of a cell is its parent's index in the grandparent `VSplit`.

When the user clicks on a cell that is next to the space, the cell swaps itself with the space:

```
PROCEDURE Mouse(v: Cell; READONLY cd: VBT.MouseRec) =
  VAR vRow, vCol, spRow, spCol: INTEGER;
  BEGIN
    IF cd.clickType = ClickType.FirstDown THEN
      GetRowCol(v, vRow, vCol);
      GetRowCol(space, spRow, spCol);
      IF vRow = spRow AND ABS(vCol - spCol) = 1
          OR vCol = spCol AND ABS(vRow - spRow) = 1 THEN
        Swap(v, space)
      END
    END
  END Mouse;
```

Swapping is possible because Trestle's splits and filters allow children to be inserted and deleted dynamically. The procedure Split.Replace(v, ch, newch) will replace the child ch of v with the new child newch. The old child ch is placed in a detached state, where it can be inserted into some other split if necessary. Two cells can be swapped using a dummy child and three replacements:

```
PROCEDURE Swap(v, w: VBT.T) =
  VAR temp := NEW(VBT.Leaf);
  BEGIN
    Split.Replace(VBT.Parent(v), v, temp);
    Split.Replace(VBT.Parent(w), w, v);
    Split.Replace(VBT.Parent(temp), temp, w)
  END Swap;
```

Swap could also have been implemented using the procedures Split.Delete and HVSplit.Insert, but it would have been messier.

One tricky bit of coding remains, which is the procedure that scrambles the puzzle:

```
PROCEDURE DoScramble(v: ButtonVBT.T; READONLY cd: VBT.MouseRec) =
  VAR j, parity: INTEGER;
  BEGIN
    parity := 0;
    FOR i := 1 TO 13 DO
      j := Random.Subrange(i, 15);
      (* This sets j to a randomly-selected element of [i..15] *)
      IF i # j THEN Swap(cell[i], cell[j]); INC(parity) END
    END;
    IF parity MOD 2 = 1 THEN Swap(cell[14], cell[15]) END
  END DoScramble;
```

Exercise 5. Explain how DoScramble selects a random solvable position. (This exercise is more about permutations than about Trestle, but you might enjoy it anyway.)

You may be wondering at this point what the window looks like when the user clicks the
Scramble button. If every call to Split.Replace updated the screen, there would be an
unpleasant flurry of painting that would show many intermediate states as well as the final
one. Trestle avoids this defect by implementing a policy of *lazy redisplay*. This means
that Trestle allows the screen to become temporarily inconsistent, and fixes it only when
the window configuration has stabilized. Here is the machinery that makes this work:

- Every VBT has a redisplay method. The call v.redisplay() is responsible for
  updating v's screen if it has become inconsistent.

- If an operation on a VBT makes its screen out-of-date, the operation *marks* the VBT.
  For example, Split.Replace marks the split as it swaps the new child for the old
  one.

- After every user event, Trestle calls the redisplay method of every marked VBT,
  simultaneously clearing its mark.

The Spot and Track programs didn't need to supply a redisplay method, because they
never allowed the screen to become inconsistent.

The built-in splits work hard to redisplay economically. For example, if two children of an
HVSplit with the same size are swapped, and then the split is redisplayed, then HVSplit
reshapes only these two children; the other children won't know that anything happened.
The DoScramble procedure might move a cell several times, but because of lazy redisplay
the cell will only be displayed in its final position.

All that remains of the Puzzle program is to declare the procedure for exiting the puzzle,
construct the main window, and install it:

```
PROCEDURE DoExit(self: ButtonVBT.T; READONLY cd: VBT.MouseRec) =
  BEGIN
    Trestle.Delete(main)
  END;

VAR
  menuBar :=
    ButtonVBT.MenuBar(
      ButtonVBT.New(TextVBT.New("Scramble"), DoScramble),
      ButtonVBT.New(TextVBT.New("Exit"), DoExit));

  main := HVSplit.Cons(Axis.Ver, menuBar, puzzle);

BEGIN
  Trestle.Install(main);
  Trestle.AwaitDelete(main)
END Puzzle.
```

7.8 Cards

Our next example program illustrates ZSplits, which are parent windows that display overlapping child windows. The program has a pulldown menu that allows you to create subwindows that look like little colored cards (see Figure 7.6).

The cards are rigid TextureVBTs with custom mouse and position methods to implement the dragging behavior:

```
TYPE Card = BorderedVBT.T OBJECT
  METHODS
    init(r, g, b: REAL): Card := Init
  OVERRIDES
    mouse := Mouse;
    position := Position
  END;

PROCEDURE Init(card: Card; r, g, b: REAL): Card =
  VAR ch := RigidVBT.FromHV(
    TextureVBT.New(PaintOp.FromRGB(r, g, b)), 20.0, 40.0);
  BEGIN
    EVAL BorderedVBT.T.init(card, ch);
    RETURN card
  END Init;
```

The parent of the card windows is a global ZSplit.T, extended with additional data fields to represent the state associated with the dragging:

```
TYPE Parent = ZSplit.T OBJECT
    dragging := FALSE;
    rect := Rect.Empty;
    pt: Point.T
  END;

VAR zSplit := NEW(Parent).init(TextureVBT.New(PaintOp.Bg));
```

When dragging is TRUE, rect is the current position of the card being dragged, and pt is the current position of the cursor.

Since Parent does not declare an init method, it inherits the method from ZSplit. ZSplit.init takes a single argument, which is a VBT to use as a "background" child. This child is below all the other children, and by default has the same shape as the parent. ZSplit.New wouldn't work here, since it would allocate a ZSplit.T, not a Parent.

The mouse and position procedures for dragging the cards use three new procedures:

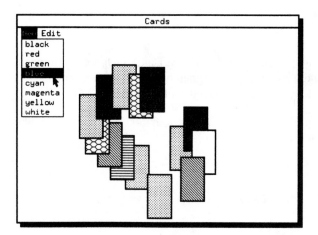

Figure 7.6: This program allows the user to create small colored cards and drag them into overlapping arrangements. A gray highlight rectangle follows a card as it is dragged. (Textures have been substituted for colors to produce a black-and-white figure.)

`ZSplit.Lift(z, ch)`

Lift the child ch to the top of the ZSplit z.

`ZSplit.Move(z, ch, rect)`

Change the domain of the child ch of the ZSplit z to the rectangle `rect`.

`HighlightVBT.SetRect(v, rect)`

Change the highlighted rectangle of the first highlight filter above the VBT v to be `rect`. This can be used to set the highlight for the first time, move the highlight, or take down the highlight (if `rect = Rect.Empty`). A third argument sets the width of the highlight; it defaults to a thin line.

A highlight filter uses `PaintOp.Swap` to complement the pixels of a rectangular outline on the screen. The highlight can be moved efficiently, without repainting the child, since the original pixel values can be restored with a second application of `PaintOp.Swap`. Solid rectangles can be highlighted by setting the highlight width to be very large.

Trestle automatically inserts a highlight filter above each top-level installed window so that any subwindow can use highlighting. For example, the feedback from the adjusting bars in the Tiling Monster all rely on the automatically-installed highlight filter.

The mouse method for the `Cards` program begins dragging on a down click, moves the child on the corresponding up click, and cancels on any chord:

```
PROCEDURE Mouse(ch: Card; READONLY cd: VBT.MouseRec) =
  VAR p: Parent := VBT.Parent(ch);
  BEGIN
    IF cd.clickType = VBT.ClickType.FirstDown THEN
      p.dragging := TRUE;
      p.rect := VBT.Domain(ch);
      p.pt := cd.cp.pt;
      ZSplit.Lift(p, ch);
      HighlightVBT.SetRect(p, rect);
      VBT.SetCage(ch, VBT.CageFromPosition(cd.cp))
    ELSE
      IF cd.clickType = ClickType.LastUp AND p.dragging THEN
        ZSplit.Move(p, ch, rect)
      END;
      HighlightVBT.SetRect(p, Rect.Empty);
      p.dragging := FALSE;
      VBT.SetCage(ch, VBT.EverywhereCage)
    END
  END Mouse;

PROCEDURE Position(ch: Card; READONLY cd: VBT.PositionRec) =
  VAR p: Parent := VBT.Parent(ch);
  BEGIN
    IF NOT p.dragging THEN
      VBT.SetCage(ch, VBT.EverywhereCage)
    ELSIF cd.cp.gone THEN
      VBT.SetCage(ch, VBT.GoneCage)
    ELSE
      IF Rect.Member(cd.cp.pt, VBT.Domain(p)) THEN
        p.rect := Rect.Add(p.rect, Point.Sub(cd.cp.pt, p.pt));
        p.pt := cd.cp.pt;
        HighlightVBT.SetRect(p, rect)
      END;
      VBT.SetCage(ch, VBT.CageFromPosition(cd.cp))
    END
  END Position;
```

The procedures illustrate two subtle points about the delivery of mouse clicks and cursor positions. First, whenever Trestle delivers a mouse click of type FirstDown to a window, it designates this window as the "mouse focus". All subsequent mouse button transitions will be delivered to the mouse focus, regardless of where they occur, up to and including the next transition of type LastUp . If it weren't for this rule the program wouldn't work: the final up transition could be delivered to the background, which would ignore it, or to another card, which would move itself instead of the card the user started dragging.

Second, the general rule that a window will receive all cursor positions outside its domain as "gone" is relaxed for the window with the mouse focus, to allow this window to track the cursor outside its domain. The card being dragged needs this freedom, since the user might drag the card far from its initial domain.

The ability to track outside your domain is useful, but not without its dangers. Suppose the user drags a card clear outside the top-level window and releases the button. Without special precautions, the card would move itself outside its parent's domain and become invisible to the user. To avoid this, the position procedure doesn't move the highlight rectangle if the position it receives is outside the parent's domain.

The position procedure still tests for the possibility cd.cp.gone, because in some unusual situations even the window with the mouse focus will receive the position "gone" (for example, if the user moves the cursor to another screen of the workstation).

Next we consider the button action procedure that inserts a new colored card:

```
TYPE
  ClrRec = RECORD r, g, b: REAL; name: TEXT END;
CONST
  Clr = ARRAY OF ClrRec{
    ClrRec{0.0, 0.0, 0.0, "black"},
    ClrRec{1.0, 0.0, 0.0, "red"},
    ClrRec{0.0, 1.0, 0.0, "green"},
    ClrRec{0.0, 0.0, 1.0, "blue"},
    ClrRec{0.0, 1.0, 1.0, "cyan"},
    ClrRec{1.0, 0.0, 1.0, "magenta"},
    ClrRec{1.0, 1.0, 0.0, "yellow"},
    ClrRec{1.0, 1.0, 1.0, "white"}};

PROCEDURE DoNewChild(b: ButtonVBT.T; READONLY cd: VBT.MouseRec) =
  VAR colorName: TEXT; card: Card; p: Point.T; dom: Rect.T;
  BEGIN
    colorName := TextVBT.Get(Filter.Child(button));
    FOR i := FIRST(Clr) TO LAST(Clr) DO
      IF Text.Equal(Clr[i].name, colorName) THEN
        card := NEW(Card).init(Clr[i].r, Clr[i].g, Clr[i].b);
        EXIT
      END
    END;
    p.h := Random.Subrange(75, 100);
    p.v := Random.Subrange(5, 40);
    dom := VBT.Domain(zSplit);
    ZSplit.InsertAt(zSplit, card, Point.Add(Rect.NorthWest(dom), p))
  END DoNewChild;
```

The interface Filter provides routines that apply to any filter, just as Split provides routines that apply to any split. To determine what color of card to create, the DoNewChild procedure uses Filter.Child(b) to get the TextVBT child out of the button, and then TextVBT.Get to get the text out of the TextVBT.

ZSplit.InsertAt(z, ch, pt) inserts ch into z with its northwest corner at pt. A small random offset is added to the position of the card, so that a new card does not totally obscure the previous card.

The program also has Exit and Erase buttons:

```
PROCEDURE DoExit(v: ButtonVBT.T; READONLY cd: VBT.MouseRec) =
  BEGIN Trestle.Delete(main) END DoExit;

PROCEDURE DoErase(v: ButtonVBT.T; READONLY cd: VBT.MouseRec) =
  VAR p, q, background: VBT.T;
  BEGIN
    p := Split.Succ(zSplit, NIL);
    background := Split.Pred(zSplit, NIL);
    WHILE p # background DO
      q := p;
      p := Split.Succ(zSplit, p);
      IF ISTYPE(q, Card) THEN Split.Delete(zSplit, q) END
    END
  END DoErase;
```

The DoErase procedure uses the Succ and Pred procedures to enumerate the children of the ZSplit and delete each one that is a card. Succ(NIL) is the first child; Pred(NIL) is the last child, which is the background. Care must be taken not to delete the background or the pull-down menu, which could be in the ZSplit when DoErase is called.

The final section of the Cards program is a bit different from our previous programs, because it uses pull-down menus. The following procedures provide the building-blocks for pull-down menus:

MenuButtonVBT.TextItem(txt, p)

Create a ButtonVBT.T with child TextVBT.New(txt) and action procedure p, suitable for including in a pop-up or pulldown menu. The item will be highlighted when the user rolls the mouse into it, and activated if he releases the mouse button over it.

AnchorButtonVBT.New(ch, m, z)

Create a button that looks like ch and that pops up the menu m in the ZSplit z when the user clicks on it. The menu will be positioned so that its northwest corner coincides with the southwest corner of ch.

```
HVSplit.AddChild(v, ch)
```

Insert ch as a new last child of v.

With these procedures the menus are easily constructed, which is all that is left of the Cards program:

```
PROCEDURE Menu1(): HVSplit.T =
  VAR res: HVSplit.T;
  BEGIN
    res := HVSplit.New(Axis.T.Ver);
    FOR i := FIRST(Clr) TO LAST(Clr) DO
      HVSplit.AddChild(res,
        MenuButtonVBT.TextItem(Clr[i].name, DoNewChild))
    END
  END Menu1;

VAR
  menu1 := BorderedVBT.New(Menu1());

  menu2 :=
    BorderedVBT.New(
      HVSplit.Cons(Axis.T.Ver,
        MenuButtonVBT.TextItem("erase", DoErase),
        MenuButtonVBT.TextItem("exit", DoExit)));

  menuBar :=
    ButtonVBT.Menubar(
      AnchorButtonVBT.New(TextVBT.New("New"), menu1, zSplit),
      AnchorButtonVBT.New(TextVBT.New("Edit"), menu2, zSplit));

  main :=
    HVSplit.Cons(Axis.T.Ver, menuBar, HighlightVBT.New(zSplit));


BEGIN
  Trestle.Install(main);
  Trestle.AwaitDelete(main)
END Cards.
```

The call to HighlightVBT.New is not absolutely necessary, because of the free highlight filter provided by Trestle.Install. But the Cards program looks sharper with a highlight filter that does not extend over the menu bar, so the program inserts one that covers only the ZSplit. (Otherwise, if the user dragged a card so that it stuck out beyond the north boundary of the ZSplit, the highlight would show up in the menu bar during dragging, while the image of the card itself would be clipped.)

7.9 Asynchronous painting

Our next example program is called `Plaid`. It draws moving plaid patterns on the display.

All of our examples so far have been synchronous: they never did anything except when Trestle prompted them by calling some VBT method. The `Plaid` program is asynchronous: it has a thread of control whose operations on the window are independent of the operations that Trestle orchestrates through method calls.

The `Plaid` program illustrates one reason for using asynchronous threads in a window application: to animate the screen. Another reason is to improve responsiveness by handling lengthy computations in the background. The point of the example is the locking protocol that must be obeyed by asynchronous threads, regardless of the reason for the asynchrony.

If an asynchronous thread were adjusting the subwindow structure of a split window at the same time that Trestle was, say, locating a mouse click in the structure, then chaos would result. To protect against this, the Trestle system is a big critical section protected by the mutex `VBT.mu`.

To deliver an event, Trestle locks `VBT.mu` and calls the event method for the root window in the tree of splits. Since `VBT.mu` is locked, the event method can access or modify the split structure. In particular, it can locate subwindows and recursively activate their event methods. When the event method for the root window returns, Trestle unlocks `VBT.mu`.

The painting thread of the `Plaid` program reads and writes the variables recording the animation state. The `reshape` method also writes these variables, to restart the animation whenever the window moves. Therefore the painting thread must synchronize with the

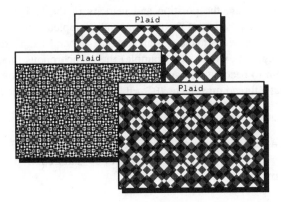

Figure 7.7: These windows are animated with varying plaid patterns. The program illustrates the locking protocol that allows asynchronous threads to operate on windows.

reshape method. It is easiest to use VBT.mu for this synchronization, since VBT.mu is automatically locked in the reshape method. The painting thread must lock VBT.mu explicitly.

Here is the animation algorithm used by the Plaid program: visualize a ball rolling on a billiard table at constant speed, bouncing when it hits the rails. A rectangle continuously expands and contracts so that it is always centered in the table with one of its corners at the position of the ball. The rectangle is sampled every few milliseconds. During the interval between an odd sample and the following even sample, the border of the rectangle acts as an "inverting paintbrush" that complements the color of the region it sweeps over, while during the alternate intervals the border of the rectangle has no effect. Voila: you have visualized Plaid (see Figure 7.7).

Here is the type declaration for the main VBT of the Plaid program:

```
TYPE
  PlaidVBT =
    VBT.Leaf OBJECT
      (* all fields protected by VBT.mu *)
      p, deltaP: Point.T;
      prevRect: Rect.T;
      oddCycle: BOOLEAN;
      c: Thread.Condition
      (* signaled when the VBT's domain becomes non-empty *)
    OVERRIDES
      repaint := Repaint;
      reshape := Reshape
    END;
```

The points p and deltaP are the position and velocity of the ball, respectively. The rectangle prevRect is the position of the most recently sampled rectangle. The boolean oddCycle is TRUE if the previous cycle was an odd one. When Plaid's domain is empty (as it is when the window is iconic, for example) the asynchronous thread blocks on c waiting for the domain to become non-empty. The comment that the fields are protected by VBT.mu means that a thread must have VBT.mu locked to read or write the fields.

Here is the code that advances p to its next sample position.

```
PROCEDURE Advance(VAR p: Point.T; delta: Point.T; dom: Rect.T) =
  (* Advance p by delta, reflecting so as to maintain p inside
     dom, which must be non-empty. *)
  BEGIN
    p := Point.Add(p, delta);
    LOOP
      IF p.h < dom.west THEN
        p.h := 2 * dom.west - p.h;
```

```
        delta.h := -delta.h
      ELSIF p.h > dom.east - 1 THEN
        p.h := 2 * (dom.east - 1) - p.h;
        delta.h := -delta.h
      ELSIF p.v < dom.north THEN
        p.v := 2 * dom.north - p.v;
        delta.v := -delta.v
      ELSIF p.v > (dom.south - 1) THEN
        p.v := 2 * (dom.south - 1) - p.v;
        delta.v := -delta.v
      ELSE
        EXIT
      END
    END
  END Advance;
```

That is, as long as p is to the west of dom, reflect it in the west edge; as long as it is to the east, reflect it in the east edge, and so on for the north and south edges. Note that in the unusual case that dom is small compared to delta, the number of bounces required to simulate a single step may be large, but the loop will eventually terminate, since each bounce decreases the distance of p from the center of dom. The -1's in the program are necessary because rectangles are closed on the west and north edges but open on the east and south edges.

The following procedure will come in handy:

```
PROCEDURE PaintDiff(v: VBT.T; r1, r2: Rect.T) =
  (* Invert the region r1 - r2 in v's domain *)
  VAR a: Rect.Partition;
  BEGIN
    Rect.Factor(r1, r2, a, 0, 0);
    a[2] := a[4];
    VBT.PolyTint(v, SUBARRAY(a, 0, 4), PaintOp.Swap)
  END PaintDiff;
```

The procedure relies on the very useful Rect.Factor routine, which computes the difference r1 - r2 of two rectangles r1 and r2. This difference will not in general be a rectangle, but it can always be expressed as a union of four disjoint rectangles; which Factor finds and stores in a[0], a[1], a[3], and a[4]. Factor also sets a[2] to the intersection of r1 and r2, so that the a[i]'s form a partition of r1. In this program we want r1 - r2 as an array of rectangles, so we replace a[2] with a[4], after which a[0] through a[3] are the desired partition. Finally, this difference is painted using VBT.PolyTint, which takes a VBT, an array of rectangles and a painting operation, and applies the operation to each pixel of the VBT's screen that lies in any of the rectangles. We could have used Region operations instead, but Rect.Factor is faster.

Here is the closure that is forked to create the asynchronous thread:

```
TYPE
  Closure = Thread.Closure OBJECT
    v: PlaidVBT
  OVERRIDES
    apply := Painter
  END;

PROCEDURE Painter(cl: Closure): REFANY =
  VAR
    v := cl.v;
    dom, rect: Rect.T;
    mid: Point.T;
  BEGIN
    LOOP
      LOCK VBT.mu DO
        WHILE Rect.IsEmpty(VBT.Domain(v)) DO
          Thread.Wait(VBT.mu, v.c)
        END;
        dom := VBT.Domain(v);
        Advance(v.p, v.deltaP, dom);
        mid := Rect.Middle(dom);
        rect := Rect.FromSize(
          2 * ABS(v.p.h - mid.h),
          2 * ABS(v.p.v - mid.v));
        (* Rect.FromSize(h, v) returns a rectangle whose width
           and height are h and v, respectively. *)
        rect := Rect.Center(rect, mid);
        (* Rect.Center(rect, mid) returns a rectangle
           congruent to rect, with middle at mid. *)
        IF v.oddCycle THEN
          PaintDiff(v, rect, v.prevRect);
          PaintDiff(v, v.prevRect, rect)
        END;
        v.oddCycle := NOT v.oddCycle;
        v.prevRect := rect
      END
    END
  END Painter;
```

Here are the repaint and reshape procedures:

```
PROCEDURE Repaint(v: PlaidVBT; READONLY rgn: Region.T) =
  BEGIN Reset(v) END Repaint;
```

```
PROCEDURE Reshape(v: PlaidVBT; READONLY cd: VBT.ReshapeRec) =
  BEGIN Reset(v) END Reshape;

PROCEDURE Reset(v: PlaidVBT) =
  VAR dom := VBT.Domain(v);
  BEGIN (* LL=VBT.mu *)
    VBT.PaintTint(v, dom, PaintOp.Bg);
    v.p := Rect.Middle(dom);
    v.prevRect := Rect.Empty;
    v.oddCycle := FALSE;
    IF NOT Rect.IsEmpty(dom) THEN Thread.Signal(v.c) END
  END Reset;
```

The comment LL=VBT.mu means that the "locking level" of the thread is VBT.mu, that is, that VBT.mu is locked. (This notation is generalized in the last section of this chapter.) Reset needs this locking level, since it writes the fields of v that are protected by VBT.mu. It also has this locking level, since it is called only from the repaint and reshape methods, which the system always calls with LL=VBT.mu.

All that remains is to fork the thread and install the window:

```
VAR v := NEW(PlaidVBT, deltaP := Point.T{1,1});
BEGIN
  EVAL Thread.Fork(NEW(Closure, v := v));
  Trestle.Install(v);
  Trestle.AwaitDelete(v)
END
```

7.10 JoinVBTs

Many window system toolkits allow clients to supply methods that define the behavior of a window in response to mouse clicks, keystrokes, exposures, and other events conveyed from the server to the client. The VBT abstraction is unusual in that it also allows clients to supply a method that defines the way a window paints.

For example, the painting method for the root window in an application address space relays the painting commands to the X server. The painting method for a child window of a horizontal or vertical split is simple: it clips to the child's domain and then paints on its parent window. The paint method for a child window of an overlapping split has more work to do: it must clip the painting operation to the child's visible region before painting on its parent window.

Overriding a paint method is more complicated than overriding, say, the mouse method, and few applications do so directly. But the flexibility of object-oriented painting is a

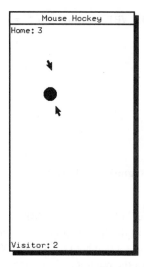

Figure 7.8: This window is visible on two workstations. Clicking on the spot propels it towards the opponent's goal. The program illustrates windows with multiple parents.

powerful tool for implementing novel interactors. In this section, we will take a look at an interactor that is based on object-oriented painting: the JoinVBT, which is a kind of inverse split.

A JoinVBT can have multiple parents: painting on the child is relayed to all the parents, and mouse clicks on any of the parents are relayed to the child. Every parent is an independent "viewer" into the child's screen. We will use JoinVBTs to program a game called mouse hockey (see Figure 7.8).

The program takes the name of a remote workstation as a command line argument and opens windows on both the local and the remote workstations. Both windows view the same playing field, which is a white rectangle containing a black spot. Each player clicks on the spot as fast and as often as he can locate it with his mouse; each click makes the spot take a random jump in the general direction of the opponent's side of the field. A player scores a point whenever the spot crosses the window boundary on the opponent's side of the field. When a point is scored the program updates the score display and moves the spot back to the middle of the field.

First the program connects to the two window servers that it will be using:

```
VAR home := Trestle.Connect(NIL);
  visitor := Trestle.Connect(Params.GetParameter(1));
```

Trestle.Connect(t) returns a handle to the window server on the workstation named t, or to the local workstation if t=NIL. The call Params.GetParameter(n) returns the nth command line parameter as a text. These handles can be passed to Trestle.Install to control the workstation on which it puts up windows.

Then the program declares two integers for counting the scores, and two VBTs for displaying them:

```
VAR
  homeScore, visitorScore := 0;
  homeScoreVBT, visitorScoreVBT := TextVBT.New("0");
```

The VBT type for the playing field is very similar to that for the old Spot program:

```
TYPE SpotVBT = VBT.Leaf OBJECT
    spot: Region.T
  OVERRIDES
    repaint := Repaint;
    reshape := Reshape;
    mouse := Mouse
  END;
```

The repaint and reshape methods are the same as for the Spot program in Section 7.5. The mouse method is the heart of the program:

```
PROCEDURE Mouse(v: SpotVBT; READONLY cd: VBT.MouseRec) =
  VAR dom := VBT.Domain(v); dv := Random.Subrange(0, 50);
    pt: Point.T;
  BEGIN
    IF cd.clickType = VBT.ClickType.FirstDown
        AND Region.Member(cd.cp.pt, v.spot) THEN
      IF Trestle.ScreenOf(v).trsl = visitor THEN
        dv := - dv
      END;
      pt.v := Rect.Middle(v.spot.r).v + dv;
      pt.h := Random.Subrange(dom.west, dom.east-1);
      IF NOT Rect.Member(pt, dom) THEN
        IF dv > 0 THEN
          INC(homeScore);
          TextVBT.Put(homeScoreVBT, Fmt.Int(homeScore))
        ELSE
          INC(visitorScore);
          TextVBT.Put(visitorScoreVBT, Fmt.Int(visitorScore))
        END;
        pt := Rect.Middle(dom)
      END;
      v.spot :=
        Region.Add(v.spot, Point.Sub(pt, Rect.Middle(v.spot.r)));
      Repaint(v, Region.Full)
    END
  END Mouse;
```

The statement res := Trestle.ScreenOf(v) sets res to a record that contains information about where the window v is installed. In particular, res.trsl is a handle to the window system on which v is installed, or NIL if v is not installed. What happens if the window is visible on two workstations, you ask? Every JoinVBT keeps track of its "current parent", which is the last one from which it received a mouse click. When Trestle.ScreenOf gets to a JoinVBT as it recurses up the tree of splits, it follows the current parent and ignores any other parent.

The mouse method of the SpotVBT can therefore determine the workstation from which the click came by testing whether the current parent is visitor or home. It uses this test to decide whether to move the spot up or down by a random displacement in the range [0..50]. The new horizontal position of the spot is randomly chosen from the window's horizontal extent. If the new position is outside the domain of the VBT, a point is scored and the spot is moved back to the middle.

The rest of the program produces the multiple views and installs them on the two workstations:

```
CONST Width = 400; Height = 700; (* size of playing field *)

VAR
  main :=
    JoinVBT.New(
      HVSplit.Cons(Axis.T.Ver,
        ButtonVBT.MenuBar(TextVBT.New("Home:"), homeScoreVBT),
        NEW(SpotVBT, spot := Circle(10.5)),
        ButtonVBT.MenuBar(
          TextVBT.New("Visitor:"), visitorScoreVBT)),
      Rect.FromSize(Width, Height));

  homeVBT, visitorVBT :=
    RigidVBT.FromHV(
      JoinVBT.NewParent(main, Point.Origin),
      Width, Height);

BEGIN
  Trestle.Install(homeVBT, trsl := home);
  Trestle.Install(visitorVBT, trsl := visitor);
  Trestle.AwaitDelete(homeVBT)
END MouseHockey.
```

JoinVBT.New(ch, rect) produces a JoinVBT.T; a filter that looks and behaves like ch, but its domain is fixed to be the rectangle rect, and it allows multiple parents. Rect.FromSize(h, v) returns the rectangle whose horizontal and vertical extent are [0..h-1] and [0..v-1].

If j is a JoinVBT.T, then JoinVBT.NewParent(j, pt) returns a new VBT that "views" the screen of j with its northwest corner at the position pt.

The home and visitor score lines are produced using `ButtonVBT.MenuBar`, which is convenient for producing one-line high left-justified `HSplits`, even if there are no buttons in them.

With the program we have presented, each player sees only his own cursor. To show both cursors, it is necessary to override the position methods of the two join parents, so that each of them tracks its cursor and paints its cursor's image. This is straightforward but tedious, so we won't present the code.

7.11 A simple filter

Many user interfaces can be constructed by programming your own leaf VBTs and connecting them together with the splits and filters that Trestle provides. But the time will come when you will want to venture into more exciting territory, and implement a split or filter class of your own. In this section we will look at the implementation of a simple filter, `ButtonVBT`.

The `ButtonVBT` interface was designed to allow two kinds of extension:

- Different kinds of buttons respond to different user gestures: command buttons are highlighted on a down click and activated on an up click; menu buttons are highlighted when the mouse rolls into them and activated on an up click; anchor buttons are activated on a down click or when the mouse rolls over them from another anchor button.

- Different user interface packages give different feedback to the user to highlight buttons: in our example program we have used `HighlightVBT` to video-reverse the button, but Marc Brown's user interface editor FormsVBT, which is built on top of Trestle, highlights buttons by shading their borders to make them look as if they were recessed into the screen [1].

To make buttons that respond to different user gestures, you override the `mouse` and `position` methods of a button.

To make buttons that highlight differently, buttons have three methods `pre`, `post`, and `cancel`, in addition to their action procedure. Regardless of the user gesture a button subtype responds to, it will call these methods in a sequence produced by the following syntax:

```
{ pre action post | pre cancel }
```

That is, every call to the `pre` method must be followed either by the `cancel` method, or by the action procedure and then the `post` method. The default `pre`, `post`, and `cancel` methods provide simple highlighting; they can be overridden to produce other effects.

We will ignore the less important procedures in the ButtonVBT interface, like MenuBar and New, and get right to the essential type declarations:

```
TYPE
  T <: Public;
  Public = Filter.T OBJECT
    action: Proc
  METHODS
    pre();
    post();
    cancel();
    init(ch: VBT.T; p: Proc; ref: REFANY := NIL): T
  END;
  Proc = PROCEDURE(self: T; READONLY cd: VBT.MouseRec);
```

The mouse and position methods of a ButtonVBT.T call the pre method on a mouse click of type FirstDown, and then call the cancel method if the user chords by clicking another mouse button or if the user moves the mouse out of the window; they call the action procedure and post method if the user releases the mouse button. This is suitable for standard command buttons. Menu buttons and anchor buttons have their own interfaces; they are subtypes of ButtonVBT.T with different mouse and position methods.

The action procedure is a field rather than a method in order to allow buttons with different action procedures to share their method suites. Any additional state required by the action procedure can be stored on the ButtonVBT's "property set". Every VBT has a property set, which is a set of non-nil traced references, all with different allocated types. VBT.PutProp(v, ref) adds ref to v's property set, replacing any existing reference of the same type. VBT.GetProp(v, tc) return the element of v's property set with typecode tc, or NIL if no such element exists.

The call v.init(ch, p, ref) initializes v with child ch and action proc p. If ref is non-nil, it is added to v's property set.

The implementation is quite straightforward:

```
REVEAL
  T = Public BRANDED OBJECT
    ready := FALSE
  OVERRIDES
    mouse := Mouse;
    position := Position;
    pre := Pre;
    post := Post;
    cancel := Post; (*sic*)
    init := Init
  END;
```

There are no surprises in the revelation of the concrete type for a ButtonVBT.T: it has one boolean data field and the expected set of methods. The only reason for naming the type Public in the interface was to use the name in this revelation.

```
PROCEDURE Init(v: T; ch: VBT.T; p: Proc; ref: REFANY := NIL): T =
  BEGIN
    v.action := p;
    IF ref # NIL THEN VBT.PutProp(v, ref) END;
    EVAL Filter.T.init(v, ch);
    RETURN v
  END Init;
```

The call Filter.T.init(v, ch) initializes v as a filter with child ch. Declaring ButtonVBT.T as a subtype of Filter.T and including the call to Filter.T.init is all that is necessary to get the default behavior of a filter: for example, reshaping the parent reshapes the child, painting on the child paints on the parent, and so on for all the other VBT methods.

The implementation is quite straightforward:

```
PROCEDURE Pre(v: T) =
  BEGIN HighlightVBT.SetRect(v, VBT.Domain(v), 99999) END Pre;

PROCEDURE Post(v: T) =
  BEGIN HighlightVBT.SetRect(v, Rect.Empty, 0) END Post;

PROCEDURE Mouse(v: T; READONLY cd: VBT.MouseRec) =
  BEGIN
    IF cd.clickType = VBT.ClickType.FirstDown THEN
      v.ready := TRUE;
      v.pre();
      VBT.SetCage(v, VBT.CageFromRect(VBT.Domain(v))
    ELSE
      IF (cd.clickType = VBT.ClickType.LastUp) AND
         v.ready AND NOT cd.cp.gone AND
         Rect.Member(cd.cp.pt, VBT.Domain(v))
      THEN
        v.action(v, cd);
        v.post()
      ELSIF v.ready THEN
        v.cancel()
      END;
      v.ready := FALSE
    END
  END Mouse;
```

```
PROCEDURE Position(v: T; READONLY cd: VBT.PositionRec) =
  BEGIN
    IF v.ready THEN
      IF cd.cp.gone OR NOT Rect.Member(cd.cp.pt, VBT.Domain(v)) THEN
        v.cancel();
        VBT.SetCage(v, VBT.GoneCage)
      ELSE
        v.pre();
        VBT.SetCage(v, VBT.CageFromRect(VBT.Domain(v)))
      END
    ELSE
      VBT.SetCage(v, VBT.EverywhereCage)
    END
  END Position;
```

The code works if the user clicks on the button and rolls in and out repeatedly.

7.12   A more complicated filter

In this section we present the implementation of TranslatedVBT, a filter that maintains
a translation between the coordinate systems of the child and parent such that the child's
coordinate system has its origin at the northwest corner of its domain. You might want
to use a TranslatedVBT filter as the root window of your application, in order to keep
your coordinate system fixed regardless of how the application is translated by the user
and window manager. The main point is to illustrate a more complicated filter than
ButtonVBT. The interface is very simple:

```
INTERFACE TranslatedVBT;
  IMPORT Filter;
  TYPE T <: Filter.T;
END TranslatedVBT.
```

TranslatedVBT.T does not need to declare its own init method; it just inherits the init
method of Filter.T. The implementation, however, is rather long, since many methods
must do some sort of translation between the child and parent coordinate systems.

The methods for splits and filters can be divided into two groups:

- The "down methods" that recurse down the tree of splits, like the repaint method.

- The "up methods" that recurse up the tree of splits, like the paint method.

Since some methods recurse up and some recurse down, a fairly sophisticated locking
strategy is required to avoid deadlock. In addition to the global lock VBT.mu, each VBT
v includes a mutex that makes operations on it atomic. These locks are revealed only to

importers of the VBTClass interface, so you don't have to worry about them until you start to implement your own VBT classes. Then you have to worry about them more than you worry about your mortgage. We introduce an order on all the locks:

- The global VBT.mu before any VBT v

- Any VBT v before Parent(v)

Each thread must acquire locks in ascending order; this rule prevents deadlock. We say that the "locking level" of a thread, or LL for short, is the highest lock that it has acquired in this order. Trestle procedure specifications always include the locking level at which a thread can legally call the procedure. For example:

- LL < v means that the only VBTs locked by the thread are a chain of proper descendants of v. The thread might or might not have VBT.mu locked.

- LL = v means that the thread has v locked, and possibly a chain of descendents of v, and possibly VBT.mu.

- LL <= VBT.mu means that the thread has no VBT locked, but it might have VBT.mu.

- LL = VBT.mu means that the thread has VBT.mu locked and doesn't have any VBT locked.

If a data field can be accessed by multiple threads, its declaration is accompanied by a comment listing the locks that protect it. To write a field, a thread must hold all its protecting locks; to read a field, a thread must hold at least one of its protecting locks. This is sufficient to ensure that no write is concurrent with any read or any other write.

The implementation of TranslatedVBT demonstrates this commenting discipline. Here is the concrete type revelation:

```
REVEAL
  T = Filter.T BRANDED OBJECT
    delta := Point.Origin
    (* child coord + delta = parent coord. *)
    (* v.delta is protected both by VBT.mu and by v.ch *)
  OVERRIDES
    reshape := Reshape;
    repaint := Repaint;
    mouse := Mouse;
    position := Position;
    setcage := SetCage;
    paintbatch := PaintBatch;
    capture := Capture;
    screenOf := ScreenOf
  END;
```

A Filter.T has a data field ch containing the filter child; this wasn't mentioned in the last section because it wasn't needed. Both v.ch and VBT.mu protect the delta field, because the field is read both by up methods and down methods. At initialization time, both v and ch have empty domains, so the value Point.Origin is correct for delta.

The mouse method simply translates the click and relays it to the child:

```
PROCEDURE Mouse(p: T; READONLY cdIn: VBT.MouseRec) =
  VAR cd: VBT.MouseRec; ch := p.ch;
  BEGIN (* LL = VBT.mu *)
    IF ch # NIL THEN
      cd := cdIn;
      IF NOT cd.cp.gone THEN
        cd.cp.pt := Point.Sub(cd.cp.pt, p.delta)
      END;
      VBTClass.PutMouseCode(ch, cd)
    END
  END Mouse;
```

Since the thread has VBT.mu, it is allowed to read the ch and delta fields. A filter child can be NIL, in which case the filter ignores all events. This is the reason for the test ch # NIL. The call VBTClass.PutMouseCode(ch, cd) is like ch.mouse(cd), but it establishes some internal invariants before and after calling the method. Clients should always use it instead of invoking the method directly. There are similar "wrapper" procedures for invoking the other down methods.

We won't list the position and repaint methods, since they are very similar to the mouse method. The last down method is the reshape method; we will save it for last.

The up methods all take the parent and child, with the child locked. We will look at the setcage and paintbatch methods; the other two are similar.

Trestle calls v.setcage(ch) to notify the split v that its child ch has changed its cage. A TranslatedVBT simply keeps its parent cage equal to its child's cage translated by delta:

```
PROCEDURE SetCage(p: T; ch: VBT.T) =
  VAR cg: VBT.Cage;
  BEGIN (* LL=ch, ch.parent = p *)
    cg := VBTClass.Cage(ch);
    CASE cg.type OF
      VBT.CageType.Gone, VBT.CageType.Everywhere => (*skip*)
    | VBT.CageType.Rectangle =>
        cg.rect := Rect.Add(cg.rect, prnt.delta);
    END;
    VBT.SetCage(p, cg)
  END SetCage;
```

VBTClass.Cage(ch) returns ch's cage; it requires that ch be locked, which follows from LL=ch. The procedure call VBT.SetCage(p, cg) requires LL < p, which follows from LL=ch and ch.parent = p. We did not mention the locking level requirement of VBT.SetCage before, since there's no way to get to a locking level that violates the requirement without importing VBTClass, which reveals the individual VBT locks.

The painting operations performed on a VBT are grouped into "batches", which are passed to the painting method as they fill up. This amortizes the cost of method invocation and saves class implementers the bother of implementing methods for each individual painting operation. Trestle calls v.paintBatch(ch, b) to paint the batch b on the child ch of the split v. Here is the paintbatch method for a TranslatedVBT:

```
PROCEDURE PaintBatch(p: T; ch: VBT.T; ba: Batch.T) =
  BEGIN (* LL = ch *)
    BatchUtil.Translate(ba, p.delta);
    VBTClass.PaintBatch(p, ba)
  END PaintBatch;
```

The PaintBatch method translates the batch using the procedure Translate from the interface BatchUtil, and then recursively paints the translated batch on the parent using VBTClass.PaintBatch, which is a wrapper procedure that invokes the parent's method.

The last method we will look at is Reshape. Recall that a ReshapeRec cd contains a field cd.saved, which is a rectangular subset of the previous domain that Trestle has preserved for the method to use in painting the new domain. TranslatedVBT's reshape method passes these saved bits on to the child if possible:

```
PROCEDURE Reshape(p: T; READONLY cd: VBT.ReshapeRec) =
  VAR
    del: Point.T;
    saved, newchdom, chsaved: Rect.T;
    ch := p.ch;
  BEGIN (* LL = VBT.mu *)
    IF ch # NIL THEN
      del :=
        Point.Sub(Rect.NorthWest(cd.new), Rect.NorthWest(cd.prev));
      saved := Rect.Meet(Rect.Add(cd.saved, del), cd.new);
      LOCK ch DO
        p.delta := Rect.NorthWest(cd.new);
        VBT.Scroll(p, saved, del)
      END;
      newchdom := Rect.Sub(cd.new, p.delta);
      chsaved := Rect.Sub(saved, p.delta);
      (* translate chdom and saved to child coordinates *)
      IF Rect.Equal(chdom, VBT.Domain(ch)) THEN
        (* Child's domain is unchanged; only need to repaint it *)
```

```
        chbad := Region.Difference(Region.FromRect(newchdom),
            Region.FromRect(chsaved));
        IF NOT Region.IsEmpty(chbad) THEN
          VBTClass.Repaint(ch, chbad)
        END
      ELSE
        VBTClass.Reshape(ch, newchdom, chsaved)
      END
    END
  END Reshape;
```

The method begins by transferring all saved bits from the old parent domain to the corresponding part of the new parent domain with the call `VBT.Scroll(p, saved, del)`, which copies from the screen of p to the screen of p, with destination rectangle `saved` and translation vector `del`. Then the method updates `p.delta` to maintain the relation between the two coordinate systems. To do this it must lock the child, which it can do legally since `LL(VBT.mu) < LL(ch)`.

The child can be painting concurrently while the reshape is happening, since painting does not require `VBT.mu`. It would be very bad if a child paint batch were processed after the assignment to `p.delta` and before the call to `VBT.Scroll`: the updated delta field would cause the batch to be routed to the parent's new domain; but then the call to `VBT.Scroll` would overwrite the parent's new domain with the now-obsolete saved bits. The effects of the batch would be lost. This race condition is avoided by keeping the child locked while the saved bits are scrolled and the `delta` field is updated.

Finally the method computes the new child domain and the saved rectangle in child coordinates; then it either repaints or reshapes the child, depending on whether the child's domain has changed. For example, if the parent moves without changing shape, and if all the bits of the parent's previous domain are saved, then the reshape method copies the old contents of the screen to the new location, updates the `delta` vector, and does not call any child methods (since `chbad` will be the empty region if everything was saved and the shape wasn't changed). Thus, the `TranslatedVBT` filter can reduce the cost of moving a window to the cost of copying its bits, which is one of its attractions.

7.13   Solutions

Solution 1. The missing lines are:

```
WITH mid = lo + hi DIV 2, vh = Axis.Other[hv] DO
  RETURN HVSplit.Cons(hv, New(lo, mid, vh),
          HVBar.New(hv, size := 3.0, texture := Pixmap.Gray),
          New(mid, hi, vh))
END
```

Solution 2. The Reshape method should initialize `delta` as follows:

```
delta :=
    Point.Sub(Rect.NorthWest(cd.new), Rect.NorthWest(cd.prev))
```

The rest of the method can be left unchanged.

The value of `Rect.NorthWest(Rect.Empty)` is defined to be `Point.Origin`, so this solution works even if `cd.new` or `cd.prev` is empty.

Solution 3. The Rescreen method should reset the spot to be centered at the origin and have the correct diameter:

```
PROCEDURE Rescreen(v: T; cd: VBT.RescreenRec);
  BEGIN
    v.spot := Circle(VBT.MMToPixels(v, 4.0, Axis.Hor))
  END;
```

A rasterized circle centered at a lattice point looks better if its diameter is odd instead of even. If you care about such details, you can use:

```
PROCEDURE Rescreen(v: T; cd: VBT.RescreenRec);
  BEGIN
    WITH r = VBT.MMToPixels(v, 4.0, Axis.Hor) DO
      v.spot := Circle(0.5 + FLOAT(ROUND(r - 0.5)))
    END
  END;
```

Solution 4. The missing code is:

```
IF NOT drawing THEN
  VBT.SetCage(v, VBT.EverywhereCage)
ELSIF cd.cp.gone THEN
  VBT.SetCage(v, VBT.GoneCage)
ELSE
  XorPQ();
  q := cd.cp.pt;
  XorPQ();
  VBT.SetCage(v, VBT.CageFromPosition(cd.cp)))
END
```

The call to set the cage to `VBT.EverywhereCage` is not really necessary, since in this case it doesn't matter whether the system continues to report cursor positions or not. (If you don't set a cage in response to the cursor position, then Trestle is free to set the cage to whatever it likes; and it naturally will tend to choose `EverywhereCage`, which minimizes its work.) But it seems good style to set the `EverywhereCage` when you don't care where the cursor is, if only to help the reader of the program.

Solution 5. To describe how `DoScramble` works, we need a few simple facts about permutations.

- A transposition is a permutation that swaps two elements.

- Every permutation is a product of transpositions.

- The parity of a permutation is even if it is a product of an even number of transpositions, odd if it is a product of an odd number of transpositions. The parity doesn't depend on how the permutation is factored into transpositions.

We also define the parity of the empty cell to be even if the sum of its row index and column index is even; odd if the sum is odd. Initially the parity of the empty cell is even, since it is on the diagonal; initially the parity of the configuration is even, since it is the product of zero transpositions. Every move of the puzzle changes the parity of the configuration, and also the parity of the empty cell. Therefore, in every solvable position, the parity of the configuration is the same as the parity of the empty cell. We leave it to the reader to establish the converse, that any configuration whose parity is the same as the parity of the empty cell is solvable.

It follows that solvability is always preserved if the position of the space is preserved and the other pieces are rearranged by an even permutation. This is the strategy of `DoScramble`: it applies a randomly-chosen even permutation to the numbered cells.

A random permutation is easily produced by selecting the first element randomly from among all the elements; the second from among the remaining elements, and so forth. Each element is swapped into its place immediately after it is selected. Thus the selected elements always form a prefix of the permutation, and each random selection is made from a suffix of decreasing size. In the last step there are only two elements in the suffix, and the random choice either transposes them or preserves them, with equal probabilities.

To produce a random even permutation, we keep track of the parity as we go, and modify the last step to transpose or not, as required to make the parity even.

Chapter 8

How the language got its spots

Anonymous

*I greatly welcomed the chance of meeting and hearing the wisdom
of many of the original language designers. I was astonished
and dismayed at the heat and even rancour of their discussions.
Apparently the original design of ALGOL 60 had not proceeded in
that spirit of dispassionate search for truth which the quality
of the language had led me to suppose.*
—*C.A.R. Hoare*

Like many programming languages, Modula-3 was designed by a committee. The meetings were held at the DEC Systems Research Center in Palo Alto, whose director, Bob Taylor, likes to record important events on videotape—including our meetings.

At first we found the whirring of the cameras distracting, but eventually we became used to it. We even started to imagine that the tapes might be useful in university courses, to teach students how real scientists approach problems of programming language design.

Unfortunately, when we reviewed the tapes at the end of the project it was obvious that to show them to students was out of the question. Such scenes would probably drive students out of computing, if not all the way out of the sciences. In fact, to show the tapes to anybody at all would be highly embarrassing. But our sense of duty to history prevailed, and we resolved to provide the world with copies of the tapes. Nobody was more disappointed than we when the secretary making the copies inadvertently turned the machine to "erase" instead of "copy", and the record was irretrievably destroyed.

As often happens with mishaps of this sort, a few sections of some of the tapes survived, of which a transcript was made for this book. However, even after the usual editing (deletion of expletives, libels, etc.) the publisher still returned the transcript with the tactful suggestion that its truths would be more appealing if they were more fully clothed. As a last resort, we have translated the material into a fictional dialogue, featuring the following characters:

> Dr. Lambdaman. (An internationally eminent authority on programming languages and their semantics.)

> Jo Programmer. (While Dr. Lambdaman lectured the committee on Abstract This and Abstract That, Jo amused herself writing microcode in her head.)

> Harry Hackwell. (He joined the committee to make sure that Modula-3 would "support his style of programming".)

> Noam Wright. (He was the most vocal member of the committee, but his remarks have been drastically abridged in the following account, since they contained almost no information.)

> Professor Pluckless. (The patron saint of committee design.)

The casting was not fixed, but varied from day to day, even from minute to minute, and every member of the committee starred at times in every role.

8.1 How the types got their identity

PLUCKLESS: The writers working on the language definition have asked us to give them a clear definition of when two types are identical.

HACKWELL: That's easy. Everyone knows that Modula uses name equivalence. Two types are the same if they have the same name.

LAMBDAMAN: The issue of type identity is too fundamental to be decided on the basis of tradition. We should explore the alternatives and decide on the basis of technical merit.

WRIGHT: Well said. All men of principle favor structural equivalence.

PLUCKLESS: Oh yeah? Don't they know the principle "if it ain't broken, don't fix it"?

JO: If you men of principle could bring yourselves to descend occasionally into the realm of specifics, we just might finish this language by the end of the century. I wonder if Hackwell really means what he says. After the declarations

```
TYPE
  A = REF INTEGER;
  B = REF INTEGER;
  C = B;
```

the types A, B, and C have distinct names. By Hackwell's definition they would be different types. But in Modula-2, B and C are the same type.

HACKWELL: I didn't mean to change the semantics from Modula-2. I want B and C to be the same, and A and B to be different. I guess "name equivalence" is a misnomer. But everyone knows what it means.

LAMBDAMAN: Should we put that in the manual?

HACKWELL: How about this: two types are the same if they have the same name, or if one of them is a renaming of the other, as in the case of TYPE C = B above.

PLUCKLESS: I suppose types can be identified by a chain of renamings.

HACKWELL: Yes, of course. The writers are good at phrasing details like that.

LAMBDAMAN: I don't like this wording because it makes a special case of renamings. It shouldn't take any extra words to say that B and C are the same after the declaration C = B. What requires explanation is that A and B are different after both have been declared to be REF INTEGER.

JO: It's also unclear what happens to anonymous types. For example, in Modula-2, after

```
TYPE R =
  RECORD
    p, q: REF INTEGER;
    r: REF INTEGER;
  END
```

the p and q fields have the same type, but the r field has a different type. I don't think this follows from Hackwell's wording, since the types involved are anonymous.

PLUCKLESS: Let me try. The way I like to think of it, every type comes in a potentially unlimited number of different "brands". Each occurrence of a type constructor puts a distinct brand on the type it creates. You can imagine there's a global counter that gets incremented each time a type constructor is applied. The value of the counter is used to generate the unique brand characterizing that application. In the declaration TYPE C = B, no type constructor is applied, no brand is created, and C becomes the same type as B. But each occurrence of REF, named or anonymous, creates its own unique brand.

LAMBDAMAN: In Modula-2, after the declarations

```
TYPE
  T = INTEGER;
  U = INTEGER
```

the types T and U are the same. But under your theory, wouldn't the two occurrences of the type constructor INTEGER produce different types?

PLUCKLESS: No. We can take the point of view that INTEGER isn't a type constructor, it's a predeclared name for a built-in type. The same goes for all the other predeclared type names.

LAMBDAMAN: Your theory seems to account for Modula-2's semantics.

HACKWELL: Well, that's that. Now about my proposal for multiple inheritance—

LAMBDAMAN: Not so fast. I agree that Pluckless has defined Modula-2 semantics, but that doesn't mean I like the semantics. Why should REF INTEGER denote a different type every place it occurs? Why make REF into a procedure with a side-effect on an invisible brand counter?

PLUCKLESS: You're proposing structural equivalence?

LAMBDAMAN: If you want to call it that. I propose that type constructors be functions from types to types: applied to equal arguments, they produce equal results. There is only one type REF INTEGER.

HACKWELL: Are you proposing that the following two types be the same?

```
TYPE
  R1 = RECORD alpha: INTEGER END;
```

```
TYPE
  R2 = RECORD beta: INTEGER END;
```

LAMBDAMAN: No. Their structure may be similar, but they're different types. The field names are arguments to the type constructor RECORD, and form a part of the type it constructs.

JO: How about the following two types:

```
TYPE
  List1 =
    REF RECORD x: INTEGER; link: List1 END;
```

```
TYPE
  List2 =
    REF RECORD
      x: INTEGER;
      link: REF RECORD x: INTEGER; link: List2 END
    END;
```

LAMBDAMAN: They are the same. They are just different ways of writing the type that intuitively is given by the infinite expression:

```
TYPE
  List =
    REF RECORD
      x: INTEGER;
      link: REF RECORD
        x: INTEGER;
        link: REF RECORD
          x: INTEGER;
          link: REF RECORD
            .
            .
            .
```

PLUCKLESS: How can the compiler test whether two types are the same?

LAMBDAMAN: There is a simple linear-time algorithm for reducing a set of type declarations to canonical form. For example, List1 is the canonical form of List2.

PLUCKLESS: What is the exact wording that you propose?

LAMBDAMAN: Two types are the same if their definitions become the same when they are expanded by replacing all names with their definitions. In the case of recursive types, the expansion is infinite.

PLUCKLESS: Are the following two types the same?

```
TYPE
  A1 = ARRAY [0..2+2] OF ARRAY [0..1] OF INTEGER;
  A2 = ARRAY [0..4], [0..1] OF INTEGER;
```

LAMBDAMAN: Yes. Constant expressions are replaced by their values in the expanded definition, and the syntactic sugar for nested arrays doesn't count.

PLUCKLESS: What's the point? Why bother with structural equivalence?

WRIGHT: Name equivalence is a flagrant violation of referential transparency.

HACKWELL: Those are just long words, not an argument.

LAMBDAMAN: Referential transparency is widely recognized as a sound semantic principle. In modern type theory, types are values in a suitable semantic domain; type constructors are maps from this domain into itself. Referential transparency is one of the foundations of this whole point of view.

HACKWELL: Be real, Lambdaman. This isn't a POPL conference.

JO: I think the referential transparency point should be taken seriously. With name equivalence, you can only ask about the identity of types that appear in the same program. But if types are values in a semantic domain that exists independently of any particular program, then you can ask about the identity of types from different programs. This seems useful for programming distributed systems.

HACKWELL: For example?

JO: When making a remote procedure call, the type of the actual and the type of the formal are types that appear in different programs. To make sense of the requirement that they be the same, you have to compare types in different programs.

HACKWELL: How about a more concrete example?

JO: Essentially the same problem arises with type-safe persistent data. Consider the call Pkl.Write(r, f), which writes the value r onto the file f. Similarly, Pkl.Read(f) reads a pickle from the file f and builds and returns the corresponding value. Now the question is: when is it type-safe for a pickle of type T written by one program to be read and assigned to a variable of type U in another?

HACKWELL: If T and U are the same type, obviously.

JO: But T and U are in different programs, so that only makes sense under structural equivalence.

HACKWELL: Why not allow the operation if the name of T in P1 is the same as the name of U in P2?

JO: That's hopeless. The types could have completely different structures.

HACKWELL: I suppose you could use structural equivalence for this special case of inter-program typechecking, and still use name equivalence within a single program.

JO: That runs into problems. Suppose that a program contains two types that are structurally equivalent to the type of a pickle that it reads. How does Pkl.Read choose the result type? For example, suppose one program is

```
    Pkl.Write(NEW(REF INTEGER), "file.pkl")
```

and the other is

```
    TYPE
      U1 = REF INTEGER;
      U2 = REF INTEGER;
    VAR v := Pkl.Read("file.pkl");
```

What's the final type of v?

HACKWELL: You could treat this as an error. After all, whether you use name equivalence or structural equivalence, it will be an error if the pickle-reading program has no type that is structurally equivalent to the type in the pickle. So it is natural also to make it an error if the program has more than one such type.

JO: It might be natural but it's a gross violation of modularity. It would mean that adding a module containing a private type REF INTEGER could break another section of the program that reads pickles. That's unacceptable.

HACKWELL: You could make the caller of Pkl.Read specify the type by supplying a typecode.

JO: That only helps for the root of the data structure. Pkl.Read will still have to come up with types for any REFANYs that are embedded inside it.

HACKWELL: But the pickles package for Modula-2+ uses name equivalence. So there must be a solution to this problem.

JO: In Modula-2+, Pkl.Write(r) puts both the name and structure of r's type into the pickle. The program reading the pickle must have a type with that name and structure.

LAMBDAMAN: What does the Modula-2+ Pkl.Write do if it encounters a type with more than one name? Or with no names? For example, after

```
TYPE T = RECORD f: REF INTEGER; g: REF INTEGER END;
VAR t: T;
...
Pkl.Write(t.g)
```

JO: If the type has more than one name, a canonical name is selected by repeatedly undoing type renamings. If the type is anonymous, a name is created for it by some rules having to do with the context in which the type expression occurs.

HACKWELL: So what's the matter with that?

WRIGHT: Can't you recognize a pile of poo when you step in it?

JO: It means that you can invalidate pickles on the disk by changing the name of a type in a program, moving a declaration from one module to another, or, in case of anonymous types, by inserting or deleting declarations that precede a declaration containing an anonymous type.

HACKWELL: Why are we worrying so much about an esoteric facility like pickles? Is it too much to ask that programmers choose a name for each pickled type, and stick to it?

JO: Type-safe persistent data is not esoteric. It's important and it's going to become more important. The current situation with name equivalence is irritating. One Modula-2+ programmer added a type declaration at the top of an interface, never dreaming that such a simple change could break the pickle reading code in a distant module. By the time it was discovered that it was broken, most of the system had been compiled against the new interface. I think it's clear that name equivalence is not quite right.

HACKWELL: Well, I think that structural equivalence is not quite right either, and my argument is based on something simpler than pickles. For example, consider these types:

```
TYPE
  Apple  = REF RECORD ... END;
  Orange = REF RECORD ... END;
```

Suppose that by coincidence, the types have the same structure. With structural equivalence, if I declare a procedure that takes an `Apple`, the type checker will also allow it to take an `Orange`; even though it's probably a programming error. Structural equivalence weakens typechecking by introducing accidental type coincidences.

LAMBDAMAN: In principle there's something to what you say, but in practice name equivalence is more lenient than you are letting on. Consider these declarations:

```
TYPE
  ExtendedChar = [0..32767];
  ProcessID    = [0..32767];
```

In Modula-2, with name equivalence, assignments between `Apples` and `Oranges` are forbidden, but assignments between `ExtendedChars` and `ProcessIDs` are allowed.

WRIGHT: Name equivalence purists preach that all types are created distinct. But some types are more distinct than others!

HACKWELL: I would be happy to explore alternatives in which assignments between `ExtendedChar` and `ProcessIDs` require explicit conversions using `ORD` and `VAL`.

PLUCKLESS: Really, Hackwell, I don't think any of us would like the result, even you. I think the point is that the danger of accidental coincidences between `Apples` and `Oranges` is not so serious a practical problem as you are making out.

LAMBDAMAN: Beside, if it does happen that a programmer erroneously assigns an `Apple` to an `Orange` and complains that the type system let it through, we have a perfectly good answer: he should have made the types opaque.

JO: Speaking of opaque types, aren't they a problem for structural equivalence?

LAMBDAMAN: How so?

JO: If a client of an opaque type knows or guesses the concrete type, then with structural equivalence, he can violate the abstraction boundary. For example, consider

```
INTERFACE Wr; TYPE T <: ROOT;  ... END Wr;

MODULE Wr; REVEAL T = OBJECT private: ... END;  ... END Wr.
```

The whole idea of opaque types is that a client of `Wr` can access variables of type `Wr.T` only through procedures that are revealed in the interface. The client is not supposed to be able to deal directly with the object's data fields. But with structural equivalence, the client can use TYPECASE to get at the private fields, like this:

```
TYPE WrRep = OBJECT private: ... END;
VAR wr := NEW(Wr.T);
   ...
TYPECASE wr OF
  WrRep (w) => ...
END
```

Since with structural equivalence the types Wr.T and WrRep are the same, the TYPECASE statement will take the first arm, and in that arm the private fields of wr will be accessible to the client via w. This is a disaster for abstraction.

LAMBDAMAN: This is a problem, but I'm sure we can easily fix it. Perhaps the abstract and concrete types shouldn't be the same. Instead they could be related by some kind of abstraction function. For example, the implementation module could contain

```
REVEAL Wr.T = ABSTRACT(OBJECT private: ... END)
```

or something of the sort.

PLUCKLESS: That doesn't solve anything. The client could declare WrRep to be ABSTRACT(OBJECT private: ... END).

JO: In general, if the concrete type is defined by the declaration REVEAL T = E, then a TYPECASE arm that contains the expression E will succeed. This is an unavoidable consequence of your beloved referential transparency principle.

LAMBDAMAN: I suppose that different occurrences of ABSTRACT could produce different types.

PLUCKLESS: Then your abstract types wouldn't be any different from my branded types.

JO: Furthermore, all the problems that name equivalence poses for distributed programming will reappear. If I write a value of type ABSTRACT(REF INTEGER) into a pickle, just which brand of ABSTRACT(REF INTEGER) will I get when I read it out?

LAMBDAMAN: Let's try another tack. Forget about these unprincipled Modula opaque types. What we need are *real* abstract types.

PLUCKLESS: What is a real abstract type?

LAMBDAMAN: It's an abstract type whose corresponding concrete type is guaranteed to be hidden at runtime as well as at compile time.

PLUCKLESS: How do you define them?

LAMBDAMAN: The basic idea is very simple. We have defined TYPECASE to classify a reference r to be a member of type T if r's allocated type is a subtype of T. But a subtype in what sense? In any module there are, in a sense, two subtype relations. There is the global subtype relation on all the types in a program. There is also a smaller relation, consisting of those subtype facts that are statically visible in the module. In our current language, we have defined TYPECASE to use the global subtype relation. If we change it to use the local relation instead, then TYPECASE will no longer be able to violate abstraction boundaries.

HACKWELL: Let me see if I understand this.   I once got burned in Modula-2+ by constructing a heterogeneous list of TEXTs and OS.ProcessIDs. These are both opaque types, and I tried to use TYPECASE to distinguish them from one another when I read the elements out of the list. Unfortunately, the concrete type of an OS.ProcessID turned out to be TEXT! Under your proposal, my program would have worked?

LAMBDAMAN: Certainly.   In the scope of your TYPECASE statement, TEXT and OS.ProcessID were unrelated in the local subtype relation. Therefore in that scope, a TEXT would narrow to a TEXT but not to an OS.ProcessID, and an OS.ProcessID would narrow to an OS.ProcessID but not to a TEXT.

HACKWELL: I like it.

PLUCKLESS: How do you implement it?

LAMBDAMAN: Instead of one table defining the subtype relation, keep one table for each module.

PLUCKLESS: Couldn't that take quadratic space? You'll have to do better than that if you expect us to sign up for this scheme.

JO: The implementation is the least of the problems with this proposal. Look at the following program:

```
INTERFACE I; TYPE T <: REFANY; END I.

INTERFACE J; PROCEDURE P(r: REF INT); END J.

MODULE I; IMPORT J; REVEAL T = REF INT; BEGIN J.P(NEW(T)) END I.
```

Is this OK so far?

LAMBDAMAN: Yes. The call to J.P typechecks, since within the scope of the module I, it is known that T = REF INT; from which it follows of course that T <: REF INT. Consequently the NEW(T) actual can be bound to the REF INT formal.

JO: Now look at the implementation of J.P:

```
PROCEDURE P(ri: REF INT) =
  VAR ra: REFANY := ri;
  BEGIN
    ri := NARROW(ra, REF INT);
    ...
  END P;
```

The programmer of J.P assumed, not unreasonably, that if he assigned a REF INT to a REFANY then he would be able to narrow that REFANY back into a REF INT. Unfortunately for him, the allocated type of the actual ri is the "real" abstract type I.T. In the scope of the call to J.P, it was known that I.T <: REF INT. But in the scope of the module J this is not known, so the NARROW will fail.

LAMBDAMAN: Your example is a bit contrived.

JO: It puts a value of type REF T into a variable of type REFANY and then narrows it back again. Admittedly this is rarely done in two consecutive assignments, but it is common to do indirectly; for example, by putting the value into a table of REFANYs. With "real" abstract types, a programmer can never trust that a parameter of type REF INT really is a REF INT.

PLUCKLESS: So much for real abstract types.

HACKWELL: And so much for structural equivalence, since it makes the world unsafe for abstraction.

JO: But Hackwell, as you found out when you blundered with TEXT and OS.ProcessID, opaque types aren't entirely safe with name equivalence either.

HACKWELL: I don't blame that problem on name equivalence. I blame it on the revelation

    REVEAL OS.ProcessID = TEXT

which should be illegal. We should require that the concrete type expression in a revelation must contain a type constructor. For example, it could be

    REVEAL OS.ProcessID = RECORD t: TEXT END

Then the automatic branding of name equivalence will make all opaque types distinct.

JO: This seems like the kind of practical approach that we need. But I'm still concerned with the problems that name equivalence poses for distributed programming. Doesn't your idea work with explicit brands as well as implicit brands?

LAMBDAMAN: An excellent point. We can add a type constructor that applies a brand. If T is a type and b is a text constant, let BRAND(b, T) be the type that is the same as T except that it is branded b.

WRIGHT: I have nothing against brands if they're explicit. Explicit brands preserve referential transparency.

LAMBDAMAN: If you write a BRAND("Wr314", REF INTEGER) into a pickle, then you get a BRAND("Wr314", REF INTEGER) when you read it out.

PLUCKLESS: But what about the conflict between structural equivalence and abstract types? If the concrete type for an opaque type is BRAND("Wr314", REF INTEGER), then a client can get at the representation by repeating that type expression in a typecase arm, brand and all.

LAMBDAMAN: We simply prohibit any brand from appearing more than once in a program. That's easy to enforce at link time.

JO: Explicit brands allow the programmer to avoid the kind of accidental type coincidences that worry Hackwell, even when the type involved is not opaque.

PLUCKLESS: All this creativity makes me nervous. How can we tell if it hangs together?

LAMBDAMAN: What could go wrong?

PLUCKLESS: Well, one thing that bothers me is the exact definition of BRAND(b, T).

LAMBDAMAN: It has all the properties of T, except its brand is b.

PLUCKLESS: Oh yeah? Is T identical with T?

LAMBDAMAN: Of course.

PLUCKLESS: Then since BRAND(b, T) has all the properties of T, one of which is to be identical with T, it follows that BRAND(b, T) is identical with T!

LAMBDAMAN: Don't be ridiculous. You know what I mean.

HACKWELL: Hah! You always get on your high horse whenever *I* say that.

PLUCKLESS: I don't think I am being ridiculous. I think your definition is nonsense. Here's another example:

```
TYPE
  T = OBJECT METHODS m() := P END;
  U = BRAND("X", T);
PROCEDURE P(self: T) = ...
```

If U has the same properties as T, then its m method is P. But P takes a T, not a U, so it can't be a method of U.

LAMBDAMAN: Oops. Good point. I suppose we could list those properties of T that are inherited by BRAND(b, T).

JO: The writers won't like that.

LAMBDAMAN: I'm not fond of it myself.

PLUCKLESS: Perhaps BRAND shouldn't be a type constructor in its own right, but an optional clause in existing type constructors.

LAMBDAMAN: That will do the trick! You would write something like this:

```
TYPE T = OBJECT fields METHODS methods BRAND b END
```

In the formal semantics, this is an application of the type constructor OBJECT to arguments that include the fields, methods, and brand. Since the brand occurs within the expanded definition, it makes the type unique.

JO: Do you propose that brands be allowed in all type constructors, or only in reference types?

HACKWELL: Can I include the keyword BRAND but omit the text literal b?

PLUCKLESS: You're not serious about that syntax, I hope?

LAMBDAMAN: I'm sure we can reach consensus on these little details.

PLUCKLESS: Maybe we could, but maybe we won't have to. Isn't it time to settle the basic question of name equivalence versus structural equivalence? I think we understand the positions as well as we are going to.

LAMBDAMAN: I vote for structural equivalence with explicit brands.

HACKWELL: I say name equivalence is simpler to think about and to implement, and that structural equivalence is evil because it allows accidental type equivalences.

WRIGHT: You all can vote for whatever you want, but I will always know what was right.

PLUCKLESS: To me this whole issue is about as exciting as whether 3.5 should round up to 4 or down to 3. The religious difference between the two proposals may be large, but the practical difference is tiny. If we go with structural equivalence, we'll be letting ourselves in for a lot of unnecessary flak. I vote for name equivalence.

JO: I agree that the practical side of the issue is small compared to the fuss everybody makes about it. Both designs will certainly work out from an engineering point of view. So we should choose on the basis of taste, not tradition. I vote for structural equivalence, since it seems better for distributed programming.

Thus the committee adopted structural equivalence, by a vote of three to two.

8.2 How the subtypes got their rules

PLUCKLESS: I have to begin today's meeting by reminding everybody that we're behind schedule. It took longer than we expected to decide the meaning of type identity. I hope it won't take so long to settle today's issue, which is type compatibility.

JO: Must we talk about types again? I have a proposal for iterators that I think you'll all like.

WRIGHT: Let's finish the foundations before we gild the gargoyles.

PLUCKLESS: Perhaps we can squeeze in iterators at the end of the meeting, if we settle compatibility quickly.

LAMBDAMAN: What exactly do you mean by type compatibility?

PLUCKLESS: When is it legal to assign x := e, or to bind the formal parameter x to the actual parameter e?

JO: It's too strict to require that x and e have the same type?

PLUCKLESS: Yes, since it should be legal to assign a [0..9] to an INTEGER, or a REF T to a REFANY.

LAMBDAMAN: It's rather obvious what the rule has to be, isn't it? Assigning e to x is legal if and only if the set of possible values of the expression e is contained in the set of values representable by the variable x. In symbols, we write T <: U (T is a subtype of U) if every value of type T is a value of type U, and define e to be assignable to x if the type of e is a subtype of the type of x.

HACKWELL: I think your rule is too strict. We should loosen up the Modula-2 straightjacket. If n is an integer and x is a real, I want to write n := x and have x automatically rounded to an integer as part of the assignment, like in Ada.

WRIGHT: You have to be a lazy typist indeed to pretend to find n := x more readable than n := ROUND(x).

PLUCKLESS: I agree with Wright. Ask the programmers who used PL/I in earnest whether implicit conversions are good or bad. In PL/I, the expression 5 < 6 < 7 evaluates to TRUE!

HACKWELL: What's the matter with that?

PLUCKLESS: Only that you might imagine it means what it looks like it means. But it doesn't. In fact the expression 7 < 6 < 5 also evaluates to TRUE, since 7 < 6 evaluates to FALSE, and FALSE < 5 is legal because of the implicit conversion of FALSE to zero, so the whole expression becomes 0 < 5, or TRUE.

HACKWELL: Cute. But I just want implicit rounding and floating. I don't want booleans to convert implicitly to integers.

PLUCKLESS: It's a slippery slope. I would much rather avoid implicit conversions completely.

LAMBDAMAN: It's not clear that we can avoid them completely. Suppose ri is a REF INTEGER and rb is a REF BOOLEAN. Then ri := NIL and rb := NIL are both legal. Similarly, NIL can be assigned to procedure types and to all the other reference types. There is nothing in the constant "NIL" to say of which type it is the null value. So it appears there must be an implicit conversion from the universal NIL to each particular NIL-for-type-T.

PLUCKLESS: Why must each type have its own NIL? The types [0..10] and [10..20] intersect in the value 10; why can't all the reference types intersect in the value NIL?

LAMBDAMAN: We might get away with that.

PLUCKLESS: Good. I still hope for a design with no implicit conversions. Is Lambdaman's rule acceptable otherwise?

JO: I have another objection. Modula-2 allows the assignment of an INTEGER value to a variable of type [10..20]. The result is a checked runtime error if the value is out of range. Lambdaman's rule would forbid this, since we don't have INTEGER <: [10..20].

LAMBDAMAN: You could get around this with an explicit VAL:

```
VAR
    e: INTEGER := ...;
    x: [10..20] := VAL(e, [10..20]);
    ...
```

This obeys the rule, and VAL will generate the checked runtime error if e is out of range.

PLUCKLESS: If we do that, we'll never hear the end of it. I see no reason to part with tradition here.

HACKWELL: You never do. My implicit conversion is bad because it's not traditional; your implicit conversion is good because it is traditional.

JO: I don't think Hackwell is being fair. If x has type [10..20] and e has type INTEGER, the assignment x := e should not be considered an implicit coercion, since if it succeeds, it changes x to the value of e, not to a different value. The value is checked, but it isn't changed.

HACKWELL: What about biased subranges? If the implementation represents a subrange value by its excess over the lower bound, then the assignment of an INTEGER to a [10..20] requires subtracting 10. If that isn't an implicit conversion, I don't know what is.

JO: That might have been relevant in the days of sixteen bit machines, but nobody uses baised subranges anymore.

LAMBDAMAN: Or to give an answer rather than dodge the question, the implementer always has a free choice over the representation. He could represent a variable of type [10..19] with four bits if the variable name begins with a vowel and with thirty-two bits if it begins with a consonant, so long as he converts the representations to make the representation invisible to the programmer. At the semantic level, which deals only in values, not their representation, there is no conversion in the assignment of an INTEGER to a subrange.

PLUCKLESS: Which leaves us with the question of how to fix the rule to allow the assignment. Perhaps we should allow the assignment of a T to a U if T <: U *or* if U <: T. In the latter case, a runtime check is required.

LAMBDAMAN: That's a nice symmetric rule.

JO: But it would still forbid the assignment of a [0..10] to a [5..15], which is also allowed by tradition.

PLUCKLESS: How about allowing the assignment of a T to a U if the sets of values of T and U overlap?

LAMBDAMAN: That would allow the assignment of a REF INTEGER to a REF BOOLEAN, since they overlap in the value NIL.

PLUCKLESS: Oops.

JO: I have a feeling that we won't get to iterators today.

HACKWELL: You all have to stop imagining that the rules will ever turn out to be as simple as you hope. Obviously there has to be a different rule for ordinal types. They are assignable if they overlap. We have to use a different assignment rule for reference types. Big deal.

LAMBDAMAN: Hackwell seems to be right. But we should keep the rules as simple as possible. Let's use the overlap rule for ordinal types, and my original rule for all other types.

JO: The overlap rule seems right for ordinal types. But for the reference types I think the symmetric rule is the right one. It is inconsistent to allow the assignment of an INTEGER to a [0..9] and forbid the assignment of a REFANY to a REF T.

PLUCKLESS: You want implicit NARROW for reference types? Isn't this a change from Modula-2+?

JO: Yes it's a change and yes I want it—like every other programmer whose has written or read Modula-2+ programs that deal with REFANYs. The experience has been that programs are more concise and readable without the explicit NARROWs.

PLUCKLESS: So we have the overlap rule for ordinals, the symmetric rule for references, and the original subtype rule for all other types. Going once. . . .

HACKWELL: You can't use the symmetric rule for all reference types. There is no way to check the assignment of an ADDRESS to, say, an UNTRACED REF INTEGER, since raw addresses won't be tagged with the type information required for a runtime check.

JO: Certainly. It's not surprising that ADDRESS is a special case. The symmetric rule holds for all reference types except ADDRESS.

PLUCKLESS: The overlap rule for ordinals, the symmetric rule for reference types other than ADDRESS, and the original subtype rule for all other types. Going twice. . . .

JO: Hold on. I also want the symmetric rule for array types. This will allow the assignment of an open array to a fixed array of the same element type, with a run-time check that the lengths are the same.

PLUCKLESS: Is this so important that we need to make a special case?

JO: Since we're already using the symmetric rule for some types, it's not a question of making a special case, it's a question of which rule is best for array types. And I think you will agree that it is rude to prohibit the following assignment:

```
PROCEDURE P(a: ARRAY OF T; ...) =
  VAR buff: ARRAY [0..BuffSize] OF T; i, n: INTEGER;
  BEGIN
    ...
    n := BuffSize; buff := SUBARRAY(a, i, n)
    ...
```

The result type of SUBARRAY is an open array, since in general the length of the result can't be determined statically. To allow the assignment we have to use the symmetric rule for array types.

PLUCKLESS: That seems convincing. So: the overlap rule for ordinals, the symmetric rule for array types and all reference types except for ADDRESS, and the original subtype rule for all other types. Gone?

LAMBDAMAN: It's not as simple as I hoped, but I can live with it.

HACKWELL: Everyone but me gets his favorite implicit conversion!

JO: On to iterators! The idea is to treat them as syntactic sugar for mapping functions—

PLUCKLESS: Excuse me, but we're not done with compatibility. We have defined the legality of x := e, assuming we can decide whether T <: U, for arbitrary types T and U. But when do we have T <: U?

LAMBDAMAN: I already told you: T <: U when the set of values of T is contained in the set of values of U. I call it the value set principle.

PLUCKLESS: That's what you *said*, and perhaps *you* understand it, but I don't know what a compiler writer or programmer will make of your definition. It's all rather hazy.

JO: How about some rules that determine whether T is a subtype of U from their syntax, instead of from the semantics of their sets of values?

LAMBDAMAN: No problem. The syntactic rules will follow from the value set principle. For example, the values of type SET OF T are the sets of values of type T. From this we conclude:

SET OF T <: SET OF U   if   T <: U

which is the syntactic rule for set subtyping. I would express it by saying that SET OF is monotonic.

JO: You can express it however you want, but I don't like it. The rule would require the compiler to produce conversion code for the assignment, since the representation of a SET OF [5..7] is different from the representation of a SET OF [0..9]. The data would have to be shifted five bits and padded with zeros. For multi-word sets, the conversion would get quite awkward.

HACKWELL: Better to write this conversion code once in the compiler than to rewrite it in every client.

JO: I expect that compiler writers have better things to do with their time than to implement conversion code that will not be used by one program in a thousand.

PLUCKLESS: Do you have an alternative rule to propose?

JO: Sure. SET OF T <: SET OF U only if T and U are the same.

LAMBDAMAN: You can't just pull subtype rules out of a hat. What principle justifies your rule?

JO: I accept half of the value set principle. If T <: U, then the set of values of T must be contained in the set of values of U or else the subtyping rule is not semantically sound. But I don't accept the other half of the principle. If the set of values of T is contained in the set of values of U, we may or may not assert T <: U, depending on whether the benefits to clients outweigh the cost to the implementation. If we expect implementations to represent T's and U's differently, then we shouldn't include the rule unless it is of obvious value and the conversion is straightforward.

LAMBDAMAN: Must we debate the utility and efficiency of every subtype rule? If you just accept the value set principle, then all the rules will follow inevitably.

JO: But the compiler will become much more complicated. For example, what are the values of type ARRAY I OF T?

LAMBDAMAN: They are the sequences of elements of T whose length is NUMBER(I).

PLUCKLESS: Why not the maps from I to T?

LAMBDAMAN: You might get away with that, but it would make it hard to explain the binding of an ARRAY CHAR OF T actual to an ARRAY OF T formal, where the domain type magically changes from CHAR to [0..255]. Defining the value of the variable to be a simple sequence avoids this problem.

JO: In either case, the value set principle would imply the rule:

```
ARRAY I OF T <: ARRAY I OF U   if   T <: U
```

LAMBDAMAN: Certainly. If every T is a U, every sequence of T's is a sequence of U's. "ARRAY OF" should be monotonic.

JO: Now look at these two arrays:

```
VAR
  a: ARRAY I OF INTEGER;
  b: ARRAY I OF [0..255];
```

Your rule would allow a := b. To implement the assignment, the elements of b have to be unpacked one by one and assigned into the elements of a. Even worse, the rule would allow b := a, since we are using the symmetric rule for array assignment. For this assignment the compiler has to lay down code to examine every element of a to check if it is in the range [0..255], and give a checked runtime error if it isn't. We should use a stricter array rule that will allow the compiler to implement array assignment simply by copying the data.

HACKWELL: But I think the monotonic array rule is very important. Suppose you're writing a general-purpose sorting routine. You make the routine take a REF ARRAY OF REFANY, together with a comparison procedure that takes two REFANYs. Now you want to pass it a REF ARRAY OF TEXT. This will require the monotonic array rule.

JO: The monotonic array rule is necessary for your example, but not sufficient. You also need a montonic rule for references:

```
REF T <: REF U   if   T <: U
```

HACKWELL: True. I think SET, ARRAY, and REF should all be monotonic.

JO: And I would rather choose subtype rules in the spirit of the Modula-2 status quo, in which the compiler writer doesn't have to perform any awkward conversions.

PLUCKLESS: I think I agree with Jo. Making SET and ARRAY monotonic is sound but seems very expensive. As for making REF monotonic, I actually think it is unsound.

HACKWELL: Why? If every value of type T is a value of type U, then a pointer to a value of type T is a pointer to a value of type U.

PLUCKLESS: Yes, but the value of type REF T is the address of a *variable* of type T, and the address of a variable of type T is not the address of a variable of type U, even if every value of T is a value of U. Look at the following program:

```
VAR
  t: REF [0..9];
  u: REF INTEGER;
  ...
u := t;    (* Allowed by the monotonic REF rule *)
u^:= 10;   (* Now t^= 10, contrary to t's type. *)
```

LAMBDAMAN: Pluckless is right. The value set principle—even just the half of it that Jo accepts—allows REF T <: REF U only if T and U are the same.

PLUCKLESS: But SET and ARRAY are still up in the air.

LAMBDAMAN: Personally I care more about PROCEDURE than about SET and ARRAY. The full value set principle leads to a nice rule for procedure subtyping, called the arrow rule.

PLUCKLESS: What is it?

LAMBDAMAN: It's easiest to see the idea by looking at the special case of a functional procedure type with one value parameter:

```
TYPE
  T = PROCEDURE(x: AT): RT;
  U = PROCEDURE(x: AU): RU;
```

The value set principle implies that T <: U whenever RT <: RU and AU <: AT. That is, the result types have to be related in the same order as the procedure types, and the argument types have to be related in the reverse order.

PLUCKLESS: It looks backwards to me.

LAMBDAMAN: The proof is easy. Let p be a procedure and suppose that RT <: RU and AU <: AT. Then

  p is in T

⇒ if x is any value in AT, then p(x) is in RT

⇒ (since RT <: RU)

  if x is any value in AT, then p(x) is in RU

⇒ (since AU <: AT)

  if x is any value in AU, then p(x) is in RU

⇒ p is in U

So p is in T implies p is in U. That is, T <: U.

PLUCKLESS: I can't argue with that proof, but I still feel uncomfortably about the rule. Can we work through an example in which the argument types are different? Let's assume Hackwell's rule for set types, and let the argument types be SET OF [5..7] and SET OF [0..9].

LAMBDAMAN: So we have a procedure

```
PROCEDURE Q(s: SET OF [0..9]): INTEGER
```

that we assign to a procedure variable

```
VAR p: PROCEDURE(s: SET OF [5..7]): INTEGER
```

The rule allows the assignment p := Q. The compiler will allow the call p(s) only when s is a subset of [5..7]. Since every subset of [5..7] is a subset of [0..9], the compile-time checking for p(s) ensures that s is also a valid parameter for Q.

PLUCKLESS: But the compiled code for Q will assume that its argument is a bit vector of length ten, while the compiled code for the call p(s) will prepare a bit vector of length three. So the computation of p := Q; p(x) will go awry, misinterpreting a three bit vector as a ten bit vector.

LAMBDAMAN: An awkward point, I admit. Perhaps upon the assignment p := Q, the implementation should construct a closure that performs the appropriate conversion before calling Q. That is, the assignment would be implemented as

```
p := (lambda s. Q(Convert(s)))
```

where Convert(s) shifts and pads the three-bit representation to the ten-bit representation.

JO: But the assignment p := Q has to achieve p = Q. The closure you construct will be a new procedure value, so the equality test will come out wrong.

LAMBDAMAN: No problem. With each generated closure you keep a pointer to the original procedure around which the closure was wrapped. Use this pointer for equality comparisons.

HACKWELL: Even I admit that this is getting too complicated.

LAMBDAMAN: I blame this on the monotonic set rule, not the arrow rule.

JO: The arrow rule interacts badly with any subtype rule that requires a change of representation on the part of the implementation, such as the monotonic set and array rules.

LAMBDAMAN: So let's pitch them and keep the arrow rule.

PLUCKLESS: The point is that we can't afford to follow the value set principle uniformly. So why should we follow it in the case of the arrow rule?

JO: I don't much like the arrow rule even without the monotonic set and array rules. Remember, we need the rule

```
ARRAY I OF T <: ARRAY OF T
```

to pass fixed arrays actuals to open array parameters. Combining this with the arrow rule, we find that p := Q is legal after

```
PROCEDURE Q(a: ARRAY OF T);
VAR p: PROCEDURE(a: ARRAY [0..9] OF T);
```

This means that the calling sequence for p must pass the length of the array, even though it's constant, since p could be bound to Q, which will expect the length.

LAMBDAMAN: Is that so terrible?

JO: Is the arrow rule so wonderful?

PLUCKLESS: What's so bad about the status quo?

Eventually, on a day when Jo exhausted herself arguing that constructors should use parentheses instead of curly braces, Hackwell got the committee to accept the monotonic set rule. The arrow rule and the monotonic array rule were both rejected. Thus the language went to press; but neither the SRC nor the Olivetti implementation teams ever got around to implementing the conversion code required by the monotonic set rule. When the language was revised after the first year of experience, the rule was dropped.

8.3   How the generics got their subsection

PLUCKLESS: Nobody, I think, will accuse me of a reckless tendency to adopt ill-considered innovations.

WRIGHT: There's a first time for everybody.

PLUCKLESS: I'm thinking of the painful absence of any generic capability in Modula-2 and Modula-2+. To write a table package, you either have to use objects or REFANYs, which can be too expensive, or you have to instantiate the interface and implementation by hand for each new element type.

HACKWELL: You don't have to apologize to me for being an advocate of progress. What's your proposal?

PLUCKLESS: Nothing elaborate or complicated. The idea is simply that some of the imported interfaces of a compilation unit can be treated as formal parameters, to be bound to actual interfaces when the unit is instantiated.

HACKWELL: Can you give an example?

PLUCKLESS: Sure. Here's a generic interface for sets:

```
GENERIC INTERFACE Set(Elem);
  TYPE T <: ROOT;
  PROCEDURE IsIn(e: Elem.T; s: T): BOOLEAN;
  PROCEDURE Empty(): T;
  PROCEDURE Insert(e: Elem.T; s: T);
  PROCEDURE Delete(e: Elem.T; s: T);
END Set.
```

To produce sets of integers, you would continue:

```
INTERFACE Integer; TYPE T = INTEGER END Integer.
INTERFACE IntSet = Set(Integer) END IntSet.
```

The interface `IntSet` is the result of expanding the generic interface `Set` with the formal import `Elem` bound to the actual interface `Integer`. `IntSet` is just like an ordinary interface, written in compressed notation.

HACKWELL: What about the implementation?

PLUCKLESS: Generic modules are very similar: they also have formal imports that are bound to actual interfaces when the generic is instantiated, and the instantiated result is like an ordinary module.

JO: Do generic modules have export clauses?

PLUCKLESS: My idea was that the generic module would not have an export clause, but its instantiation would. That is, we would have

```
GENERIC MODULE Set(...); ... END Set.
MODULE IntSet EXPORTS IntSet = Set(...); END IntSet.
```

The "EXPORTS IntSet" could be omitted in the second line, since by default a module exports the interface of the same name.

JO: Why not have the export be a parameter to the generic module?

PLUCKLESS: I don't feel strongly about the issue.

LAMBDAMAN: In the `IntSet` example, what would happen if the actual interface `Integer` did not contain a type `Integer.T`?

PLUCKLESS: An error would occur when the compiler expanded and processed `IntSet = Set(Integer)`.

LAMBDAMAN: You mean the constraints on the generic parameter are implicit in the uses of the parameter within the generic's body? That seems contrary to the spirit of static typechecking. Surely it would be better if the constraints were explicit in the generic's header. For example, `IntSet` might look something like this:

```
GENERIC INTERFACE Set(Elem);
  WHERE Elem.T: TYPE;
  ...
```

Then a reader of the generic interface can see that `Elem` can be bound to any interface that defines a type named T.

PLUCKLESS: But where does this lead? Suppose a generic module implements `Set(Elem)` by means of a hash table, and that it imports the hash function from the `Elem` interface. It would begin something like this, I suppose:

```
GENERIC MODULE Set(Elem);
  WHERE Elem.T: TYPE; Elem.Hash(e: Elem.T): INTEGER;
  ...
```

LAMBDAMAN: That seems sound. The constraints give names to the relevant types and give names and signatures to the relevant procedures.

PLUCKLESS: It won't stop there. Suppose the module uses `Elem.T` as the domain type for an array. Then `Elem.T` must be constrained to be an ordinal type, not just any type.

LAMBDAMAN: We could add meta-types, or type classes, like `ORDINALTYPE`.

PLUCKLESS: And then again the constraint might be that `Elem.T` is a record type that contains a "clip" field, or an enumeration that contains elements named A and B. You can't just answer the objections one by one, you have to find a unifying principle.

LAMBDAMAN: CLU and ML have principled ways to define the constraints on generic parameters. The basic idea in both languages is to express all constraints on type parameters as requirements that the types support certain operations. For example, you can't directly express the constraint "T must be an ordinal type", but you can express, "T must be a type that supports the operation `T.FIRST`". Similarly, you don't say "T is a record type with a `clip` field", but you can say "T is a type that supports the `get-clip` and `set-clip` operations".

PLUCKLESS: You have a long row to hoe if you think you can make that strategy work with Modula-3. The type systems of CLU and ML are much more uniform than Modula-3's.

LAMBDAMAN: Can you give a particular example of what will go wrong?

JO: I think I can. Consider a generic implementation of `Set(Elem)` that includes the expression:

```
s := NEW(REF ARRAY OF Elem.T, 2 * NUMBER(s^))
```

This will work as long as `Elem.T` is not an open array type; otherwise the call to `NEW` will not compile because it has too few parameters. The philosophy used in CLU and ML doesn't work, since the constraint is not that the type `Elem.T` supports a certain operation. The constraint is that a certain type produced from `Elem.T` by applying certain other type constructors supports a `NEW` operation with a certain number of parameters.

LAMBDAMAN: CLU and ML don't have this particular problem because they don't have open array types.

PLUCKLESS: We're not going to give up open array types, or purchase a beautiful type system at the cost of wholesale heap allocation.

LAMBDAMAN: If the generic parameters were object types instead of interfaces, then the CLU/ML approach would work.

PLUCKLESS: If you're willing to live with a Table package in which the key is an object type with hash and compare methods, then you don't need generics at all. You can already build such a package with object types. The idea of the generics proposal is to avoid the unnecessary allocations and method calls when the keys have a simple scalar type like INTEGER.

LAMBDAMAN: Aren't there other Algol-like languages with type-checked generics?

PLUCKLESS: Ada is the only one that comes to mind. I think you'll find its rules for generics more complicated than you'll like.

LAMBDAMAN: Can't we alter Modula-3's type system to preserve its efficiency and at the same time arrange that the CLU/ML principle suffices for typechecking generics?

PLUCKLESS: No doubt you can succeed where so many others have failed, but in the half an hour that remains of this meeting I would prefer to aim at terrestrial targets.

LAMBDAMAN: Perhaps if we can't add generics properly, we shouldn't add them at all.

JO: I think it's unfair to imply that there is anything improper about a generics proposal in which the typechecking is performed after the generic is expanded. It's still static checking, after all, performed before the program is executed, and from the point of view of achieving program reliability static checking is what matters. The Pluckless proposal may offend a type theorist who enjoys the challenge of polymorphic type systems, but to me it looks like a simple and useful facility.

LAMBDAMAN: I'm willing to concede the point for today. But I haven't given up on Poly-M3.

HACKWELL: I have a different objection. Why restrict generics to interfaces and modules, and generic parameters to interfaces? I want to be able to write things like this:

```
GENERIC TYPE Table(Key, Value: TYPE) = ...;
TYPE IntToIntTable = Table(INTEGER, INTEGER);
VAR tbl: IntToIntTable;
```

This is much nicer than having to declare a whole new Table interface.

JO: Do you plan to use the table, or just declare it? If so you will need Table.Put and Table.Get, and Table will end up as an interface, not a type, just as in the original proposal.

HACKWELL: Table could be an object type, with Get and Put methods.

JO: Even if it is an object type, where would you put it, in the Thread interface? If you don't like using interfaces to organize your program, you shouldn't be using Modula.

HACKWELL: I guess I don't mind treating Table as a generic interface. But I want its parameters to be types, not interfaces, so that I can say Table(INTEGER, INTEGER) instead of writing the stupid Integer interface just to get the type Integer.T = INTEGER.

JO: But the generic table implementation will probably require that the `Key` interface provide a procedure `Key.Hash`. It really is an interface that `Table` requires, not just a type.

HACKWELL: I still think it's crufty.

JO: One of the things I like about the Pluckless proposal is that generics only interact with interfaces and modules, not with the type system. Its semantics can be defined in a sentence or two, by a simple rewriting in terms of renamed imports. You seem to be proposing that every construct should be accept every kind of entity as a parameter, which is bound to be get complicated. Pluckless generics give ninety percent of the value for ten percent of the cost.

HACKWELL: I'd certainly rather have Pluckless generics than no generics at all. But I have another question about the design. Can I use generic expressions? For example, can I write this:

```
INTERFACE IntSetSet = Set(Set(Integer)) END IntSetSet.
```

Or do I have to do laboriously instantiate interface by interface:

```
INTERFACE IntSet = Set(Integer) END IntSet.
INTERFACE IntSetSet = Set(IntSet) END IntSetSet.
```

WRIGHT: Of course you can use generic expressions. The principle of referential transparency tells us that the two definitions of `IntSetSet` must be the same, since `IntSet` is defined to be the same as `Set(Integer)`.

PLUCKLESS: I'm not entirely comfortable with this last twist. What does the compiler do when confronted with `Set(Set(Integer))`?

HACKWELL: It just expands it by inventing temporary interfaces. A definition like

```
INTERFACE IntSetSet = Set(Set(Integer)) END IntSetSet.
```

is just shorthand for something like this:

```
INTERFACE Temp = Set(Integer) END Temp.
INTERFACE IntSetSet = Set(Temp) END IntSetSet.
```

PLUCKLESS: And the name of the temporary doesn't matter?

HACKWELL: Of course not, by the referential transparency principle, which seems to be on my side of the argument for a change.

PLUCKLESS: Let me get this straight: after

```
INTERFACE Temp = Set(Integer) END Temp.
INTERFACE IntSet = Set(Integer) END IntSet.
```

Your view is that `Temp.T` and `IntSet.T` are the same type?

HACKWELL: Surely they are just different names for the type that could be written `Set(Integer).T`, if we allowed it.

PLUCKLESS: Now forget about generics and answer me this: after the ordinary interface declarations

```
INTERFACE I; TYPE T <: ROOT; END I.
INTERFACE J; TYPE T <: ROOT; END J.
```

are the types `I.T` and `J.T` the same?

HACKWELL: Now that you mention it, we took considerable pains to guarantee that they would be different.

PLUCKLESS: Yet the interfaces I and J are identical except for their names?

HACKWELL: It would seem so.

PLUCKLESS: If the identical contents of `Temp` and `IntSet` cause `Temp.T` and `IntSet.T` to be the same, why don't the identical contents of I and J cause `I.T` and `J.T` to be the same?

HACKWELL: This makes my head hurt.

JO: I have another example program that might be relevant:

```
INTERFACE IntSet1 = Set(Integer) END IntSet1.
INTERFACE IntSet2 = Set(Integer) END IntSet2.
MODULE ListSet EXPORTS IntSet1;
  REVEAL T = BRANDED OBJECT n: INTEGER; link: T END;
  ...
END ListSet.
MODULE HashSet EXPORTS IntSet2;
  REVEAL T = BRANDED OBJECT a: REF ARRAY OF INTEGER; ...
  ...
END HashSet.
```

The generic interface `Set` is instantiated twice, both times with argument `Integer`, and the two instances are implemented differently: one using lists and one using hash tables. I used ordinary modules for the implementations, but they could just as well be generics. `IntSet1.T` and `IntSet2.T` are obviously different, even though the interfaces are identical except for their names. This is inconsistent with Hackwell's strategy for unfolding generic expressions.

PLUCKLESS: Obviously `Set(Set(Integer))` doesn't work, but I don't see clearly what goes wrong. And I confess this makes me nervous about the soundness of the whole proposal.

LAMBDAMAN: Your simple, non-polymorphic generics proposal? Really, establishing its soundness would be an elementary exercise in the theory of dependent types.

PLUCKLESS: Then I'm extremely willing to have *you* do the exercise.

LAMBDAMAN: I'll be glad to. The basic idea is to move up from the level of ordinary Modula-3 values like integers and references, and think instead of a whole module as a single value, like a big record containing procedures, variables, exceptions, types, and so on. Just as ordinary values have ordinary types and can be stored in ordinary variables, these new module values have "module types" and can be stored in "module variables".

PLUCKLESS: Can you give an example?

LAMBDAMAN: Sure. Here's a Modula-3 interface:

```
INTERFACE I; VAR x, y: INTEGER END I.
```

When we translate this into the formal semantics it turns into a declaration of a module-variable:

```
MODULE-VAR I: MODULE-RECORD x, y: INTEGER END;
```

Here `MODULE-VAR I: T` declares a module variable `I` of module-type `T`, sort of like the ordinary `VAR I: T`. Similarly, `MODULE-RECORD` is like `RECORD`, except that it produces a module-type instead of an ordinary type.

JO: The name of the interface is the name of the variable, not the type?

LAMBDAMAN: Exactly.

PLUCKLESS: What if the interface contains an opaque type?

LAMBDAMAN: That's the big difference between `MODULE-RECORD` and ordinary `RECORD`. An ordinary record type specifies the component types independently, but a module record type can be a "dependent type"—that is, it can specify the types of later components as functions of the values of earlier components. For example, this interface

```
INTERFACE I; TYPE T <: REFANY; PROCEDURE P(x: T): T END I.
```

translates to this declaration:

```
MODULE-VAR I: MODULE-RECORD T: TYPE; P: PROCEDURE(x: T): T END.
```

PLUCKLESS: What happened to the "`<: REFANY`"?

LAMBDAMAN: I suppose the field in the module record should be something like "`T: REFTYPE`" instead of `T: TYPE`, but that's a boggish detail I'd rather avoid. It's not important to the basic idea.

PLUCKLESS: What is the semantic meaning of `IMPORT`?

LAMBDAMAN: Nothing special. It's just a scoping discipline that allows one interface to mention another one.

PLUCKLESS: Is that all there is to interfaces?

LAMBDAMAN: That's it.

PLUCKLESS: And I suppose you're going to tell us that a Modula-3 MODULE translates into a constructor for one of your module values?

LAMBDAMAN: If you ignore the export clause, then you're correct. The export clause specifies which module variable is to be initialized with the constructed module value. For example, look at the these two interfaces and modules:

```
INTERFACE I; TYPE T <: REFANY; PROCEDURE P(x: T): T END I.
INTERFACE J; TYPE T <: REFANY; PROCEDURE P(x: T): T END J.
MODULE M EXPORTS I;
  REVEAL I.T = BRANDED REF INTEGER;
  PROCEDURE P(x: T): T = BEGIN RETURN NIL END P;
END M.
MODULE N EXPORTS J;
  REVEAL J.T = BRANDED REF BOOLEAN;
  PROCEDURE P(x: T): T = BEGIN RETURN x END P;
END N.
```

Here's a loose formal translation of the two interfaces:

```
MODULE-TYPE S = MODULE-RECORD T: TYPE; P: PROCEDURE(x: T): T END;
MODULE-VAR I, J: S;
```

The interfaces have different names but are otherwise identical, so in the formal semantics, the two module variables I and J have the same module type. I named the module-type S for convenience.

PLUCKLESS: What about M and N?

LAMBDAMAN: The body of M constructs a module value of type S from the type BRANDED REF INTEGER and the procedure (Lambda x. NIL). The export clause says that this module-value is to be used to initialize the module-variable I. If we use the module-type S as a constructor, by analogy with an ordinary record constructor, then the semantic effect of M is the following assignment:

```
I := S{BRANDED REF INTEGER, (Lambda x. NIL)}
```

Similarly, N initializes J:

```
J := S{BRANDED REF BOOLEAN, (Lambda x. x)}
```

JO: And now we see why I.T and J.T are different, even though the interfaces are the same except for the names. It's because the module-variables I and J have different module-values, even though they have the same module-type.

LAMBDAMAN: Exactly.

PLUCKLESS: What happened to the names M and N?

LAMBDAMAN: They disappear in the translation. The syntax for a module name is pretty useless semantically. What matters is the name the module exports. Of course, the export name is usually defaulted to the module name.

JO: What about a module that exports more than one interface?

LAMBDAMAN: It constructs a module value for each interface that it exports.

JO: And an interface that is exported by more than one module?

LAMBDAMAN: The corresponding module variable is initialized in pieces, one piece coming from each exporter. These details aren't important to the basic idea. Let's assume a one-to-one correspondence between interfaces and the syntactic modules that export them.

PLUCKLESS: How do generics fit into this model?

LAMBDAMAN: A generic interface is a function from module-values to module-types. For example, consider

```
GENERIC INTERFACE GI(X) = PROCEDURE P(): X.T; END GI.
```

Semantically, GI is a function that takes a module-value X and produces the module-type GI(X):

```
GI(X) = MODULE-RECORD P: PROCEDURE(): X.T END
```

An ordinary interface I declares a module-variable I with an explicit module-type. An instance I of a generic interface is similar: it declares a module-variable I whose module-type is obtained by applying the generic function. For example,

```
INTERFACE I = GI(X) END I.
```

has the meaning

```
MODULE-VAR I: GI(X);
```

PLUCKLESS: What about generic modules?

LAMBDAMAN: A generic module is a function from module-values to module-values. For example,

```
GENERIC MODULE GM(X) =
  PROCEDURE P(): X.T = RETURN NIL END P; END P;
END GM.
```

Semantically, GM is a function that takes a module-value X and produces a module-value GM(X), which in this case is a module-value with just one component, P.

An ordinary module that exports M initializes the module-variable M with an explicit module-value. An instance M of a generic module is similar: it initializes the module-variable M to a module-value obtained by applying the generic function. For example, the instantiation

```
MODULE M EXPORTS I = GM(X) END M.
```

rewrites to

```
I := GM(X);
```

PLUCKLESS: What happened to the M?

LAMBDAMAN: Just like in an ordinary module, its the export that matters. In practice you would default the export clause by writing "`MODULE I = GM(X) END I`".

JO: When Pluckless first introduced his proposal I was bothered that the exported interface wasn't a parameter to the generic, but now I'm content. When you instantiate a generic interface, the result of the function is only the module-type, not the name of the module-variable to be declared. When you instantiate a generic module, the result of the function is only the module-value, not the name of the module-variable to be initialized. This is nicely parallel.

PLUCKLESS: I do like formal semantics, when it justifies my designs.

JO: This also explains why `Set(Set(Integer))` doesn't work. The generic `Set` is a function from module-values to module-types. The outer application, of `Set` to `Set(Integer)`, is nonsense because `Set(Integer)` is a module type, not a module-value.

WRIGHT: Whew! Referential transparency is saved.

JO: I have only one more question.

LAMBDAMAN: Yes?

JO: The only fundamental difference between module variables and ordinary variables seems to be that module variables can have dependent types. If dependent types are good, why restrict them to the module level? It seems to me that we could sweep away all the special syntax and semantics for modules and interfaces simply by adding a constructor for dependent types.

Lambdaman found a truly remarkable answer to this question, but unfortunately this book is not thick enough to contain it.

8.4 How the parameters got their modes

HACKWELL: Modula-2 has two parameters modes: value and variable parameters. I would like to make the case that Modula-3 should also support VAR IN parameters.

PLUCKLESS: What is a VAR IN parameter?.

HACKWELL: It's like a VAR parameter, except the procedure isn't allowed to modify it, and the actual can be any expression, not just a designator.

PLUCKLESS: When you say that it's like a VAR parameter, do you mean that it's passed by reference? How can you pass an expression by reference?

HACKWELL: If the actual is an expression, the calling sequence passes the address of an anonymous temporary containing the expression's value.

PLUCKLESS: What's the point?

HACKWELL: The point is that it's generally more efficient to pass records by reference than by value. For example, look at the following fragment of code from a window system:

```
IF Rect.Overlap(highlightRect,
      Rect.Join(badRect,
        Rect.Move(Rect.Meet(target, clip),
          Point.Minus(toPoint, fromPoint))))
THEN ...
```

These geometry procedures are defined as functions, so that they can be used in expressions. If the functions take their arguments by value, the calls will be needlessly slow, since points and rectangles are large enough to be expensive to copy. If they take their arguments by VAR, expressions like the one above will be illegal. You would have to rewrite the expression like this:

```
temp1 := Point.Minus(ToPoint, FromPoint);
temp2 := Rect.Meet(target, clip);
temp2 := Rect.Move(temp2, temp1);
temp2 := Rect.Join(badRect, temp2);
IF Rect.Overlap(highlightRect, temp2) THEN ...
```

This gets boring fast. The solution is for the procedure formals to be VAR IN.

PLUCKLESS: Why not define points and rectangles to be references to records?

HACKWELL: It's too expensive to allocate them.

LAMBDAMAN: Are you also going to propose VAR OUT?

HACKWELL: Why not?

JO: VAR IN and VAR OUT do make programs more readable. And in the case of an RPC interface, VAR IN and VAR OUT convey information to the stub generator that would otherwise have to be embedded in comments or pragmas.

PLUCKLESS: Hackwell's proposal seems to be getting some support. Any objections?

LAMBDAMAN: I don't have any objections, but I do have a related proposal. I hope that nobody will call me Don Quixote, but I believe that a programming language should be defined by a set of proof rules, in the style that Hoare and Wirth defined Pascal. I think we should avoid constructs that are difficult to axiomatize. In general I think we have succeeded, but I have one request: could we please forbid the aliasing of VAR parameters?

WRIGHT: Oh no. Here comes another tirade against aliasing from the axiomatic semantics quarter.

LAMBDAMAN: When parameter aliasing occurs it is usually an error. For example, given the procedure declaration

```
PROCEDURE Multiply(VAR a, b, c: Matrix);
(* c := a * b *)
```

an attempt to square a matrix m by calling

```
Multiply(m, m, m)
```

is unlikely to work correctly. We could fault the specification, and say that it should have been:

```
PROCEDURE Multiply(VAR a, b, c: Matrix);
(* c := a * b.  c must not be aliased with a or b. *)
```

But I argue that it should be an implicit part of the specification of all procedures that VAR parameters cannot be aliased.

HACKWELL: But this would needlessly forbid the aliasing of a and b.

LAMBDAMAN: Yes, but this can be fixed by declaring the routine properly:

```
PROCEDURE Multiply(VAR IN a, b: Matrix; VAR OUT c: Matrix)
(* c := a * b *)
```

The rule is that two parameters may be aliased only if both are VAR IN.

WRIGHT: Anybody want to take my bet that we have not yet seen the final form of the rule?

LAMBDAMAN: There's really only one additional technicality, which is that if a routine accesses a global variable, then that global variable must be considered as an implicit parameter: a VAR parameter if the routine modifies the global, and a VAR IN parameter otherwise.

JO: This makes the rule rather difficult to enforce.

LAMBDAMAN: We wouldn't *require* that an implementation detect aliasing. But we would *allow* it to put in static or dynamic checks and reject programs that fail them. It would be fairly easy to catch common errors like `Multiply(m, m, m)`. The key point is that the language define the aliasing of `VAR` parameters to be an error.

HACKWELL: Doesn't this completely forbid the use of pointers, since if two pointers are equal, their referents are aliased?

LAMBDAMAN: Not at all. The issue is only the semantics of `VAR` parameters.

PLUCKLESS: Do you have an exact wording to propose?

LAMBDAMAN: The wording in Section 7.4 of the Euclid report is precise.

PLUCKLESS: But somewhat daunting.

LAMBDAMAN: Perhaps. If you don't like that, I have a sentence we could add to the manual that is equivalent to the Euclid rules, and very easy to understand.

PLUCKLESS: Do tell.

LAMBDAMAN: "`VAR` parameters may be passed either by reference or by value-result".

WRIGHT: Ah ha, the rule has changed yet again.

LAMBDAMAN: This is the same rule expressed in a different way. With the new wording, a program that violates the Euclid aliasing restriction will have an implementation-dependent effect; a program that obeys the restriction will be unable to tell the difference between the two implementations.

WRIGHT: Well I say it's different, and I say it's worse. Now you are mixing up `VAR` parameters with value-result parameters.

LAMBDAMAN: A point of terminology: I propose that we use "`VAR` parameter" to denote the mode of declaration in the language, and use "by reference" and "by value-result" to denote two possible implementations of that mode. We must be careful to avoid confusing implementations and specifications.

WRIGHT: You can point your terminology wherever you like, but I say a `VAR` parameter is a `VAR` parameter.

JO: I like the freedom that your rule would give to the implementation. Compilers for modern machines keep more and more local variables in registers, where they have no addresses, and are consequently easier to pass by value-result than by reference.

HACKWELL: I have never heard of or seen a modern language implementation that used value-result instead of by-reference.

JO: That just proves you're ignorant of half the world's Modula-2+ implementations. The Acorn implementation used value-result to get the most out of their proprietary RISC architecture.

HACKWELL: Suppose two threads communicate via a global variable, and that one of the threads passes the global variable to a procedure as a VAR parameter. This works fine with the by-reference implementation, but it doesn't work with value-result.

JO: We should provide what good programmers need, not what bad programmers want. Your example only shows that it is possible to write multi-threaded programs that depend on aliasing, not that it is necessary or desirable.

HACKWELL: I am thinking of how many times I have passed a record containing a mutex by VAR in Modula-2+. That wouldn't work with value-result. In fact, the whole idea of assigning mutexes seems suspicious.

JO: This is the same line of reasoning that led us to conclude that Modula-2+ was wrong to make a mutex a non-reference type. We fixed that problem. Passing Modula-3 mutexes by value-result works fine.

PLUCKLESS: Whatever the language definition says, programmers will write code that depends on the semantics of their implementation, and these hidden bugs will surface when the program is ported to a different implementation.

JO: Remember that real programmers write portable code in C, in spite of all its implementation-dependent features. No self-respecting programmer is going to complain that he can't write portable Modula-3 code because he keeps accidentally aliasing his VAR parameters. Most of these accidents crash quickly, anyway.

HACKWELL: I'm sure I've written multi-threaded code that depends on the aliasing of VAR parameters.

JO: That may well be.

PLUCKLESS: Remember our rule that we are assembling and selecting proven features, and excluding untried ideas of our own.

LAMBDAMAN: FORTRAN forbids the aliasing of VAR parameters. Ada effectively forbids it for many types, by allowing inout parameters to be passed either by reference or by value-result.

PLUCKLESS: Even so, I sense that your rule would be unpopular, and my gut feeling is to vote with the people instead of with the proof rules.

WRIGHT: Hooray! Vote, vote!

LAMBDAMAN: I cannot believe that this committee will vote to legitimize a monstrosity like Multiply(a, a, a).

HACKWELL: Why not? Your proof rules might not be able to handle such calls, but denotational semantics has been used to give a precise semantics of aliasing.

LAMBDAMAN: If VAR parameters are required to be passed by reference, then the semantic difference between VAR and VAR OUT vanishes, since the initial value of the parameter is available to the callee, whether he wants it or not.

HACKWELL: So we'll remove VAR OUT.

LAMBDAMAN: It is asymmetric to have VAR IN and not VAR OUT.

HACKWELL: So we'll change VAR IN to READONLY.

WRIGHT: Vote, vote!

PLUCKLESS: Really, Wright, a roll call is hardly necessary. Anybody want to recant? I thought not. A VAR parameter is a VAR parameter, three to two.

> *No more good must be attempted than the people can bear.*
> *—Solon*

About the Authors

Andrew Birrell got his Ph.D. at the University of Cambridge, where he worked on Algol 68 and the CAP operating system. From 1978 to 1983 he explored distributed systems at Xerox PARC, developing the Grapevine system, Cedar, and one of the earliest RPC systems. Since then at DEC SRC he has continued to work on distributed systems, mostly in the areas of file systems, naming, communication, concurrency, and security.

Mark R. Brown earned a B.S. in Mathematics and Computer Science from Yale College (1974) and a Ph.D. in Computer Science from Stanford (1977). He taught at Yale and worked at the Xerox PARC Computer Science Laboratory before joining DEC SRC in 1984. His technical interests include reliable distributed computing and programming tools.

Luca Cardelli was an undergraduate in Pisa and has a Ph.D. in Computer Science from the University of Edinburgh (1982). He worked at AT&T Bell Labs, Murray Hill, from 1982 to 1985 before assuming his current position at DEC SRC. His main interests are in constructive logic, type theory, and language design and implementation.

Jim Donahue received his Ph.D. in Computer Science at the University of Toronto (1975). He was an Assistant Professor at Cornell University from 1975 to 1981. In 1981, he joined the Computer Science Laboratory of the Xerox Palo Alto Research Center. In 1986, he established the Olivetti Research Center and was its Director until 1990. He is now a Senior Scientist and Product Manager for Teknekron Software Systems. His interests include programming language design, distributed system design, and database systems and applications.

Lucille Glassman is a technical writer for DEC SRC.

John Guttag is a Professor of Computer Science and Engineering at MIT and a member of MIT's Laboratory for Computer Science. He has a Ph.D. from the University of Toronto and an MA and MS from Brown University. Professor Guttag has taught undergraduate, graduate, and professional development courses in the areas of programming languages, compiler design, software engineering and operating systems. His research centers around the investigation of ways to improve the quality of software and the efficiency with which software is produced. His publications in this area include a book, written with Barbara Liskov, "Abstraction and Specification in Program Development".

Jim Horning has been a member of DEC SRC since 1984. After receiving his Ph.D. from Stanford in 1969 he became a member of the University of Toronto Computer Systems Research Group and then the Xerox PARC Computer Science Laboratory. He is active in the Larch Project, which is developing methods, tools, and languages for formal specifications of program interfaces. He participated in the design of the languages XPL, SUE System Language, Euclid, and Cedar.

Bill Kalsow received his Ph.D. in Computer Science from the University of Wisconsin at Madison (1986). Since then he has worked as DEC SRC. His primary interests are programming languages and their implementations.

Roy Levin holds a B.S. in Mathematics from Yale University and a Ph.D. in Computer Science from Carnegie-Mellon University. He is presently a Senior Consulting Engineer at Digital Equipment Corporation's Systems Research Center. He has been a principal contributor to the Hydra/C.mmp project at CMU, the Grapevine and Cedar systems at Xerox PARC, and the Topaz distributed programming environment and Vesta software development system at SRC.

Greg Nelson got his Ph.D. from Stanford in 1980, where he worked on program verification and algorithms for mechanical theorem proving. He was the author of the Juno constraint-based graphics system at Xerox PARC's Computer Science Laboratory, has taught at Princeton University, and is now a member of DEC SRC. Currently his active interests are window systems, programming language design, and the semantic theory of guarded commands.

Bibliography

[1] Gideon Avrahami, Kenneth P. Brooks, and Marc H. Brown. A two-view approach to constructing user interfaces. *SIGGRAPH Proceedings*, 29(3), July 1989.

[2] A. Birrell and B. Nelson. Implementing remote procedure calls. *ACM Trans. Comput. Syst.*, 2(1), February 1984.

[3] Graham M. Birtwistle, Ole-Johan Dahl, Bjorn Myhrhaug, and Kristen Nygaard. *Simula Begin*. Auerbach, Philadelphia PA, 1973.

[4] D. Clark. The structuring of systems using up-calls. *Proceedings of the 10th Symposium on Operating System Principles*, December 1985.

[5] Edsger W. Dijkstra. The structure of the 'THE'—multiprogramming system. *Communications of the ACM*, 11(5):341–346, 1968.

[6] J. V. Guttag and J. J. Horning. A Larch Shared Language handbook. *Science of Computer Programming*, 6:135–156, 1986.

[7] J. V. Guttag, J. J. Horning, and Andrés Modet. Report on the Larch Shared Language, version 2.3. Research Report 58, Digital Systems Research Center, 1990.

[8] J. V. Guttag, J. J. Horning, and J. M. Wing. Larch in five easy pieces. Research Report 5, Digital Systems Research Center, July 1985.

[9] John V. Guttag, James J. Horning, and Jeannette M. Wing. The Larch family of specification languages. *IEEE Software*, 2(5):24–36, 1985.

[10] B. Haddon. Nested monitor calls. *Operating Systems Review*, 11(4), October 1977.

[11] C.A.R. Hoare. *Procedures and Parameters: An Axiomatic Approach*, pages 102–116. Springer-Verlag, 1971.

[12] C.A.R. Hoare. Monitors: An operating system structuring concept. *Communications of the ACM*, 17(10), October 1974.

[13] Sun Microsystems Inc. *System Services Overview*, May 1988. Chapter 6.

[14] Sun Microsystems Inc. *Sun OS 4.0 Reference Manual*, November 1987. Section 3L.

[15] C. B. Jones. Specification and design of (parallel) programs. *Proceedings IFIP Congress*, 83.

[16] Leslie Lamport. Specifying concurrent program modules. *ACM TOPLAS*, 5(2):190–222, 1983.

[17] Leslie Lamport. A simple approach to specifying concurrent systems. *Communications of the ACM*, 32(1):32–45, January 1989.

[18] Butler W. Lampson and David D. Redell. Experience with processes and monitors in Mesa. *Communications of the ACM*, 23(2), February 1980.

[19] Barbara Liskov and John Guttag. *Abstraction and Specification in Program Development*. MIT Press/McGraw-Hill, 1986.

[20] Mark Manasse and Greg Nelson. Performance analysis of a multiprocessor window system. Research Report 69, Digital Systems Research Center, 1991.

[21] Mark Manasse and Greg Nelson. Trestle reference manual. Research Report 68, Digital Systems Research Center, 1991.

[22] P. McJones and G. Swart. Evolving the UNIX system interface to support multi-threaded programs. *Proceedings of the Winter 1989 USENIX Conference*, February 1989.

[23] Eric S. Roberts and Mark T. Vandevoorde. Workcrews: An Abstraction for Controlling Parallelism. Research Report 42, Digital Systems Research Center, April 1989.

[24] Paul Rovner. Extending Modula-2 to build large, integrated systems. *IEEE Software*, 3(6), November 1986.

[25] Paul Rovner, Roy Levin, and John Wick. On extending Modula-2 for building large, integrated systems. Research Report 3, Digital Systems Research Center, January 1985.

[26] J. Saltzer. Traffic control in a multiplexed computer system. Thesis. Technical Report MAC-TR-30, MIT, Cambridge, MA, July 1966.

[27] J. E. Stoy and C. Strachey. OS6—an experimental operating system for a small computer. Part 2: input/output and filing system. *The Computer Journal*, 15(3), 1972.

[28] Charles P. Thacker and Lawrence C. Stewart. Firefly: a multiprocessor workstation. *IEEE Transactions on Computers*, 37(8):909–920, August 1988.

[29] Jeannette M. Wing. Writing Larch interface language specifications. Thesis. *ACM Transactions on Programing Languages and Systems*, 9(1):1–24, 1987.

[30] Jeannette Marie Wing. A two-tiered approach to specifying programs. Technical Report LCS-TR-299, MIT, Cambridge, MA, 1983.

Index